To Mr. Avery

George W. Seevers

Happily Ever After

December 7, 1941
Surprise! in Hawaii
No Surprise in the White House

F.D.R.'s Policies for World War II
Never Say "No" to Stalin; but
Often "No" to Our Friends

George W. Seevers

School Source
Van Alstyne, Texas 75495

 Published by School Source, 1204 Wild Road, Van Alstyne, Texas 75495.

Printed in the United States of America.

Publisher's Cataloging-in-Publication
(Provided by Quality Books, Inc.)

Seevers, George W.
Happily ever after : December 7, 1941 : surprise! in Hawaii, no surprise in the White House / George W. Seevers—1st ed.
p. cm.
Include bibliographical references and index.
SUMMARY : Describes the breaking of the Japanese code in 1941, the Japanese attack on Pearl Harbor, FDR's foreign policy for WWII, the report of the Joint Congressional Committee (1946) to investigate the Pearl Harbor attack, and U.S. pro-Soviet foreign policy during the war.
LCCN: 99-73796
ISBN: 0-9658278-2-8

1. Pearl Harbor (Hawaii), Attack on, 1941—Juvenile literature I. Title.

D767.92 S44 1999 940.54'26
QB199-660

Note to the reader: For information on School Group Discounts, please contact the publisher, School Source, 1204 Wild Road, Van Alstyne, Texas 75495

Dedicated to our Unwarned Pearl Harbor Servicemen—both Dead and Survivors—including their heroic Commanders, Admiral Husband E. Kimmel and General Walter C. Short, shamefully and unjustly saddled by F.D.R. with the Attack's Blame; and to untold millions of innocent Friends, betrayed by cavalier F.D.R. decisions to Slavery and Death behind Curtains of Iron.

The author of a recent Book-of-the-Month-Club novel had been working on it for half a century. I cannot claim such notability. I have been laboring on—but enjoying—this opus for only some twenty-five years.

One distinction which I share with Shakespeare is that we both write everything out in longhand. My good wife, Jean, does the family typing and serves as a sounding board off whom I can bounce trial passages. I read them to her when I need another opinion. If she frowns, it's back to the drawing board.

By the way, I've always wondered who's really done all that typing for Avon's bard.

TABLE OF CONTENTS

FOREWORD

After the war when I returned from more than three and a half years with the infantry in the Southwest Pacific, my mother told me of the radio newscaster Kaltenborn who in his regular broadcasts often brought a bit of lift to war-weary listeners with his cheery "Well, there's good news tonight!" I'm sure that every mother, every wife or sweetheart, every child, could visualize that a serviceman somewhere was almost on his way home. In recent years now, after a bloody and heinous half century since the dawning of the pretensions of peace in that war, it would be quite fitting for Kaltenborn to be here to reiterate that comforting phrase.

I believe that two cornerstone events set the stage for these late developments. First was the election in 1980 of President Reagan—by landslide—and his subsequent reelection in 1984 by a greater avalanche of United States voters. There had been times when leaders held our policies and our values up to question. Reagan was perceived by friend and foe as one who was intensely proud of our nation and its strengths, and was resolved that our people and the rest of the world should continue so to evaluate him and those determinations. Love?—Perhaps not; but respect—Yes.

Second was the coming of Gorbachev to his role of leadership in the Soviet Union. It would seem that Gorbachev was by no means a hardline Marxist-Leninist. He was a pragmatist, as it appears were many recent-day European Communists and their overlords. Two factors contended as final determinants in all those countries: the quality of economic livelihood and the level of oppression. Some people might abide some degree of oppression if they enjoy ready supplies of food and consumer goods; others, wanting in those latter comforts, would be mollified—yea, satisfied if their lot were cast in the areas of basic freedoms and individual rights. Indeed, the Marxists of Europe and Asia for half—even three quarters of a century—held that it was their aim and destiny to provide the best of both worlds for their peoples. Neither of those good results has been realized, and the leaders well know it —and the gray "today" is the roseate "tomorrow" the disciples of Marxism had misled their followers toward as decade followed decade into the drab graveyard of years.

How long will peoples suffer the double curse of poverty and dearth of freedom? And leaders surely have nervously awaited inevitable explosions—some relatively sympathetically or with relief; others, as in Rumania, unrelentingly, with bared teeth. And, where it is true, those leaders must be thankful that the rumblings have occurred and they are still alive!

Perestroika, or the reconstruction of the Soviet system, was Gorbachev's pragmatic recognition that the place where something was rotten was not in

Denmark, but in Russia. And since such a massive program of rectification had no possibility of being carried off in secret, he wisely adopted the policy of glasnost, or openness, for the undertaking - undoubtedly fearful at stages that the "old guard" might make a personal utilization of that word for someone who dared to attempt such changes.

Lech Walesa and the Solidarity Labor Union had been shining names in Poland for years, standing staunchly against the Communist government. Arrested, imprisoned, his union outlawed, Walesa's wife accepted the 1983 Nobel Peace Prize for him when he was not allowed to do so himself. As late as January 1, 1989, Solidarity had no legal standing. Eight months later they were running the government of Poland, the Red masters in disordered retreat.

In May of 1989 Hungary cut down the Communists' wire fence which had long constituted a barrier with neutral Austria. Ere long East Germans by the thousands were streaming through, presently actively given a "leg up" on their way to West Germany by the Hungarian government. With the effectiveness of their "prison" negated, the East German Red government under ailing and aging (77) Erich Honecker, stopped all effective maintenance of the Berlin Wall. Hacking huge hunks out of that edifice became a popular pastime as scores of thousands went over it,through it, and around it to the West—and the house of Honecker fell amid charges of graft and scandal.

The Czechoslovakian Democratic Party came to power with President Vaclav Havel, though the Communist Party did not disappear as opposition—as yet. In Bulgaria, Parliament has elected a democratic President, and the Communists have changed their party name in disgrace. Rumania, oppressed long by the unrelenting and unrepentant dictator Ceausescu, his family, and his brutal secret police, finally exploded in wrath, trying him and his wife in untimely haste and punctuating him and his wife and the 1989 Holiday season with shots from a "democratic" firing squad one man (or woman), one bullet.

All Russian troops were withdrawn from the Baltic States (Lithuania, Estonia, and Latvia) by 1993 and 1994, and stirrings of independence and democracy stand on unsteady legs. In Beijing, China's Tiananmen Square in May of 1989 a million young Chinese students and others demonstrated for democracy, but Owen Lattimore's heroes didn't quite get into the mood of things. In early June they brought the proceedings to a very bloody adjournment with tanks, machine guns, and many many bullets. The world, nonetheless, watched with thrilled interest and bated breath—then retched in disgust.

The Ayatollah Khomeini in Iran ruled with sick rage for ten years, then did the world a favor on June 3, 1989—he died. In South Africa some consider advances—questionably—to be in the offing making. Castro still rants in Cuba—lonely. Scandalous, arrogant Noriega is less arrogant in a Miami jail than in Panama, and Violeta Chamorro trounced the Sandanista's Ortega to become Nicaraugua's President, in spite of everything Representative Boland and the U.S. Congress could do to prevent it.

Yes—there's good news tonight!

But hold on a bit. Let us hark back to the great Victory of 1945.

How did it happen that in that magnificent moment of triumph the foundations had already been laid—in concrete—for the more than half a century we are only now, hopefully, perceiving as beginning to erode—half a century—at the gateway to two generations? Note, if you will, that the curse of Hitler's depredations beyond his own national boundaries was just two months in excess of seven years. Stalin and his Red heirs have wielded their tyranny over blameless non-Russian victims for more than six times that long!—Over many scores of millions of inhabitants of our fellow democratic nations (as well as over millions of their own unwilling peoples), with despotism and death, terror, torture, and tears, poverty and imprisonment, slaughter and slave labor, and the crushing of all pride and free will.

Emily Dickinson eloquently wrote more than a century ago:

'Hope' is the thing with feathers –
That perches in the soul –
And sings the tune without the words –
And never stops - at all –

The Communists found ways—malevolent ways—to cease the irrepressible song of hope and replace it with anguish and fear.

It is my intent in this writing to throw light upon the reasons the United States entered the Second World War and the methods that were painstakingly utilized to accomplish that end—and the person responsible. To those cognizant of the particulars, the expression "Day of Infamy" assumes a darker, more dastardly connotation. I intend also to spell out in detail the plans this powerful person had for the directions and aims in the uses of the great powers of our nation. The personage, of course, was President Franklin Delano Roosevelt. The President's activities leading to our wartime participation have been outlined by a number of historians—some in broader detail and some in treatments confined to more specific and limited aspects of the story. Some raconteurs have indeed told the story (or stories) well, while the attempts of others to enlighten (if such was truly their purpose) have been,indeed, far less than salutary. These appraisals are quite fitting as well for the diverse reactions and writings of those who have made, and reported for, the various boards and Congressional Committees commissioned to study and investigate some of these events.

I am, by the way, disgusted with writers of textbooks for high schools, colleges, and graduate schools who have failed to utilize "historical method" in dealing with the data—even if only to take note that the "controversy" existed—but rather have completely ignored events that have been the center for numerous high-level Congressional and other investigations.

However, no one to my knowledge has endeavored to fathom why President Roosevelt worked with such pertinacity to get us into the war, why and to what ends he utilized his own and the nation's great resources and might during the conflict, and what was the ultimate design for all of these activities. That is the additional distinctive task I have set for myself in the writing of this volume. As an additional additional assignment I am dealing with the compounded ramifications and bitter tragedies that have cursed our human family as a direct legacy of those ill conceived conceptions. Some readers will be made angry; some will be made to think. I trust that when the totals are in, the latter will outnumber the former.

There cometh now—parenthetically—an illuminating historical "weather report" that highlights the realities of Pre-Domino Southeast Asia: There has been a STORM IN THE DESERT—Mighty and Devastating and Liberating! It was pursued basically with the weapons and know-how we have possessed for more than a quarter of a century—but sans the obstructions of the Jane Fondas, the professional Communist-sympathizers, and the Peace-at-any-Price-holy-ones in and out of our government and our churches that characterized the Vietnam era. (We will presently be dealing in depth with those dark days.) Weeks of deft air war; four days of lightning war on the ground. It would be hard to mount arguments that a somewhat similar campaign would not have been possible had it not been for the pious—or the timorous foot-draggers who sapped our national spirit, energy, and resolve. And how many thousands of names of Vietnam dead would never have found themselves among the more than 58,000 that adorn a memorial wall in our nation's capital! (Too bad we didn't finish Saddam Hussein!)

Comes now a Russian General Volkogonov, prompted by a die-hard American supporter of that great secret document larcenist Alger Hiss. He reports that Hiss did no such thing. Oh—? I submit that anyone with a modicum of knowledge of Hiss's 1950 perjury trial would find that impossible to swallow. The best account is De Toledano and Lasky's monumental *Seeds of Treason*. Knowledge of the trial revelations leave a myriad damning facts that cry "guilty." Those who remember hark back to the lies of Hiss—all crushingly smashed by the truth: the documents in Hiss's own handwriting, the microfilm, the old Ford coupe, the prothonotary warbler. I think the thunderbolt—one of them—was the old Woodstock typewriter which Hiss and his wife wrapped in a mountain of falsehoods. It was proved that Hiss owned it, that Priscilla Hiss had typing lessons in college (she had sworn she could not type), that 200 pages of stolen documents had been typed on his typewriter in his home while he had it in his possession. Hiss's testimony in court was:

> 'I am amazed; and until my dying day I shall wonder how Whittaker Chambers [the accuser] got into my home to use my typewriter.' The jurors laughed out loud.

It may be noted that your author has utilized the area to interject several postscripts—or should the word be "afterject?" I have heard and read references to the "death of Communism," and I will acknowledge that the Red face as presented to the world has been displayed on occasion during the past numerous months as a "red face" as the Union of Soviet Socialist Republics has in large measure disintegrated. Certainly for most of us this has brought more relief than grief—to quote Shakespeare: "tis a consummation devoutly to be wished." (And this, too, highlights the genius of the great dramatist in that he could envision across nearly four centuries the downfall of the "Evil Empire!")

The race is often to the swift. Aesop, however, reminds us that persistent tortoises on occasion may take blue ribbons slowly home. It is well to bear in mind, however, that victors share one attribute: they are ready.

It is still to be noted that fledgling democratic reforms in Russia are not winners by default; many leaders and citizens in that erstwhile mighty domain will continue to probe with hesitant—and diverse—toes into the enigmatic waters of a new and uncertain experiment in popular government. We, ourselves, are prone to changes as adverse twists in economic fates bedevil us; and more than one and a quarter billion people in China, Vietnam, North Korea, and Cuba (to enumerate some areas) are still under the thrall of Communist taskmasters who view with decided animosity any toe-testing in the waters of freedom. They are not convinced of Communism's demise.

My contentions in my final chapter as to the urgent necessity for a vital moral code founded in the experience of the Judeo-Christian Tradition, principally, are still as relevant and as powerful as when ruthless Red dictators cracked the Kremlin whip over minions throughout the world. What alternatives, indeed, are there?

We have been beset with politicians, editorials, school leaders, columnists, and church voices who loudly decry violence on television. Two teenagers robbing a bank execute a middle-aged teller who doesn't lie down on the floor quickly enough for them. Two more hold up a minimarket and kill the woman clerk "just for kicks." Dan Rolling slays and mutilates five University of Florida students he doesn't even know. A couple of drifters beat a boy to death and rape his sister. The loathsome, nauseating ledger unfolds before us every day. The reason that some T.V. stories and some movies and books and magazine and news accounts—and some brutal original "inspirations"—may lead to dastardly acts is that no moral code—no "Thou shalt nots"— have been instilled into the minds and souls of the potential wrong-doers; there is no conscience that restrains. The suggestives write upon a blank page.

We must—all mankind and nations—wherever such bleak and vacuous voids prevail, put a moral code where the blank pages plague and curse our existence. Only then may we approach the threshold of living "Happily Ever After."

George W. Seevers

INTRODUCTION

The Easter Bunny Is Not Dead

There is a phrase in vogue these days among those columnists and commentators who are deemed to be—or who deem themselves to be—"correct." That phrase is "revisionist history." The expression comes hurtling down from the exclusive, unattainable heights of Mount Olympus where its framers thunder with Thor and presumably cohabit with their fellow gods in overseeing the approved correctity (There—I've coined a word!) of things terrestrial. I know—I've misplaced a Scandinavian deity in Greece, but I couldn't resist the allure of alliteration (I've done it again)—and who is to say with certainty that the gods don't get around today as much as we mere mortals—or swallows—do?

However, history is truth, fact, reality, as established by reliable—if possible, unquestionable—primary sources. Secondary sources who have authenticated themselves as honest, accurate, and discriminating observers may give weight to alternative choices when they are found in agreement. Ancient mariners who charted their voyages in the fear of sea dragons and monsters and the dread falling-off place at the end of the world were revealed to be in error when Columbus and Magellan, with faith and courage, demonstrated that it wasn't so. It never had been so. It was myth, not history.

Then there was that story given currency during the twelfth and thirteenth centuries, particularly among the Crusaders, of a wonderful fountain of youth. The location was speculated to be in various places, and its seekers were numerous and avid—and always disappointed. Reports of those miraculous waters seem to have died out until the beginning of the 1500's. It was then that the Spanish explorers at their early bases in the Caribbean began to get exciting reports from the Indians about just such a fountain in the lands to the north of them. The intrepid Ponce de Leon thenceforth led an intrepid expedition in that direction. They discovered and named Florida, and they searched intrepidly for the fabled stream. They might just as well have been trepid, for their explorations revealed no such fountain. It simply wasn't so. It never had been so. It was myth, not history.

There is a parallel to our chic "history" writers to be found in our "authoritics" on times prehistoric—the embarrassing episode of the Piltdown Man. Evolutionary scientists tripped all over each other in concocting the details of the life and times of this Eanthropus, or "Dawn Man," as construed from some skull fragments found at Piltdown in England in 1912. They ascertained that he was from the pleistocene age, more than a quarter of a million years old. They "discovered" the crude stone tools that he used and many other "facts" about his life and times. Webster's 1947 Dictionary referred to him as: "An extinct species of man characterized by a retreating, apelike chin and thin cranial bones, but a human like cranium." They found what they very much wished to find. But, alas, when the fairy tales were all in place, skeptical analysis proved it wasn't so. A more recent Random House College Dictionary describes it as:

> A hypothetical early modern man whose existence, inferred from skull fragments found at Piltdown in SE England, in 1912, has now been completely discredited, the fragments being of modern origin.

(Come now—a quarter of a million years!?) The wish was father to the "discovery." It wasn't so. It never had been so. It was myth, not history.

Time and space would fail me to recount all the myths that men have credited as fact—or have been led by "authoritics" to believe were—or are—true. Now, that title, for example. "The Easter Bunny is Not Dead." The Easter Bunny could not be dead, of course, because there never was an Easter Bunny. I do not intend to split hares over this. He is just a myth, not history.

Now back to the term "revisionist history." It would appear plausible—nay, I would postulate that the only creditable history on the two areas of my research which follow is that which is supported by primary sources.

On the subject of Pearl Harbor, I submit that our intelligence services had cracked the Japanese code system long before December 7, 1941, and we—including the Commander-in-Chief, President Franklin D. Roosevelt—were following Japan's every move for many weeks as they worked toward that fatal day. And that the President did not endeavor to warn the sitting ducks at Pearl Harbor two months ahead of time—nor two weeks—nor two days—nor two hours.

On the subject of the conduct of United States foreign policy during World War II, we have President Roosevelt's personal plan, the "Great Design;" and we have the inexorable, tragic results for our nation and our world including, of course, Asia and Vietnam. Apologists who say that Roosevelt was constrained by desperate uncompromising circumstances to make the decisions he made disregard the fact that those choices were the ones he had at the outset announced his intentions of making.

We are going to survey some vital points of history—"revisionist" though it may be labeled—and in the process unmask some illusions which disinformation has relentlessly utilized to becloud truth. And we will find that some tales which have been miscast as fact simply were not so. They never had been so.

They were myth, not history.

Once Upon A Time . . . .

Once upon a time, longer ago than most people now living can recall, the Japanese government had a high security diplomatic message code called the Purple Code. This employed a machine to do all its enciphering and deciphering. And, behold, heroic young Americans broke this code so completely that they were able to build such machines and thus to intercept and decipher all such messages daily. Lo, more than ten months before the Japanese attack on Pearl Harbor the American ambassador to Tokyo had warned Washington of possible Japanese plans to make just such an attack in case of war between our countries—in accord with historic practice utilized by warriors of the Land of the Rising Sun to initiate at least three of their wars within less than half a century. And, hark! Our President's name was on the Navy Department list to receive every Japanese message on the day it was decoded; and, behold, he was one who read the "bomb plot" message two months before the attack and followed with eager interest as the spies in Hawaii sent messages replying to Tokyo's requests for the specific locations of ships in the harbor. And, alas, he told not the Army and Navy leaders at Pearl Harbor of this vital information.

And it came to pass that our brave soldiers and sailors suffered 3435 casualties, of whom 2326 were slain, and it was deemed necessary to cover up the fact that our President had known. And, lo, messages disappeared, and witnesses were brow-beaten into "forgetting" or changing stories. And once upon a time and twice upon a time and more—friendly investigations "found" that our President and his Washington deputies were "innocent" of any foreknowledge of the attack; and hapless leaders in Hawaii were removed from their commands and allowed unjustly to shoulder the blame and the shame in the eyes of an angry public.

And, yea, long years passed, and so did the President; and another Congressional committee—mostly friends of the President—looked at all the intercepted Japanese messages and the facts of the failure to warn Pearl Harbor—and said it wasn't so!

And once upon an earlier time, that self-same President, avowing to voters his hatred for war, plotted secretly, prior to the Japanese attack, to involve our nation in that which he professed to hate by endeavoring to goad Germany into attacking our ships. And at the very threshold of Pearl Harbor he was evidently going at it from another angle. The *Tampa Tribune* for December 4, 1987, had a UPI story from New York which said in part:

> President Franklin D. Roosevelt probably engineered the sensational leak of America's military-preparedness plans on the eve of World War II, even though it 'embarrassed and made a liar out of him,' *American Heritage* magazine reported Wednesday.

> The top-secret plans, headlined in front-page stories in *The Chicago Tribune* and *The Washington Times Herald* on Dec. 4, 1941, detailed top-secret plans for an army of 10 million, including an expeditionary force of 5 million men that would invade Europe to defeat Hitler.
>
> Code-named 'Rainbow Five,' the plans were drawn up at Roosevelt's order by the Joint Board of the Army and Navy.
>
> The stories were printed three days before the Japanese bombed Pearl Harbor and pulled the United States into World War II.
>
> 'Why would Roosevelt have deliberately leaked a sensitive military document that embarrassed and made a liar of him?' the magazine asked and then presented historian Thomas Fleming's theory that, frustrated by isolationist sentiments, the President wanted to 'goad Hitler' into declaring war before Britain and the Soviet Union were defeated.
>
> Fleming said the leak was so extensive and detailed that no other explanation fills all the holes in the puzzle as completely as FDR's complicity.
>
> 'Would a president who had already used faked maps and concealed from Congress the truth about the naval war in the Atlantic hesitate at one more deception—especially if he believed that war with Japan was imminent?' Fleming asked.

And more than once upon a time after our nation was in the war, this President worked secretly behind the scenes to undermine the leadership of nations that had traditionally been our friends and shared our interests in freedom and democracy—the British leader, Winston Churchill, the French leader, Charles DeGaulle, the Christian leader of China, Chiang Kai-shek, the leaders of Poland and the Baltic and other East European countries.

And verily—yea, verily—the President labored mightily and long, using all the resources of our nation available to him to build up the power of the cardinal Communist, that despicable dictator, Josef Stalin, erstwhile collaborator with Adolf Hitler in the infamous Nonaggression Pact, invader of Poland and Finland, appropriator of the Baltic States of Bessarabia, Latvia, and Lithuania, murderer of millions of small farmers in his own Russian Ukraine, master of millions of living dead in his slave-labor camps, and the herdsman of hotbeds of spies working in our government to steal diplomatic and military secrets for the Soviet Union—all of which the President well knew.

Once upon a time . . . .

Relying upon a preponderance of primary sources, I have gone behind the scenes and under the covers to attempt to interpret the implications and amplifications of these events. Why did President Roosevelt do these things? What have been the effects of this orientation of amorality on our nation, on the Soviet Union, on Europe, on Asia, and on the world? Are we trapped, or have we alternatives?

It would oft appear that the prevailing counsel is to hit the ejection seat and let the plane crash while we float away at leisure, dangling from our merry parachute. Now, I've never parachuted, and I've really never been all that eager to. I'll grant that if conditions necessitate jumping from a plane it's probably better to do it with a parachute than without one—unless speed is a paramount objective. However, we shall attempt to survey some more responsible—and palatable—choices that may serve to keep us and the plane together without a crash.

Thus there starkly stand three startling facets of history and its accounting which burst like atomic detonations from the war's lurid legend:

1. F.D.R. certainly tricked—and prevaricated—our nation into the war, including advance knowledge of the coming Japanese attack on Pearl Harbor.

2. F.D.R. collaborated with Stalin in the attainment of the Red tyrant's wartime and longtime objectives, as distinctly at cross-purposes with the democratic and freedom-loving aims of the President's own people and all the like aims and aspirations of our traditional allies. No other individual was so powerful an architect, shaping drastically and fatefully the destiny of Earth and its billions for the years during and since the war—and conceivably for ensuing centuries.

3. The dominant drafters of history and armadas of academe have denied—or unaccountably, been ignorant of the aforementioned facts, and have carried on as though these readily ascertainable data were nonexistent. This strange state of affairs seems to result from academic timidity or from impelling desire not to look facts in the face. "I don't want to believe it—and it's more comfortable this way," with the prostrate sleeping dogs. The building's not really on fire even though the alarm is sounding. The skunk has been demusked—surely it's been demusked!

Or the timidity may be academic and political gall.

Historical and political powers of great weight have contrived—with vast success—to keep FDR's activities and aims concealed from the world and from the American people - even at this late date beyond half a century since those events transpired.

From 1985 to 1991 upon the stage of Russian Communism rose a dictator with a new face—or so it seemed. General Secretary Mikhail S. Gorbachev could not be said to have "found religion," but he was a realist when he contemplated the shortcomings of Marxism as a system of supplying of consumer goods—and, mayhap, defense goods—for a vast population in a modern world. He was also the first real "politician" to present a "winning" face to world-wide Kremlin watchers. He galloped over Western leaders when public opinion polling took place in Western Europe. Indeed, there was certainly no comparison to be made between him and the evil Stalin and his line. We all wanted very much to hear the herald angels sing, proclaiming a great new day of peace and brotherhood.

But, alas, those of you who sing the strains of unilateral disarmament have chanted the same refrain about every single Communist dictator -including Stalin! The boy who cried "wolf" too often has, in this century, learned to intone soothingly "lamb" and "peace."

And, alack, other Red leaders there were for whom Mr. G's puncturing assumptions or presumptions about traditional Marxist-Leninist dogma possessed all the quaint charm of ham sandwiches at a bar mitzvah. Alas, Mr. Gorbachev was not a permanent fixture in his exalted position.

And the reform had its limits. Lithuanian citizens loudly voiced their resentments at the crushing of their nation by Stalin on the fiftieth anniversary of the Hitler-Stalin pact. And the Associated Press on August 29, 1989, reported that Gorbachev had warned Lithuanian leaders that they "have gone too far" in their demands for freedom and independence.

We must ever be mindful of the massacres in Beijing's Tiananmen Square when the impulse presents itself to make gratuitous assumptions as to benevolence manifested toward us by the leaders of international Communism. Indeed, even for so prosaic a chore as changing the wiring in one's home one would not assume that someone else had turned off the electricity.

Book I

President Roosevelt and the Pearl of Great Price

Chapter I
Preludes to Infamy—Sequels

U.S. Ambassador Grew, in Tokyo, to the State Department, January 27, 1941:

> The Peruvian Minister has informed a member of my staff that he has heard from many sources, including a Japanese source, that in the event of trouble breaking out between the United States and Japan, the Japanese intended to make a surprise attack against Pearl Harbor with all their strength and employing all their equipment. The Peruvian Minister considers the rumors fantastic. Nevertheless, he considered them of sufficient importance to convey the information to a member of my staff.

Secretary of War Stimson, Diary, November 25, 1941:

> Then at 12 o'clock we (viz., General Marshall and I) went to the White House where we were until nearly half past one. At the meeting were Hull, Knox, Marshall, Stark, and myself. There the President . . . brought up entirely the relations with the Japanese. He brought up the event that we were likely to be attacked perhaps (as soon as) next Monday, for the Japanese are notorious for making an attack without warning, and the question was what we should do. The question was how we should maneuver them into the position of firing the first shot without allowing too much danger to ourselves. It was a difficult proposition.

For the tragedy of December 7, 1941, there have developed two quite different theses as to responsibility among American leaders. The official wartime version—of, by, and for the ruling administration—portrayed infamous and bloodthirsty Japanese striking a totally unexpected blow at a base commanded by two criminally inept officers, General Short and Admiral Kimmel, who refused to cooperate with Washington or with each other to maintain an adequate defense and alertness in spite of the administration's best efforts to warn them and to prepare them. Postwar revelations, however, have outlined a version dramatically different and copiously documented with materials not even considered in the earlier portrayal.

This more up-to-date accounting possesses connotations more shocking than Halloween's most gruesome goblins; and it has a tendency to evoke foot stamping four letter word anger, frantic evasions and unconvincing denials.

This was somewhat the case some years ago when the father of one of my high school American history pupils called me—at the top of his voice—because his son had complained that I had presented documents in class relative to President Franklin D. Roosevelt's prior knowledge of the Japanese attack on Pearl Harbor and his "maneuverings" designed to that end. It was wrong, I was told, for a teacher to refer to such a subject, particularly since it was "all a lie." Furthermore, he was going to report me to higher authorities, a move which I agreed would be welcome on my part. I did, however, voice some dissent to the insinuation that I must be a "Communist" to suggest such things about "the greatest president we've ever had."

True to his word, the gentleman gave lurid accounts to our congressman, the State Superintendent of Public Instruction, the county school board, and the County Superintendent of Public Instruction. Then came the most amazing revelation of the entire episode, for none of them seemed even aware of the existence of the documentation nor of the facts of the case. And when one supervisor learned that relevant books were in the school library he forcefully suggested that they be removed from the shelves. The congressman indicated ignorance of the subject and checked with the Library of Congress. To his surprise he discovered, as he later wrote: "It seems that some historians have raised this question."

The dedicated historian and teacher of history is committed to the proposition that wisdom for the present and future is predicated upon an accurate knowledge of the past. From time to time those who have a vested interest in the events of history quite understandably find it to their advantage to manipulate the record so that incomplete or even erroneous conceptions are a temporary result. Many sincere persons, such as those mentioned heretofore and a host of their contemporaries, have thus been left with a wholly inadequate and misleading picture of the Pearl Harbor story. In the long run, it has never been found to be beneficial to a nation that its citizens and its leaders should build on a false interpretation of the past. The clarion call of the muse of history is found in the Biblical injunction, "You shall know the truth and the truth shall make you free." It is after a contemplation of these factors that I have decided to compose the following digest of theses and documents in a capsule form.

The principal lines of the story as it has developed from the series of investigations during and since the war are these:

1. Despite his many public declarations to the contrary, President Roosevelt devoted much effort during the late 1930's and early 1940's toward involvement of the United States in the war then beginning in Europe, and finally toward our participation in the

Pacific. For the President this was a radical departure from his erstwhile isolationist position which had caused him to boycott the London Economic Conference and in a 1932 speech before the New York State Grange to declare: "American participation in the League would not serve the highest purpose of the prevention of war and a settlement of international difficulties in accordance with fundamental American ideals. Because of these facts, therefore, I do not favor American participation."
(Public Papers of Franklin D. Roosevelt, Forty-Eighth Governor of the State of New York, p. 551)

2. After a succession of moves in the Atlantic theater, in great measure kept secret from the American Public, the President turned his major attention to the Pacific as a more promising gateway to U.S. involvement.

3. The President provided for the Japanese a tempting target for an attack, then he baited their government by incendiary diplomacy.

4. President Roosevelt was aware well in advance of the interest of Japan in Pearl Harbor as a surprise raid target, and for nearly twenty-four hours before the attack he and his top aides in Washington knew when and where it would come.

I shall present the documents and evidence relative to these points. Unfortunately, it is impossible to go much beyond speculation as to President Roosevelt's motivations in all of these matters. On no occasion did he make them public, and his private papers have in large measure been kept just that. The minority report of the Joint Congressional Committee in 1946 (p. 501) commented on the obvious:

> President Roosevelt's secretary, Miss Grace Tully, was permitted to determine for herself and the Committee and the country what portions of the official correspondence of the late President had any relevancy to Pearl Harbor. This could hardly be a satisfactory substitute for the responsibility placed upon the committee.

We do know from a number of sources (e.g. Charles A. Beard, Justice Hugo Black, and Ambassador William E. Dodd, as reported in Tansill's *Back Door to War*) of Roosevelt's concern over the 1938 Recession and his political reverses in the Congressional elections of that year, and we have testimony as to current discussions within the administration anent the economic effect of wartime production and conscription. We are also aware that at least by the summer of 1940 many Americans were sincerely fearful of the power of the Axis as a possible threat to U.S. security.

The Gallup Poll indicated in October 1940 an overwhelming desire by Americans that we stay out of war, with only 17% favoring entry on the eve of that year's election. Perhaps this gives some explanation of the President's concurrent public statements that were so at odds with the policies we shall review. On October 30 he included in a campaign speech these phrases well calculated to reassure the majority of voters:

> While I am talking to you, mothers and fathers, I give you one more assurance. I have said this before, but I shall say it again and again and again. Your boys are not going to be sent into any foreign wars.

On November 2 he said, "Your President says this nation is not going to war." On the next day he added, "The first purpose of our foreign policy is to keep our country out of war."

More honest than those who ignore the facts we shall be treating and who blandly deny any foreknowledge on President Roosevelt's part is Dr. Thomas A. Bailey of Stanford University. With approval, he says in his *The Man In The Street* (pp. 11-13):

> Franklin Roosevelt repeatedly deceived the American people during the period before Pearl Harbor . . . . He was like the physician who must tell the patient lies for the patient's own good . . . . The country was overwhelmingly noninterventionist to the very day of Pearl Harbor, and an overt attempt to lead the people into war would have resulted in certain failure and an almost certain ousting of Roosevelt in 1940, with a consequent defeat of his ultimate aims.
>
> A president who cannot trust the people with the truth betrays a certain lack of faith in the basic tenets of democracy. But because the masses are notoriously shortsighted and generally cannot see danger until it is at their throats, our statesmen are forced to deceive them into an awareness of their own long run interests. This is clearly what Roosevelt had to do, and who shall say that posterity will not thank him for it?

Now I shall proceed to the listing of documentation, some from reputable secondary sources, the great majority from primary sources.

LOSSES

Theobald, *The Final Secret of Pearl Harbor*, pp. 7-8:

> The results of the Japanese air attacks upon the U.S. Pacific fleet in Pearl Harbor on December 7, 1941, were as follows:
>
> **Battleships:**
> Arizona, total loss . . . ; Oklahoma, total loss . . . ; California, West Virginia, sank in upright position at their berths . . . much later raised, repaired, and returned to active war service; Nevada, beached . . . to prevent sinking in deep

water after extensive bomb damage—repaired and returned to active war service; Pennsylvania, Maryland, and Tennessee, all received damage but of a less severe character.

Smaller Ships:
Cruisers: Helena, Honolulu, and Raleigh were all damaged, but were repaired and returned to active war service;

Destroyers: Two damaged beyond repair; two others damaged but repaired and returned to active war service . . . .

Target Ship: Utah, former battleship, sank at her berth . . . .

Report of the Joint Committee on the Investigation of the Pearl Harbor Attack; Congress of the United States, pp. 64-5 (summarized)

U.S. military personnel casualties were: Navy, including Marine Corps, 2086 officers and enlisted men killed, 749 wounded; Army, including the Army Air Corps, 240 officers and enlisted men killed, 360 wounded. Total 3435. *Report of the Joint Committee on the Investigation of the Pearl Harbor Attack, Congress of the United States*, p. 553 (minority report):

> The fatal error of Washington authorities in this matter was to undertake a world campaign and world responsibilities without first making provision for the security of the United States, which was their prime constitutional obligation.

STEPS TOWARD WAR : OPEN AND SECRET

The wisdom of some of the following steps may be argued by proponents and opponents of U.S. neutrality at the time; there could be little controversy as to the direction they were taking us. It was not consistent with the President's statement: "The first purpose of our foreign policy is to keep our country out of war." On page 47 of W. H. Chamberlin's *America's Second Crusade* we find the following moves outlined as steps into war by President Roosevelt:

1. November, 1939–repeal of the arms embargo
2. September, 1940–fifty destroyer trade with Britain
3. March, 1940–Lend-Lease Act
4. January-March 1941–Secret American-British staff talks
5. April 24, 1941–institution of "patrols" in the North Atlantic
6. Sending American laborers to build a naval base in Northern Ireland
7. Early summer, 1941–blocking German credits in the U.S. and closing of consulates
8. July 7, 1941–occupation of Iceland by American troops

9. August 9-12, 1941–The Atlantic Conference
10. September 11, 1941—"shoot on sight" orders to American warships announced
11. November, 1941–authorization for arming of merchant ships and sending of merchant ships into war zones

Morgenstern, *Pearl Harbor,* pp. 109-111:

Lieut. Col. Henry C. Clausen, who had taken a world tour in 1944 to look for evidence in support of Secretary Stimson's thesis that blame for the Pearl Harbor disaster solely attached to the commanders on the spot, told the Congressional committee that his inquiries led him to the White House, but that he was discouraged from entering.

Clausen said that the statements of Army leaders convinced him there was 'an informal agreement but not a binding agreement' on the part of the United States to fight Japan if the British or Dutch were attacked.

'That may make sense to you; it didn't to me,' he told the committee.

'I suggested that the inquiry would lead to the White House, but I was told that it was beyond the scope of my function to investigate there.' He said that he was so informed by Col. William J. Hughes, assistant to the Army judge advocate general.

However strenuously it might be denied that the intention of Roosevelt was to circumvent constitutional limitations, the indisputable fact is that as soon as the staff agreements were drafted the Army and Navy drew up supplementary Pacific war plans of their own designed to carry out master strategy in concert with the British and Dutch. The joint Army and Navy basic war plan, which bore the short title 'Rainbow No. 5,' was approved by Stimson and Knox on the same dates upon which they approved the report on the Washington staff conversations, which bore the short title 'A B C -1.'

On the basis of Rainbow 5, the Navy basic war plan, known as 'WPL-46,' was promulgated May 25. The Pacific fleet's plan to support the basic Navy plan was distributed on July 25 and approved September 9 by the chief of naval operations. It was known as 'W P Pac - 26.' The Army also drew up a plan of operations to supplement Rainbow 5. This was approved by Chief of Staff Marshall on August 19.

The objectives of the joint Army-Navy plan were described by Adm. Turner, Navy war plans officer, in the following words:

'The plan contemplated a major effort on the part of both the principal associated powers against Germany initially. It was felt in the Navy Department that there might be a possibility of war with Japan without the involvement of Germany, but at some length and over a considerable period this matter was discussed and it was determined that in such a case the United States would, if possible, initiate efforts to bring Germany into the war against

> us in order that we would be able to give strong support to the United Kingdom in Europe. We felt that it was incumbent on our side to defeat Germany, to launch our principal efforts against Germany first, and to conduct a limited offensive in the Central Pacific, and a strictly defensive effort in the Asiatic.'

Courting War in the Atlantic

Report of the Joint Committee, Op. Cit., p 168 (majority report) May 24, 1941. Admiral Stark to Admiral Kimmel:

> Day before yesterday afternoon the President gave me an overall limit of 30 days to prepare and have ready an expedition of 25,000 men to sail for, and take the Azores. Whether or not there would be opposition I do not know but we have to be fully prepared for strenuous opposition. You can visualize the job particularly when I tell you that the Azores recently have been greatly reinforced. The Army, of course, will be in on this but the Navy and the Marines will bear the brunt. (This never materialized.)

The following materials may be best appreciated when it is remembered that ship sinkings have been instrumental on several occasions in propelling the United States into war. The sinking of the *Maine* prior to the Spanish American War and the loss of 114 Americans on the *Lusitania* during World War I are dramatic cases in point. Tansill's *Back Door to War*, pp. 608 and 614, provides accounts of relevant events:

> But this German policy of conciliation was sorely tried by incidents arising out of the establishment of a neutrality zone announced by the Panama Conference, October 3, 1939. This safety belt around the Americas south of Canada varied in width from 300 to 1000 miles. Belligerents were warned to refrain from naval action within that area, but no armed forces were stationed along the safety belt to enforce this legislation.
>
> In order to conciliate America the German Admiralty issued orders designed to prevent naval engagements within this safety belt. When the Admiralty wished to recede from this position, Hitler refused to permit any change of orders. Moreover, the Fuhrer adhered to this conciliatory policy even when American vessels adopted a course that must have enraged him. In December 1939 the German liner *Columbus* left Veracruz and was closely trailed by the U.S.S. *Tuscaloosa* which constantly broadcasted her position. This action compelled the Nazi captain to scuttle his ship some 450 miles east of Cape May. The same tactics were pursued by the U.S.S. *Broome* in trailing the *Rhein*, which also was scuttled by her captain. The freighter *Idarwild* was followed by the *Broome* until it was destroyed by H.M.S. *Diomede* (November 1940) with the *Broome* standing by to watch the result of her pursuit. The German government refrained from filing any protest at these actions.
>
> On November 13, 1941, the directives for conduct of German warships when encountering American naval vessels remained pacific: 'Engagements

with American naval or air forces are not to be sought deliberately; they are to be avoided as far as possible . . . If it is observed before a convoy is attacked that it is being escorted by American forces, the attack is not to be carried out.

Theobald, *The Final Secret of Pearl Harbor*, pp. 23-24:

Furthermore, in March, 1941, the already inferior Pacific fleet was further weakened by the detachment of three battleships, one aircraft carrier, four light cruisers, and eighteen destroyers for duty in the Atlantic; and in June, 1941, Washington gave serious consideration to the transfer of three additional battleships to the Atlantic. Such changes in fleet dispositions, in those critical diplomatic days, would never have been made without the President's approval.

Beard, *President Roosevelt and the Coming of the War 1941*, pp. 87-89, gives a copy of a letter from Senator Tobey of New Hampshire to President Roosevelt dated April 17, 1941. I include here some relevant excerpts:

On March 31 I introduced a joint resolution (S.J. Res, 62) to prohibit convoys. Later on that day, a man who has close contacts with the Government came to my office and asked me if I would be surprised to learn that United States convoys were already being employed. I replied that I could not believe that the President would for a moment permit this practice, in view of his statement that:

'Convoys mean shooting and shooting means war.'

This man left my office, and from then on I received a series of persistent reports that convoys were being employed . . . .

Mr. President, these persistent rumors have come to me repeatedly in the past few days from various sources, and yesterday I received a letter the contents of which I feel forced, as a public duty, to bring to the American people, and to the Congress. It comes from the Atlantic Seaboard, and reads as follows:

April 15
'My Dear Senator Tobey: I know you are against convoying by our Navy. Some information has come to me which has shocked me. I think I should pass it on to you.
'A young relative is in the Navy. He has been at sea on service. He was taken ill and put ashore in order to go to a hospital. I cannot tell you the name of the port. In fact, I should not write this at all, but I think you should know.

'He tells me that the United States Navy has been convoying ships for about 1 month. His ship was one of the convoys. If I tell you the name of the ship or the lad's name I would perhaps get him in trouble. He has been worried and thinks someone should know.

'He says that they in the service know that the President's delay on the subject of convoying—the "put off" as he expresses it, is because it is secretly going on.
'I trust you to use this information as you see fit, and only wish I could have given more details.'

Beard, Ibid, pp. 138-142:

The hopes of those who were working to speed up American participation in the war by aiding the Allies were raised to a high pitch in September, 1941, not by an Executive appeal to Congress for a declaration of war on Hitler, but by events at sea. On September 4, the Navy Department announced that a submarine of undetermined nationality had attacked the American destroyer *Greer* that morning in the Atlantic on its way to Iceland; that torpedoes had been fired at the vessel; that the *Greer* had counterattacked by dropping depth charges, with unknown results. The destroyer, the department explained, was operating as a part of the Atlantic patrol established during the summer by President Roosevelt and was carrying mail. Was this the 'attack' that would emancipate President Roosevelt from his commitment to the Democratic plank of 1940 against participating in foreign wars 'except in case of attack?' . . . .

For days the war of words went on in the press, American and Axis, while anxious observers in the United States waited for an official statement by President Roosevelt. The statement came on September 11 in the form of a radio broadcast.

'The *Greer*', the President said, 'was carrying American mail to Iceland. She was flying the American flag. Her identity as an American ship was unmistakable. She was then and there attacked by a German submarine. Germany admits that it was a German submarine . . . . I tell you the blunt fact that the German submarine fired first upon this American destroyer without warning, and with deliberate design to sink her'—at a point southeast of Greenland . . . .

Admiral Stark's report to the Senate Committee, which filled several typewritten pages presented an account of the *Greer* affair which made the President's statement of the case to the nation on September 11 appear in some respects inadequate, and in others, incorrect. The following summary gives the essential facts of the *Greer* incident as supplied by Admiral Stark to the Senate Committee:

While en route to Iceland with mail, passengers, and some freight, the *Greer* was informed by a British plane of the presence of a submerged submarine about ten miles directly ahead.

Acting on this information from the British plane, the *Greer* proceeded to trail the submarine, broadcasting its position.

This chase of the submarine went on for over three hours; the British plane dropped four depth charges in the vicinity of the submarine and departed, leaving the *Greer* to continue the hunt, zigzagging and searching.

The *Greer* thus had held contact with the submarine for three hours and twenty-eight minutes; the submarine fired a torpedo which crossed the *Greer* about 100 yards astern.

Then the *Greer* 'attacked the submarine with a pattern of eight depth charges;" to which the submarine replied with another torpedo that missed the Greer.

After losing sound contact at this time with the submarine, the *Greer* started searching for it, made contact again about two hours later, and 'attacked immediately with depth charges,' without discoverable results.

The *Greer* thereupon continued its search for about three hours more and proceeded to its destination, Iceland.

Beard, Ibid. pp. 430-431:

September 22, 1941. Admiral Stark to Admiral Thomas Hart, Commander of the Asiatic Fleet:

. . . So far as the Atlantic is concerned we are all but, if not actually, in it. The President's speech of September 11, 1941 put the matter squarely before the country and outlined what he expected of the Navy. We were ready for this; in fact our orders had been issued . . . . In a nutshell, we are now escorting convoys regularly from the United States to points in the Iceland area, where these convoys are picked up by the British and escorted to the British Isles. In addition to our own escort vessels, the Canadians are participating. Both forces (Canadian and our own) are operating under King's direction . . . .

September 23, 1941. Admiral Stark to Admiral Kimmel on the 'shooting orders' for the Atlantic and the Southeast Pacific sub-area:

At the present time the President has issued "shooting orders" only for the Atlantic and Southeast Pacific sub-area.'

Beard, Ibid., pp. 434-442, begins with questioning before the Joint Congressional Committee on Pearl Harbor:

Mr. Gearhart. Now you described the conditions as existing on the 7th day of November 1941 as indicating a condition of war. Now, I am asking you when did the condition come into being?

Admiral Stark. I think perhaps I might read a brief which I had made up thinking it might be of use to the Committee—primarily I wanted it for myself to get the sequence—of the hemispheric defense orders . . .

Mr. Gearhart. Was there an order commanding commanders of American ships in the Atlantic to fire upon German submarines or surface ships under any conditions?

Admiral Stark. There was.

Mr. Gearhart. Who issued that order?

Admiral Stark. I did, by direction of the President.

Mr. Gearhart. And when was it issued?

Admiral Stark (reading): "'On October 8, 1941 by dispatch 082335 the Chief of Naval Operations ordered the above outlined plan executed at 1400 G.C.T.' that is Greenwich Civil Time—

'11 October 1941. The plan remained in effect until December 11, 1941, at which time the Chief of Naval Operations by dispatch 111550 ordered the above outlined plan canceled and replaced by WPL 46, Navy Basic War Plan Rainbow No.5.' . . . .

Admiral Stark's digest of war orders, or instructions, between April 21, 1941, and September 26, 1941, may be summarized as follows:

I. The first plan described by Admiral Stark, promulgated at the direction of the President, April 21, 1941, and made effective in the Atlantic on April 24, if cautious and limited in form, was explicit in its direction . . . .

The text of Admiral Stark's digest of this project follows Navy Hemisphere Defense Plan #2 (WPL-49), promulgated April 21, 1941, issued by the Chief of Naval Operations at the direction of the President, was based on the general concept:

Entrance into the Western Hemisphere by Naval vessels and aircraft of belligerent Powers, other than of those powers which have sovereignty over Western Hemisphere Territory, will be viewed as actuated by a possibly unfriendly intent toward territory or shipping within the Western Hemisphere.

[–thus covering territory and shipping belonging to other countries with possessions in the hemisphere as well as the United States.]

The specific tasks assigned the Naval Operating Forces were:

(a) Trail naval vessels and aircraft of belligerent Powers (other than of those Powers which have sovereignty over Western Hemisphere Territory), and broadcast in plain language their movements at four hour intervals, or oftener if necessary.' . . . .

II. The second plan listed by Admiral Stark, called Hemisphere Defense Plan #4 (WPL-51)1 was issued on July 11, 1941, at the direction of the President . . . .

When the order to execute this plan was issued, Change #1 had been incorporated. The tasks assigned to the Atlantic Fleet were:

(a) Protect United States and Iceland flag shipping against hostile attack, by escorting, covering, and patrolling, as required by circumstances, and by destroying hostile forces which threaten such shipping.

(b) Escort convoys of United States and Iceland flag shipping (including shipping of any nationality which may join such convoys, between United States ports and bases and Iceland).

(c) Provide protection and sea transportation for the initial movements and continued support of United States overseas garrisons.

(d) Trail naval vessels and aircraft of belligerent Powers (other than of those Powers which have sovereignty over Western Hemisphere Territory and other than belligerent vessels and aircraft involved in encounters in executing 2, b, and c): and broadcast in plain language their movements at four hour intervals, or oftener if necessary. Amplify such broadcasts by encrypted dispatch to the Chief of Naval Operations.

Trail merchant vessels of belligerent Powers (other than those Powers which have sovereignty over Western Hemisphere Territory), if suspected of acting as supply ships for, or otherwise assisting the operations of, the naval vessels or aircraft of such belligerents. Report the movements of such vessels to the Chief of Naval Operations . . . .

September 13, Chief of Naval Operations informed the Commander in Chief of the Atlantic Fleet that 'the President had modified previous instructions regarding convoy and escort, and that the United States Naval vessels could escort convoys in which there was no United States or Iceland flag vessels and that United States flag vessels could be escorted by Canadian ships.' . . . .

Admiral Stark's digest of Plan #5-WPL-52, issued September 26, and in force from October 11, to December 11, 1941, follows:

The tasks assigned the Atlantic Fleet were:

. . . (d) Trail merchant vessels suspected of supplying or otherwise assisting operations of German or Italian naval vessels or aircraft. Report the movements of such vessels to the Chief of Naval Operations.' . . . .

After Admiral Stark had finished reading Plan #5, Mr. Gearhart resumed his questioning:

Mr. Gearhart. Now, is this the order that you made pursuant to the direction of the President under which the Navy began to wage war in the Atlantic?

Admiral Stark. It is the order under which we operated and under which we told the Germans, and Italians in the later stages, that if they came to the westward of the 26 Meridian, as I recall, that their intent would be regarded as hostile and they would be dealt with accordingly, and regarding which the President had previously informed the country.

Mr. Gearhart. Then pursuant to this order shells were exchanged by American surface warships carrying American flags and German submarines?

Admiral Stark. Yes, sir; we attacked German submarines under this order.

THE TURN TO JAPAN: WE'D RATHER FIGHT THAN NOT SWITCH

It should be remembered that modern Japan since its opening by Commodore Perry in 1854 has displayed a penchant for initiating its wars by surprise attacks—particularly against the opponent's navy—prior to the formal declaration of war. The most dramatic example of this tactic was the attack on the Russian fleet at Port Arthur in February of 1904. In the case of Pearl Harbor, our own air arms had conducted dry run simulated attacks over the base, and predictions had been made that Japan would strike there in the event of hostilities between her and the United States. In October of 1941, the Russian spy Sorge reported to the Kremlin Japanese plans for an attack on Pearl Harbor within 60 days should hostilities appear imminent. This report was transmitted to President Roosevelt and his top commanders in Washington.

Theobald, Op. Cit., p. 43:

> Ambassador Grew, Tokyo, to State Department, January 27, 1941: 'The Peruvian Minister has informed a member of my staff that he has heard from many sources, including a Japanese source, that in the event of trouble breaking out between the United States and Japan, the Japanese intended to make a surprise attack against Pearl Harbor with all their equipment. The Peruvian Minister considers the rumors fantastic. Nevertheless, he considered them of sufficient importance to convey the information to a member of my staff.'

Report of the Joint Committee (Congress), Op. Cit., p. 506 (minority report):

> At least as early as October 8, 1940, President Roosevelt believed that affairs had reached such a state that the United States would become involved in a war with Japan. On that day Admiral Richardson asked the President 'if we were going to enter the war.' According to the Admiral's account the President replied—'that if the Japanese attacked Thailand, or the Kra Peninsula, or the Dutch East Indies we would not enter the war, that if they even attacked the Philippines he doubted whether we would enter the war, but that they (the Japanese) could not always avoid making mistakes and that as the war continued and the area of operations expanded sooner or later they would make a mistake and we would enter the war.'

Beard, Op. Cit., p. 293, quotes from an October 8, 1944, *New York Times* account of an interview with Mrs. Eleanor Roosevelt:

> Dec. 7 was just like any of the other D-days to us. We clustered at the radio and waited for more details—but it was far from the shock it proved to the country in general. We had expected something of the sort for a long time.

Report of the Joint Committee (Congress), Op. Cit., pp. 522-523 (minority report):

High authorities in Washington definitely knew from a message received from Ambassador Winant at 10:40 A.M. December 6, 1941 (Washington time) that two large Japanese forces had been seen sailing toward the Kra Peninsula and were distant only fourteen hours in time. Washington authorities should have known, therefore, that this would bring the strategic principle of what to do about Hawaii into immediate military calculations. They took no steps to alert Hawaii.

Congress, Ibid., p. 521:

There is no evidence in the record before the Committee that President Roosevelt, Secretary Hull, Secretary Stimson, and/or Secretary Knox expected at any time prior to December 7 a formal declaration of war on the United States by Japan in case the diplomatic negotiations came to a break. Indeed, all the evidence bearing on expectations in Washington as to Japan's probable methods of making war point to the belief of the Administration that Japan would begin with a surprise attack.

For example, Secretary Hull on November 25 and November 28 at a meeting of 'high officials' when he stated that the matter of safeguarding our national security was in the hands of the Army and Navy, 'expressed his judgment that any plans for our military defense would include the assumption that the Japanese might make the element of surprise a central point in their strategy, and also might attack at various points simultaneously with a view to demoralizing efforts of defense and of coordination for purposes thereof' (*Peace and War*, p. 144).

Speaking to Ambassador Halifax on November 29, Secretary Hull said that it would be a—'serious mistake . . . to make plans of resistance without including the possibility that Japan may move suddenly and with every possible element of surprise . . . that the Japanese recognize that their course of unlimited conquest . . . is a desperate gamble and requires the utmost boldness and risk.' (*Peace and War*, 1943, pp. 144-145).

Ambassador Grew reported to Hull on November 3–

'Japan may resort with dangerous and dramatic suddenness to measures which might make inevitable war with the United States.' (*Peace and War*, p. 775).

Dangling The Bait

Congress, Ibid., p. 543:

The decision to base the fleet at Pearl Harbor was made by the President in March 1940, over the protest of Admiral Richardson.

Congress, Ibid., pp. 521-522:

Neither the diplomatic negotiations nor the intercepts and other information respecting Japanese designs and operations in the hands of the United States authorities warranted those authorities in excluding from defense measures or from orders to the Hawaiian commanders the probability of an attack on Hawaii. On the contrary, there is evidence to the effect that such an attack was, in terms of strategy, necessary from the Japanese point of view and in fact highly probable, and that President Roosevelt was taking the probability into account—before December 7.

The fleet was stationed at Pearl Harbor in a large measure, if not entirely, for the purpose of exercising a deterring effect on the aggressive propensities of the Japanese Government during the diplomatic negotiations and of making the Government more likely to yield to the diplomatic representations of the United States in matters of policy. This was done contrary to the advice of the Commander in Chief of the U.S. Fleet, Admiral Richardson (who was removed because of protest on that issue), and with which Admiral William D. Leahy, former Chief of Naval Operations, agreed. (Tr. vol. 6, p.916). The fleet could produce this effect only as an instrument of war that constituted a potential threat to the Japanese; that is, a powerful instrument which could be used effectively to strike Japanese armed forces if they moved too far southward in the direction of British, Dutch, and/or American possessions in that region.

Having determined to move far southward and having moved far on the way early in December toward that region, the Japanese were warned by every principle of sound naval strategy to destroy, if possible, the American fleet at Hawaii on their left flank.

As Prime Minister Churchill said, in an address to the House of Commons on January 27, 1942, with reference to the Atlantic Conference and British strategic decisions as time went on after that Conference:

It must also be remembered that over the whole Pacific scene brooded the great power of the United States Fleet, concentrated at Hawaii. It seemed very unlikely that Japan would attempt the distant invasion of the Malay Peninsula, the assault upon Singapore, and the attack upon the Dutch East Indies, while leaving behind them in their rear this great American Fleet.'

President Roosevelt recognized this strategic consideration as shown by his message to Chiang Kai-shek as follows:

'Meanwhile we are exchanging views with the British Government in regard to the entire situation and the tremendous problems which are presented, with a view to effective coordinating of efforts in the most practicable way possible . . . .

'Indirectly influencing that situation: American military and naval defensive forces in the Philippine Islands, which are being steadily increased, and the United States Fleet at Hawaii, lying as they do along the flank of any

Japanese military movement into China from Indo-China, are ever present and significant factors in the whole situation.'

Beard, Op. Cit., p. 415:

Apparently Admiral Richardson was removed from his command of the Pacific Fleet by President Roosevelt on the ground that he opposed basing the fleet at Pearl Harbor. Admiral Richardson was convinced that this policy was dangerous to the security of the United States, as, in fact, it proved to be, tragically.

Report of the Joint Committee (Congress), Op. Cit., pp. 266B-266C—"Additional Views of Mr. Keefe" (a member of the majority):

During the year 1941 the United States Pacific Fleet was based in Pearl Harbor in the Hawaiian island of Oahu . . . . There gradually emerged evidence of the President's decision to retain the Fleet in the Hawaiian area to deter Japan from aggression in the Far East. The Commander in Chief of the Fleet, Admiral J.O. Richardson, protested the decision with a vigor which caused him to be relieved of command. He believed that the readiness of man and ships of the Fleet for war operations would impress Japan rather than its presence in Hawaii, where facilities to render it ready for war were greatly inferior to those available on the west coast. Richardson was succeeded in command by Admiral H.E. Kimmel in February 1941 . . . Pearl Harbor was the only anchorage in the Hawaiian area offering any security. It was then, however, an extremely deficient naval base. Its exposed position rendered concealment of fleet movements practically impossible in an area filled with Japanese agents. The Army's equipment for antiaircraft defense was meager. The local Army-Navy defense forces did not have sufficient long-range patrol planes to perform effective distant reconnaissance, even if the patrol planes of the fleet were made available to augment the handful of Army reconnaissance planes.

Under these circumstances, the position of the Fleet in the Hawaiian area was inherently untenable and dangerous . . . . Once the ships were in Pearl Harbor, with its single channel, they were a target for any successfully launched air attack from carrier-borne planes . . . .

Although the Fleet was placed by the President in the Hawaiian area in 1940 as an implement of diplomacy and as a deterrent to Japan, its strength was appreciably reduced in April and May of 1941. At that time, one aircraft carrier, three battleships, four cruisers and eighteen destroyers were detached from the Pacific Fleet and transferred to the Atlantic.

Thumbing Our Nose At Japan

Congress, Ibid., pp. 266N-2660:

The concept of an 'incident' as a factor which would unify public opinion behind an all-out war effort either in the Atlantic or Pacific had influenced the thinking of officials in Washington for a long time. Many plans which might have produced an incident were from time to time discussed and considered. As early as October 10, 1940, Secretary Knox had advised Admiral Richardson, then Commander-in-Chief of the Pacific Fleet, of a plan the President was considering to shut off all trade between Japan and North and South America. This would be accomplished by means of a patrol of American ships in two lines extending from Hawaii westward to the Philippines, and from Samoa toward the Dutch East Indies (R. 792). This plan was to be instituted in the event Japan retaliated against Great Britain upon the reopening of the Burma Road scheduled for October 17, 1940 (R.792). Admiral Richardson was amazed at this proposal and stated that the Fleet was not prepared to put such a plan into effect, nor for the war which would certainly result from such a course of action (R. 793).

On February 11, 1941, the Chief of Naval Operations in a Memorandum for the President, described the President as considering a plan to send a detachment of vessels to the Far East and perhaps to permit a 'leak' that they were going out there (exhibit 106). He quoted the President in the same memorandum as stating that he would not mind losing one or two cruisers, but that he did not want to take a chance on losing five or six. Again, in a letter of April 19, 1941 the Chief of Naval Operations quoted the President as saying to him:

> Betty, just as soon as those ships come back from Australia and New Zealand, or perhaps a little before, I want to send some more out. I just want to keep them popping up here and there and keep the Japs guessing (exhibit 106) . . . .

On July 25, 1941 the chief of Naval Operations wrote Admiral Kimmel to the effect that he might be called upon to send a carrier-load of planes to Russia via one of the Asiatic Russian ports (exhibit 106). 'I don't know that you will, but the President has told me to be prepared for it, and I want you to have the thought.' Admiral Kimmel replied to this suggestion as follows:

> I entertain no doubt that such an operation, if discovered (as is highly probable), will be tantamount to initiation of a Japanese-American war. If we are going to take the initiative in commencing such a war, I can think of more effective ways for gaining initial advantage. In short, it is my earnest conviction that use of a carrier to deliver aircraft to Asiatic Russian ports in the present period of strained relations is to invite war. If we have decided upon war it would be far better to take direct offensive action. If for reasons of political expediency, it has been determined to force Japan to fire the first shot, let us choose a method which will be more advantageous to ourselves'(exhibit 106).

On July 31, 1941, Admiral Stark sent Admiral Kimmel a copy of a letter to Captain Charles N. Cooke as follows:

> . . . The Iceland situation may produce an 'incident.' You are as familiar with that and the President's statements and answers at press conferences as I am. Whether or not we will get an 'incident' because of the protection we are giving Iceland and the shipping which we must send in support of Iceland and our troops, I do not know.

After his return from the Atlantic Conference with Churchill in August of 1941, President Roosevelt presented to Japan a shoulder bearing a prominent chip. (*Congress*, Op. Cit., (minority report), p. 509:

> In his statement to the Japanese Ambassador on Sunday, August 17, 1941 . . . President Roosevelt warned Japan against further attempts to dominate 'neighboring countries,' not merely the possessions of the United States, and used diplomatic language which, according to long-established usages, had only one meaning, namely, that such further attempts would result in a conflict with the United States. His statement read: this Government (of the United States) now finds it necessary to say to the Government of Japan that if the Japanese Government takes any further steps in pursuance of a policy or program of military domination by force or threat of force of neighboring countries, the Government of the United States will be compelled to take any and all steps which it may deem necessary toward safeguarding the legitimate rights and interests of the United States and American nationals and toward insuring the safety and security of the United States. [Foreign Relations of the United States: Japan, vol.11, pp. 556-557.]

Congress, Op. Cit., (minority report) pp. 501-502:

> A modus vivendi was under discussion with Japan in November 1941 to run for 3 months. This had been strongly urged by the War and Navy authorities in order to supply absolutely essential time for preparation. Secretary Stimson and Knox went over the terms of this document and advised Secretary Hull that it adequately protected our interest.
>
> Suddenly the modus vivendi was dropped from the agenda and there was substituted the Hull message which was followed shortly after by the attack on Pearl Harbor. *Congress*, Op. Cit., (minority report), pp. 509-510:
>
> On November 26, 1941, Secretary Hull, with the approval of President Roosevelt, rejected the Japanese proposal of November 20 for a temporary agreement, sometimes called a modus vivendi . . . and presented to Japan his memorandum of that date, the Secretary recognized, and said, that there was then 'practically no possibility of an agreement being achieved with Japan.' Having reached this conclusion, the Secretary, according to his account of what happened, declared on November 25 and on November 28, at meetings of high officials of the Government, 'that the matter of safeguarding our national security was in the hands of the Army and Navy.' (*Peace and War*, 1943, p. 144.) This was presumptively a warning to the War Department and

the Navy Department to make ready for war.

The circumstances and details of the August 17 message were concealed from the public, as was the case with the subsequent November 26 ultimatum outlined below from Theobald, *The Final Secret of Pearl Harbor*, pp. 20-22:

> On November 26, 1941, Secretary Hull handed the Japanese Ambassadors the note which purported to set forth the American proposals for resolving the issues between the two countries. Stripped of its diplomatic verbiage and plainly stated, the note suggested that, in exchange for a new trade agreement and the unfreezing of each other's assets, Japan agree to: (1) the acceptance of complete defeat in the Sino-Japanese war, by the withdrawal of all her forces from China; (2) her tacit surrender to the economic encirclement, by a similar withdrawal from French Indo-China, whose inviolability would thereafter be respected; (3) her participation in a nonaggression treaty, whose practical effect would be to guarantee the following lands from attack: the Philippines, Siberia, the Dutch East Indies, China, Thai; (4) the abolition of the Japanese-created puppet governments in China and Manchukuo, by promising with the United States to support no government in China but that of Chiang Kai-shek; (5) the practical abrogation of Japanese obligations to Germany and Italy under the provisions of the Tripartite Treaty . . . .
>
> These American proposals were absolutely devoid of diplomatic finesse . . . . The only possible conclusion is that President Roosevelt wanted to be absolutely sure that Japan's answer would be a declaration of war. He used an iron-shod club instead of a diplomatic rapier to attain his purpose.
>
> Everyone concerned recognized that this note put an end to the Kurusu-Nomura negotiations, and that war was inevitable. Secretary Hull at once informed the heads of the Army and Navy that diplomatic negotiations had failed, and that further action must be the responsibility of the Armed Forces. Tokyo, by secret dispatch . . . immediately told the Japanese Ambassadors that the American proposals were totally unsuited as a basis for future negotiations.

Congress, Op. Cit., p.559:

> Secretary Stimson called up Secretary Hull early in the morning of November 27 and Secretary Hull declared positively: 'I have washed my hands of it and it is now in the hands of you and Knox—the Army and the Navy.'

On pages 520-521 Beard gives a transcript from a hearing of a Congressional Committee on April 9, 1946:

> Senator Ferguson. Then I go to page 27 (page 46) of his (Diary of Secretary Stimson) memorandum. This is on November 25. This is the day before the Secretary of State sent his message to the Japanese. He is quoting the President:
>
> 'Then at 12 o'clock, General Marshall and I went to the White House where we were until nearly half-past one. At the meeting were Hull, Knox, Marshall, Stark, and myself. There the President, instead of bringing up the

Victory Parade . . . brought up entirely the relations with the Japanese. He brought up the event that we were likely to be attacked perhaps (as soon as) next Monday, for the Japanese are notorious for making an attack without warning, and the question was what we should do. The question was how we should maneuver them into the position of firing the first shot without allowing too much danger to ourselves. It was a difficult position.'

Do you recall that discussion with the President?

General Marshall. Yes Sir . . . .

Senator Ferguson. This takes place before we sent the message of the 26th.

General Marshall. Yes, sir.

Beard, Ibid., pp. 522-23, continuing the same hearing:

Senator Ferguson . . . . Mr. Stimson said at the bottom of page 47:

I pointed out to the President that he had already taken the first steps toward an ultimatum in notifying Japan way back last summer that if she crossed the border into Thailand, she was violating our safety, and therefore he had only to point out (to Japan) that to follow any such expedition was a violation of a warning we had already given. So Hull is to go to work on preparing that.'

Now, I take it he was talking about the memorandum and the conversation he had on the 27th (17th) of August. That is when the President returned from the Atlantic Conference.

We had taken, as Mr. Stimson defines it, the first step in an ultimatum, and that if America wanted to, we could rely upon that particular message as saying–

We have warned you. Therefore if you do anything you take the first step and fire the first shot.

Is that correct? Is that a fair analysis?

General Marshall. I think that is the rough idea of the thing; yes.

Beard, Ibid., p. 519:

Hence, as Mr. Stimson later told the Congressional Committee in 1946, the War Cabinet confronted a delicate situation on November 25, 1941:

One problem troubled us very much. If you know that your enemy is going to strike you, it is not usually wise to wait until he gets the jump on you by taking the initiative. In spite of the risk involved, however, in letting the Japanese fire the first shot, we realized that in order to have the full support of the American people it was desirable to make sure that the Japanese be the ones to do this so that there should remain no doubt in anyone's mind as to who were the aggressors. We discussed at this meeting the basis on which this country's position could be most clearly explained to our own people and to the world, in case we had to go into the fight quickly because of some sudden move on the part of the Japanese.'

Congress, Op. Cit., (minority report), pp. 498 and 500:

These difficulties were supplemented by even greater ones stemming from Presidential restraints on the Committee and from the partisan character of the Committee itself.

Even before the Committee commenced its work, it was confronted with an order issued on August 28, 1945, and signed by President Truman, which severely limited the power of the Committee to gain access to the full facts. The order is as follows (Tr., Vol. 1, p. 26):

August 28, 1945

Memorandum for—

The Secretary of State.

The Secretary of War.

The Secretary of the Navy.

The Attorney General.

The Joint Chiefs of Staff.

The Director of the Budget.

The Director of the Office of War Information.

Appropriate departments of the Government and the Joint Chiefs of Staff are hereby directed to take such steps as are necessary to prevent release to the public, except with the specific approval of the President in each case, of — Information regarding the past or present status, technique or procedures, degree of success attained, or any specific results of any crypt analytic unit acting under the authority of the United States Government or any department thereof.

Restricted . . . Harry S. Truman

It was not until October 23, 1945, that President Truman made the order less stringent by a new order. The modification left much to be desired . . . .

This firm refusal by the Committee majority, consisting of six Democrats as against four Republicans, at the very outset to allow the scope to individual members even with every safeguard proposed against the alleged danger of abuse was both unfortunate and disquieting.

Everything that has since developed must be viewed in the light of this iron curtain that was then imposed.

Chapter II

Infamy—Infinitely Itemized

Breaking of the Japanese Code

The Library of Congress, Washington, D.C., Legislative Reference Service, D 521 U.S. B Main File Copy

> *The Breaking of the Japanese Code.* Sometime before July 1941 the War and Navy Departments succeeded in breaking the Japanese diplomatic (Purple) code. The result of this successful crypt analysis was part of the mass of intercepted and decoded Japanese messages which were known by the code name of "Magic."

Theobald, Op. Cit., p. 32:

> The Japanese Purple Code
>
> The Japanese high-security communication systems were all enciphered codes. The Purple Code differed from the others in that it employed a machine to accomplish its enciphering and deciphering.
>
> Washington broke this Purple Code so completely that not only was the code recovered and the cipher recognized as machine controlled, but the mechanics of the machine were also fully diagnosed. As a consequence, a number of Purple cipher machines were fabricated for use by American and British decrypting units.

Keeping Hawaii In The Dark About Japanese Messages And Plans, Theobald, Ibid., pp. 36-37:

> When the Purple machines became available in Washington, at least one was shipped to London. Two machines were retained by the Communications Intelligence Unit in the Navy Department, and two by the Signal Intelligence Service in the War Department. This permitted each of the Washington decrypting units to have one machine always set for the cipher of the current twenty-four hours, with the other at hand for use on the traffic of the preceding and other earlier such periods.

In April, 1941, the last machine available in the Navy Department was shipped to the Commandant of the Sixteenth Naval District in the Philippines; additional personnel, required to fill out a complete decrypting unit, accompanied the machine. The organization was established in the caves on Corregidor Island. The information contained in the outgoing Tokyo diplomatic messages was thus assured to the Commander-in-Chief of the Asiatic Fleet and the Commanding General of the U.S. Army Forces in the Philippines. There was no Purple Machine for Hawaii.

Several thoughts immediately come to mind. First, when orders for the manufacture of these machines were placed in Washington, why did they not provide for two or three spares? If the thought of the spares had been overlooked, the later fabrication of an additional machine could not have been too lengthy a job. In any event, why not take care of American needs, including Hawaii, before giving any of these Purple machines to the British, who were not our allies at the time? There is one assured fact: these self-evident solutions to the problem of providing one or more Purple machines for the Hawaiian Commanders are too obvious to have been overlooked when the decisions regarding the allocation of the machines were being made.

Report of the Joint Committee (Congress), Op. Cit., p. 521 (minority report):

The dissemination of magic materials did not include the commanders at Hawaii, but on a few occasions materials derived therefrom was dispatched by the Navy Department to Admiral Kimmel. The War Department did not send the magic to the field. A large amount of other intelligence obtained from various sources within and without the country was not sent to either of the commanders in Hawaii.

Theobald, Op. Cit., pp. 25-26:

In August, 1945, certain opinions of the Naval Court of Inquiry and the action of the Secretary of the Navy on those opinions were published. The Court criticized Admiral Stark's judgment because: he failed, during the critical period between November 26 and December 7, 1941, to transmit to Admiral Kimmel important information which he had regarding the Japanese situation; he did not immediately transmit, on December 7, the fact that a message had been received which appeared to indicate that a break in diplomatic relations was imminent, and that an attack in the Hawaiian area might be expected soon . . . .

The next day, at least one Washington, D.C., newspaper carried the Admiral's reply to these strictures. He said that his conscience was entirely clear, because all his official actions in the days before Pearl Harbor had been governed by 'higher authority.' Admiral Stark repeated that statement, at least once, in private correspondence. During those days, President Roosevelt was the only naval authority higher in rank than Admiral Stark.

Report of the Joint Committee (Congress), Op. Cit., pp. 229-230 (majority report):

The fact that General Marshall decided on the basis of the intercepts of Japanese messages made available on or before 11:25 o'clock on the morning of December 7, to send an urgent war warning to the outpost commanders is itself evidence that, despite previous messages to outpost commanders, Washington authorities recognized that their knowledge of these intercepts and their minute direction of affairs placed an obligation on them to convey precise information to outpost commanders, and to make sure that they were on an all-out alert for war. Owing to inexcusable delays in Washington this final warning to General Short did not reach him until after the Japanese attack.

General Marshall failed to use the scrambler telephone on his desk to call General Short in Hawaii on Sunday morning, December 7, nearly 2 hours before the attack, and give him the same information which he sent in the delayed telegram which reached General Short after the attack.

Congress, Ibid., "Additional Views of Mr. Keefe" pp. 266L-266M:

(Quoting from Committee records)

Mr. Keefe: Well, now let me put it in another way. You have now stated that it was your responsibility as Chief of Staff to see to it that General Short out there in Hawaii, which you have described as being your bastion of defense, to see that he was alerted, and if he misinterpreted your order to see that that order was carried out.

General Marshall. That is my responsibility, sir.

Mr. Keefe. Now, I have stated it correctly, haven't I?

Mr. Keefe continues his commentary:

It was the responsibility of General Marshall to see that General Short was properly alerted. General Short, after being ordered to report his state of readiness to General Marshall, was entitled to assume that this state of readiness was satisfactory to the Chief of Staff unless he heard to the contrary. Neither General Marshall, General Gerow nor Secretary of War Stimson made any criticism or suggestion to General Short about the condition of his alert in Hawaii in the ten-day period prior to the attack. Because of their silence General Short was led to believe that the Chief of Staff approved his alert against sabotage.

Who Regularly Received All The Intercepted Japanese Messages?

Theobald, Op. Cit., p. 34

There were seven recipients of Magic on the Navy Department Distribution list, and six on that of the War Department. Fourteen finished copies of each message were prepared, and OP-20 GZ and the Signal Intelligence Service each supplied the other with seven copies of every message which it processed. The recipients were:

Navy Department Distribution	War Department Distribution
President Roosevelt	Secretary Hull
Secretary Knox	Secretary Stimson
Admiral Stark	General Marshall
Rear Admiral Noyes	Brig. General Gerow
Rear Admiral Turner	Brig. General Miles
Captain Wilkinson	Colonel Bratton
Commander McCollum	

Report of the Joint Committee (Congress), Op. Cit. pp. 520-521 (The quote here is taken from the report of the Minority. With the exception of the final sentence, the identical text is found in the report of the Majority, p.180):

> The 'magic' intelligence was regarded as preeminently confidential and the policy with respect to its restricted distribution was dictated by a desire to safeguard the secret that the Japanese diplomatic codes were being broken. Delivery of the English texts of the intercepted messages was limited, within the War Department, to the Secretary of War, the Chief of Staff, the Chief of the War Plans Division, and the Chief of the Military Intelligence Division; within the Navy, to the Secretary of the Navy, the Chief of Naval Operations, the Chief of the War Plans Division, and the Director of Naval Intelligence; to the State Department; and to the President's naval aide for transmittal to the President. By agreement within the Army and Navy in Washington, the Army was responsible for the distribution of magic within the War department and to the State Department; the Navy for distribution within the Navy Department and to the White House.
>
> The President requested the original raw messages in English examining them personally and on December 6 had his naval aide on special night duty to receive and deliver them to him.

Congress, Ibid., p. 183, footnote 133 (majority report):

> The practice of preparing gists is indicated to have been discontinued during the month of November 1941, for the reason that the President insisted on seeing the original messages 'because he was afraid when they tried to condense them, someone would change the meaning.' See testimony of Captain Safford, Hewitt Inquiry Record, p. 408; also Clarke Inquiry Exhibit No. 23.

Beard, Op. Cit., pp. 286-294, presents an interesting account of the explosiveness of the Pearl Harbor issue in the 1944 Presidential campaign and of the strategic role played by Roosevelt's Chief of Staff, General Marshall, in persuading Governor Dewey, the Republican candidate, not to reveal what he had learned of the Administration's foreknowledge of and responsibility in the devastating defeat of some three years before.

In a footnote on p. 291 Beard notes that

> General Marshall's account of his negotiations with Governor Dewey . . . . is to be

found in the Hearings of the Congressional Committee on Pearl Harbor, December 6, 1945, Part 3, pp. 1127 ff.

What Roosevelt And His Staff Knew From The Japanese Intercepts

Report of the Joint Committee (Congress), Op. Cit., p. 526 (minority report):

> Colonel Otis Sadtler testified before the Army Pearl Harbor Board that about November 20, 1941, a Japanese message was intercepted notifying nationals that another message was to come indicating whether war, if launched, would be against the United States, Great Britain, or Russia or any combination of them. The first message stated that the second or 'activating' message to come would indicate by reference to the directions of the winds and weather the names of the countries against which war would be started. The Army Pearl Harbor Board also had evidence to the effect that the second or 'activating' message from Japan had come and that it meant 'War with England, War with America, Peace with Russia.
>
> According to the Board's report:
>
> This original message has now disappeared from the Navy files and cannot be found. It was in existence just after Pearl Harbor and was collected with other messages for submission to the Roberts Commission. Copies were in existence in various places but they have all disappeared (Top Secret, p. 8).'

Beard, Op. Cit., p. 532, adds an additional sentence from the "Top Secret Report of the Pearl Harbor Board" (1944): "There, therefore, can be no question that between the dates of December 4 and December 6, the imminence of war on the following Saturday and Sunday, December 6 and 7, was clear-cut and definite."

Congress Op. Cit., (minority report), pp. 514-515:

> Four volumes laid before the Committee contain hundreds of the messages—including in some cases comment and interpretations:
>
> (1) Pearl Harbor: Intercepted Diplomatic Messages, Ex.1 (253 pp.);
>
> (2) Japanese Messages Concerning Military Installations, Ship Movements, etc. (of the United States) (mimeograph, Ex. 2); and
>
> (3) Army Pearl Harbor Board: Top Secret Testimony, Report, and Official Memoranda (mimeograph).
>
> (4) The Navy Court of Inquiry Top Secret Testimony and Report.
>
> No person has any intellectual or moral right to pass judgment on the question of responsibility for Pearl Harbor who has not read, compared, studied, and interpreted all of these documents.

Congress, Ibid, pp. 515-516:

> A message from the Japanese Government to its Ambassador in Berlin, sent on November 30, was intercepted and translated by the Navy in

Washington on December 1 (exhibit 1, p. 204). In this message the Japanese Ambassador was instructed to—'immediately interview Chancellor Hitler and Foreign Minister Ribbentrop and confidentially communicate to them a summary of developments***. Say very secretly to them that there is extreme danger that war may suddenly break out between the Anglo-Saxon nations and Japan through some clash of arms and add thc timc of the breaking out of this war may come quicker than anyone dreams.'

The President regarded this message as of such interest that he retained a copy of it, contrary to the usual practice in handling the intercepted messages . . . .On December 2, 1941, elaborate instructions from Japan were intercepted dealing in precise detail with the method of internment of American and British nationals in Asia 'on the outbreak of war with England and the United States.'

Texts of Japanese Messages About Pearl Harbor Report of the Joint Committee (Congress) Op. Cit., pp. 516-517 (minority report):

The probability that the Pacific Fleet would be attacked at Pearl Harbor was clear from the 'bomb plot' available in Washington as early as October 9, 1941, and related Japanese messages. It will aid in obtaining a clear understanding of these important messages if the principal intercepted communications are set forth in full.

They are:
From: Tokyo (Toyoda)
To: Honolulu
September 24, 1941
#83
Strictly secret.
Henceforth, we would like to have you make reports concerning vessels along the following lines insofar as possible:
1. The waters (of Pearl Harbor) are to be divided roughly into five subareas. (We have no objections to your abbreviating as much as you like.)
Area A. Water between Ford Island and the Arsenal.
Area B. Waters adjacent to the Island south and west of Ford Island. (This area is on the opposite side of the Island from Area A.)
Area C. East Loch.
Area D. Middle Loch.
Area E. West Loch and the communicating water routes.
2. With regard to warships and aircraft carriers, we would like to have you report on those at anchor, (these are not so important) tied up at wharves, buoys and in the docks. (Designate types and classes briefly. If possible we would like to have you make mention of the fact when there are two or more vessels along side the same wharf.)

ARMY Trans. 10/9/41 (S)

From: Honolulu (Xita)
To: Washington
September 29, 1941
Circular #041
Honolulu to Tokyo #178
Re your #083
(Strictly secret)
The following codes will be used hereafter to designate the location of vessels:

1. Repair dock in Navy Yard (The repair basin referred to in my message to Washington #48):KS.
2. Navy Dock in the Navy Yard (The Ten Ten Pier): KT
3. Moorings in the vicinity of Ford Island: FV.
4. Alongside in Ford Island: FG. (East and west sides will be differentiated by A and B respectively.)

Relayed to Washington, San Francisco.
JD-l 5730 23312 (D) Navy Trans. 10-10-41 (x)

From: Tokyo (Togo)
To: Honolulu (Riyoji)
November 15, 1941
#111
As relations between Japan and the United States are most critical, make your "ships in harbor report" irregular, but at a rate of twice a week. Although you already are no doubt aware, please take extra care to maintain secrecy.
JD-l 6991 25644 (Y) Navy Trans. 12-3-41 (S)

From: Tokyo (Togo)
To: Honolulu
November 18, 1941 #113
Please report on the following areas as to vessels anchored therein: Area "N", Pearl Harbor, Mamala Bay, and the Areas Adjacent thereto. (Make your investigation with great secrecy.)
Army 25773 Trans. 12-5-41 (S)

From:Tokyo (Togo)
To: Honolulu
November 20, 1941
#111 Strictly secret
Please investigate comprehensively the fleet–bases in the neighborhood of the Hawaiian military reservation.
ARMY 25694 JD 7029 Trans. 12-4-41 (S)

From: Tokyo
To: Honolulu

November 29, 1941 #122
We have been receiving reports from you on ship movements, but in future will you also report even when there are no movements.
JD-1 7086 25823 (Y) Navy Trans. 12-5-41 (2)
From: Honolulu (Kita).
To: Tokyo November 18, 1941.
#222.
1. The warship at anchor in the harbor on the 15th were as I told you in my #219 on that day.
Area A–A battleship of the Oklahoma class entered and one tanker left port.
Area C–Three warships of the heavy cruiser class were at anchor.

2. On the 17th the Saratoga was not in the harbor. The carrier Enterprise, or some other vessel, was in area C. Two heavy cruisers of the Chicago Class, one of the Pensacola Class were tied up at docks KS. Four merchant vessels were at anchor in Area D.

3. At 10 a.m. on the morning of the 17th, eight destroyers were observed entering the harbor. Their course was as follows: In a single file at a distance of 1,000 meters apart at a speed of 3 knots per hour, they moved into Pearl Harbor. From the entrance of the harbor through area B to the buoys in area C, to which they were moored, they changed course five times, each time roughly 30 degrees. The elapsed time was 1 hour: however, one of these destroyers entered area A after passing the water reservoir on the eastern side.
ARMY 25817 Trans. 12-6-41

Congress, Ibid., pp. 228-229 (majority report):

One of the most unfortunate circumstances attending the handling of Magic is the fact that several very significant messages were not translated until after the attack . . . . The . . . message dated December 2 (translated December 30) read:

In view of the present situation, the presence in port of warships, airplane carriers, and cruisers is of utmost importance. Hereafter, to the utmost of your ability, let me know day by day. Wire me in each case whether or not there are any observation balloons above Pearl Harbor or if there are any indications that they will be sent up. Also advise me whether or not the warships are provided with antimine nets.

. . . Of extreme significance are two messages of December 6 (both translated December 8) one of which reads as follows: . . . Insofar as Hawaii is concerned . . . . At the present time there are no signs of barrage balloon equipment. In addition, it is difficult to imagine that they have actually any. However . . . there are limits in the balloon defense of Pearl Harbor. I imagine that in all probability there is considerable opportunity left to take advantage for a surprise attack against these places.

2. In my opinion the battleships do not have torpedo nets. The details are not known. I will report the results of my investigation.

Morgenstern, Op. Cit., pp. 249-250, re the other message alluded to above:.

At 7:22 P.M., December 6, the night before the Japanese carrier assault on Pearl Harbor, American intelligence intercepted this report by the spies to Tokyo:

The following ships were observed at anchor: nine battleships, three light cruisers, three submarine tenders, seventeen destroyers, and in addition there were four light cruisers and two destroyers lying at the docks. The heavy cruisers and airplane carriers have all left. It appears that no air reconnaissance is being conducted by the fleet air arm.

Report of the Joint Committee (Congress), Op. Cit., pp. 526-528 (minority report):

From a message from Tokyo to Washington, dated December 2 and translated December 3, high authorities in Washington learned that the Japanese Government had ordered its Washington Embassy to destroy all codes except one and all secret documents. (One code machine was to be kept for use in the final negotiations which ended in the rupture of relations on December 7.)

From a message dated December 6 and translated on December 6, sometime in the afternoon, Washington authorities learned that the Japanese Government had notified the Japanese Embassy in Washington that a memorandum for the United States would be sent in 14 parts and to be prepared to present it—the memorandum that would make a rupture in relations with the United States.

Messages serving as guides to procedure in the matter of this 14 part message follow:

(Secret)
From: Tokyo
To: Washington
December 7, 1941
(Urgent–Very Important)
#907 to be handled in Government Code
Re my #902.a
Will the ambassador please submit to the United States Government (if possible to the Secretary of State) our reply to the United States at 1:00 p.m. on the 7th, your time.
Trans. 12/7/41 (5)
Army 25850
a.S.I.S. #25843-text of Japanese reply

(Secret)

From: Tokyo
To: Washington
December 6, 1941
#904
Re my #902
There is really no need to tell you this, but in the preparation of the aide memoire be absolutely sure not to use a typist or any other person. Be most extremely cautious in preserving secrecy.
Trans. 12-6-41 (S)

Army 25844
JD: 7144

Secret
From: Tokyo
To: Washington
December 7, 1941
(Extremely Urgent)
#910

After deciphering part 14 of my #902a and also #907b, #908c and 909d, please destroy at once the remaining cipher machine and all machine codes. Dispose in like manner also secret documents. Trans. 12/7/41 (S)

The 'pilot message' was filed in Tokyo at 6:56 a.m. Washington time December 6; it was intercepted by the Navy by 7:20 a.m. Washington time December 6, and forwarded to the Navy Department. It was sent by the Navy to the Army for decryption and translation about noon, Washington time, on December 6 (exhibit 41.) It was decrypted, translated, and distributed about 3 p.m., Washington time, by the Army, to Mr. Hull, Mr. Stimson, General Marshall, the Chief of the War Plans Division, General Gerow, and the Chief of Military Intelligence, General Miles (Tr., Vol. 62, p. 12050). In the Navy Department the Director of Naval Intelligence—Admiral Wilkinson—received the so-called 'pilot message' prior to 6 p.m., Washington time, on December 6 (Tr., Vol. 26, p. 4662). Admiral Turner, Chief of the War Plans Division in the Office of the Chief of Naval Operations, received the 'pilot message' in the evening of December 6 (Tr., Vol. 30, pp. 5440-5442). Admiral Stark and General Marshall each denies that on December 6 he had knowledge of the 'pilot message' (Tr., Vol. 21, p. 3473, and Vol. 32, p. 5813). We find on the testimony of General Miles and Colonel Bratton that the 'pilot message' was delivered to General Marshall during the afternoon of December 6, 1941 (Tr., Vol. 21, pp. 3589-3590, and Vol. 62, pp. 12049-12050).

F.D.R.'s Reaction

In late afternoon or early evening of December 6, American Naval Communications intercepted, decoded, and translated the first 13 parts of this memorandum from the Japanese Government to the State Department—the answer to the United States note to Japan on November 26. The translation of these 13 parts was presented to President Roosevelt between 9 and 10 o'clock that evening. After he had read the 13 parts, the President said in substance, 'This means war.'

The evidence indicated that the first 13 parts were read on the evening of December 6 by particularly, the President, Mr. Harry Hopkins, Secretary Knox, Admiral Ingersoll, Admiral Turner, Admiral Wilkinson, Admiral Beardall, General Miles, Captain Kramer, and Colonel Bratton.

Evaluations of Intercepts

Congress, Ibid., pp. 183-185 (majority report):

In endeavoring to evaluate the intercepted dispatch of September 24 and related dispatches, it is to be borne in mind that the Japanese were insistent in their desire to secure information concerning the location and movements of American vessels everywhere and not merely at Pearl Harbor. There are no other dispatches before the committee, however, in which *Tokyo* manifested an interest concerning the disposition of ships within a harbor, as in the case of the 'berthing plan,' as distinguished from the desire to know whether a vessel was at a particular harbor. Viewing the September 24 instructions to her Honolulu consul in this light, it would appear that Tokyo was manifesting an unusual interest in the presence of our Pacific Fleet and the detailed location thereof in Pearl Harbor . . . .

On the other hand, Admiral Stark, who stated he had no recollection of having seen the berthing plan and accompanying messages prior to the attack, testified:

'These messages are of a class of message which gives positions of ships in harbor, gives locations. The message, however, is distinctly different from the usual type of ship report, which simply would say, 'So many ships' or give their names, in Pearl Harbor. This dispatch is different in that it calls for the location of a ship in the harbor in her particular berth.

'I recall no such request from Tokyo to the field; that is, to the Japanese people, to report like that except for Pearl Harbor.'

Congress, Ibid., pp. 518-520 (minority report):

The 'bomb plot' message, and those messages relating to Pearl Harbor which followed it, meant that the ships of the Pacific Fleet in Pearl Harbor were marked for a Japanese attack. No other American harbor was divided into subareas by Japan. And no other American harbor had such a large share of the fleet to protect.

In no other area did Japan seek information as to whether two or more vessels were alongside the same wharf. Prior to the 'bomb plot' message Japanese espionage was directed to ascertain the general whereabouts of the American Fleet, whether at sea or in port. With the 'bomb plot' message Japan inaugurated a new policy directed to Pearl Harbor and to no other place, in which information was no longer sought merely as to the general whereabouts of the fleet, but as to the presence of particular ships in particular areas of the harbor. In the period immediately preceding the attack Japan required such reports even when there was no movement of ships in and out of Pearl Harbor. The reports which Japan thus sought and received had a useful purpose only in planning and executing an attack upon the ships in port. These reports were not just the work of enthusiastic local spies gathering meticulous details in an excess of zeal. They were the product of instructions emanating from the Government of Japan in Tokyo. Officers of the high command in Washington have admitted before us that the 'bomb plot' message, if correctly evaluated, meant an attack on ships of the Pacific Fleet in Pearl Harbor . . . .

Simple reason in evaluating these bomb plot messages should have discovered their significance.

1. Such meticulous detail was not needed to enable Japan to keep track of the American fleet for general purposes.

2. The messages were sent to Tokyo obviously for use originating from there—air or sea attack.

3. The messages couldn't be for sabotage. Sabotage is an on-the-spot affair. Saboteurs have to be in Hawaii. They get their information direct by local observation. Therefore, they needed no bomb plot.

4. The only purpose could be for air attack, submarine attack, direct invasion—all external operations.

5. Had Washington so evaluated this bomb plot, it could have seen this significance and warned the commanders at Hawaii. Washington authorities failed to do so or if they did in fact evaluate it, they failed to pass the information on to the Hawaiian commanders . . . .

Washington Plays "I've Got a Secret"

In Washington, long prior to December 7, 1941, Army and Navy intelligence officers, the Chief of Naval Operations, the Army Chief of Staff, and other high authorities gained vital information (the bomb plot messages) from intercepted Japanese communications affecting the fleet and the defense of the naval base at Hawaii. They gained it from sources of information not available to Admiral Kimmel and General Short.

In these circumstances it was the express duty of the Washington authorities to pass this information in its original form on to Admiral Kimmel and

General Short. The information was of such a specific character and so directly related to the fleet and naval base that Washington authorities were not justified in keeping it to themselves or in evaluating it in any manner which would dilute or generalize the significance of the messages in their original form. Washington authorities failed in this, a prime responsibility in their relations with the outpost commanders.

In the days immediately preceding Pearl Harbor, Japan made no effort to conceal the movements or presence of her naval forces in South East Asia (Tr., Vol. 3, p. 453). The movements of her troops in Indo-China at that time were the subject of diplomatic exchanges between the United States and Japan (*Foreign Relations of the United States*, Japan, 1931-41, vol. II, p. 779). Yet the intercepts showed that some Japanese plan went into effect automatically on November 29, from which Japan hoped to divert American suspicion by a pretext of continued negotiations. The Pearl Harbor 'bomb plot' messages gave some hint of what might follow 'automatically.'

Only the President and his top advisors in Washington had this information.

Congress, Ibid., "Additional Views of Mr. Keefe," p. 266 F:

[Rep. Keefe includes four sentences from the preceding report, but with more specific comments on Washington's deception.]

Despite the fact that the 'bomb plot' message and related intercepts dealing with the berthing of ships in Pearl Harbor were delivered to General Marshall and Admiral Stark, they testified before the Committee that they have no recollection of ever seeing them (R.2911-2912: 5787-5792). No intimation of these messages was given to General Short or Admiral Kimmel in Hawaii. On the contrary, Admiral Kimmel had been advised by the Navy Department on February 1, 1941:

> . . . no move against Pearl Harbor appears imminent or planned for in the foreseeable future (exhibit 15).'

In the days immediately preceding Pearl Harbor, Japan made no effort to conceal the movements or presence of her naval forces in Southeast Asia (r.453). The movements of her troops in Indo-China at that time were the subject of diplomatic exchanges between the United States and Japan

> (*Foreign Relations of the United States, Japan, 1931-41*, vol. II, p. 779)
>
> Yet the intercepts showed that some Japanese plan went into effect automatically on November 29, from which Japan hoped to divert American suspicion by a pretext of continued negotiations. What was its nature? Only the President and his top advisors in Washington had this information.

Despite the elaborate and labored arguments in the report and despite the statements of high ranking military and naval officers to the contrary, I must conclude that the intercepted messages received and distributed in Washington on the afternoon and evening of December 6 and the early hours of December 7, pointed to an attack on Pearl Harbor.

Morgenstern, Op. Cit., pp/ 252-253:

The irony of Kimmel's predicament was that the information which the Roosevelt administration denied the commander-in-chief of the United States fleet was being freely given to the British all through 1941. Gen. Miles testified that the secret American process for decoding Japanese communications was given to Britain as early as January . . . .

Significance of 1 O'clock

The Hawaiian commanders, as has been seen, were also denied knowledge of the final Jap diplomatic note of December 6-7, followed by the pilot message directing that the statement be handed in to Hull at 1:00 P.M. The Army Board has shown that there could have been no misconception as to the meaning to be read into these dispatches. 'It was well known,' the report states, 'that Japan's entry into all wars of the past has been characterized by the first overt act of war coming simultaneously with the declaration. The services, both Army and Navy, were well aware of this Japanese characteristic. It was, therefore, to be expected that an unexpected attack would be made by Japan as the first indication of a breach of relations.'

The breach of relations would come at 1:00 P.M., Washington time. Therefore, that was the hour for war and the first overt act.

Congress, Ibid., "Majority Report," pp. 223-4:

Captain Kramer testified that upon his return to the Navy Department at 10:20 a.m. he found the 'one o'clock' message and thereafter, between 10:30 and 10:35 a.m., delivered it to the office of the Chief of Naval Operations, where a meeting was in progress. Delivery was then made within approximately 10 minutes to an aide to Secretary Hull at the State Department and thereafter within roughly another 10 minutes, to a Presidential aide at the White House. In the course of delivery to the office of the Chief of Naval Operations and to Secretary Hull's aide mention was made of the fact that 1 p.m., Washington time, was about dawn at Honolulu and about the middle of the night in the Far East. No mention was made that the time indicated an attack at Pearl Harbor . . .

After completion of his reading of the memorandum, General Marshall came to the 'one o'clock' message and appears to have attached immediate significance to it. He testified that he and the officers present in his office were certain the hour fixed in the 'one o'clock' message had 'some definite significance,' that 'something was going to happen at 1 o'clock;' that 'when they specified a day, that of course had significance, but not comparable to an hour;' and, again, that it was 'a new item of information of a peculiar character.'

Congress, Ibid., p. 228, from the Majority Report:

We believe, however, that the 'one-o'clock' intercept should have been recognized as indicating the distinct possibility that some Japanese military action would occur somewhere at 1 p.m., December 7, Washington time. *Marshall And Stark: The Lost Weekend*

Congress, Ibid., "Minority Report," pp. 568-570:

Apparently the President did communicate with Admiral Stark later that evening, but the evidence before the committee is indirect, for Admiral Stark's mind seems to be a complete blank as to his whereabouts and doings on the evening of December 6, 1941. When he testified before the Committee at its regular hearings, the admiral was under the firm impression that he did not talk with the President over the telephone that evening, but then confessed that he might be mistaken. Later, however, at a special session of the Committee on May 31, 1946, Admiral Stark testified that a friend, Cap. H. D. Krick, had recently given him some information on the point. Captain Krick had informed Admiral Stark that they had been together on the evening of December 6, 1941 and that the admiral had been in communication with the President over the telephone. But this recent information did not refresh the admiral's memory, for he declared at the special session of the Committee that he still had 'no recollection whatever of any events of that evening' . . . .

F.D.R.'s Responsibility

During the hours from 10 o'clock Saturday night to 11 o'clock Sunday morning, President Roosevelt had at his command not only the latest intercepts and his own knowledge of diplomatic negotiations with Great Britain and Japan but also special knowledge that had come to him before the evening of December 6; for example:

(1) The message from Tokyo to the Japanese Ambassador in Berlin telling him to see Hitler and Ribbentrop and—'say very secretly to them that there is extreme danger that war may suddenly break out between the Anglo-Saxon nations and Japan through some clash of arms and add that the time of the breaking out of this war may come quicker than anyone dreams (Ex.l, p.204).'

This message, received in Washington on November 30, so moved President Roosevelt that he expressed a desire to retain or have a copy of it (Tr., Vol. 57, pp. 10887-10888).

(2) The message transmitted at 10:40 o'clock in the morning of December 6 by Ambassador Winant in London from the British Admiralty, stating that large Japanese expeditionary forces were moving swiftly toward Kra—a threat which was to bring into play American-British war plans for combined action against Japan unless the President refused to give official sanction to the plans he had approved 'except officially.'

Knowing all these things and more besides, including the zero hour of 1 o'clock fixed by the Japanese Government for the delivery of the message that meant a de facto rupture of relations, unable under the Constitution to commit the overt act of striking Japan at once, waiting for the Japanese to fire 'the first shot without allowing too much danger to ourselves,' President Roosevelt was under direct and immediate obligation to make certain that urgent messages be sent to the outpost commanders, including General Short and Admiral Kimmel, and sent not later than 11 o'clock on Sunday morning by the swiftest possible means of communication.

For his failure to take this action Saturday night, December 6, or early Sunday morning, December 7, President Roosevelt must bear a responsibility commensurate with his powers and duties under the Constitution, with his position as Commander in Chief of the Army and Navy, and with the trust vested in him as the Chief Executive by the people of the United States.

More Evaluations of Intercepts And Responsibilities A La F.D.R.

Beard, Op. Cit., p. 373:

In his secret report to President Roosevelt after his return from a visit to Hawaii in December, 1941, shortly after the Japanese attack, Secretary Knox stated: 'Neither Short nor Kimmel, at the time of the attack, had any knowledge of the plain intimations of some surprise move, made clear in Washington, through the interception of Japanese instructions to Nomura, in which a surprise move of some kind was clearly indicated by the insistence upon the precise time of Nomura's reply to Hull, at one o'clock on Sunday.'

Theobald, Op. Cit., PP. 120-121:

Another astonishing feature connected with this last denial (of Magic to Hawaii) was that the time-of-delivery message definitely established that Pearl Harbor would be the scene of the attack. Added to the earlier evidence, there was no other plausible deduction. We have seen that there were only two attractive objectives for a Japanese surprise attack in the Pacific—the Fleet in Pearl Harbor and the Panama Canal. On the other hand, it was 7:30 in Hawaii, the exact time that the planes would reach their objectives, based upon the assumption of a launching area about 150 miles from Pearl Harbor and a morning twilight take-off. Furthermore, 7:30 was the time that the crews of American ships were habitually piped to breakfast. An attack upon Pearl Harbor, shortly after that time,would thus conform in every particular to the accepted technique of those days for a surprise attack by carrier-based planes.

To deliver a mid-day attack on Panama, the carriers would have had to advance to the launching area during six hours of daylight through the crowded focal waters of the western approaches to the Canal—an operation that would never be considered in connection with a surprise attack.

It is difficult to believe that these inescapable facts were completely overlooked in the continuous conference in Admiral Stark's office during that forenoon.

> There was never any military reason for preserving to the Japanese the opportunity of a surprise attack through the denial of information to the Hawaiian Commanders. Free to act, it is an absolute certainty that both Admiral Stark and General Marshall would have done everything in their power to prevent such an attack. And yet, on the morning of December 7, Washington refused to send one short message to Hawaii in time to cushion the effects of the Japanese attack!
>
> That is the most revealing fact of the entire Pearl Harbor story. There is only one conceivable reason for it—nothing must be done to prejudice the chances of the attack, even at the last moment. Japan was about to bring war to the United States, and President Roosevelt did not intend that any American action should cause them to change their plans at the last minute.

I am indebted to Dr. Harry Elmer Barnes for his kindness in sending me a generous supply of his own writings in the area of Pearl Harbor and World War II in general. It is appropriate that I quote here from his article, "The End of the Old America" which appeared originally in *Modern Age, A Conservative Review*, Vol. 2, No. 2, (Spring 1958). On pp. 145-14 he says:

> As Stark knew by about 8:30 on the morning of the 7th that the Japanese were in all probability going to make an immediate attack on Pearl Harbor, presumably at 1:00 P.M. Washington time, and yet never warned Kimmel, such action on the part of an intelligent and patriotic officer can only be explained on the basis of his having been ordered by Roosevelt not to send any warning.
>
> When, between 8:30 and 9:00 A.M. on the morning of December 7, Stark received the Japanese message indicating the attack at 1:00 P.M., he 'cried out in great alarm' and exclaimed: 'My God, this means war! I must get word to Kimmel at once!' He did nothing of the kind and his astounding failure to do so has never been explained. It may be that his exclamation was the automatic response of a trained naval officer, and that his later lapse was the result of recalling his phone conversation with Roosevelt the previous night. Anyone with a better explanation is welcome to produce it.
>
> If Stark had been free to act in an independent and unhampered manner, there is no doubt that he would have remained awake and alert all night on December 6, seeking all possible information as to the time of the Japanese attack. At least, he would have demanded that all information of this sort be brought to him immediately. The Japanese message which indicated that the attack on Pearl Harbor would come at 1:00 P.M. Washington time was available at the Navy Department at 5:00 A.M . . . .No evidence has been produced to prove that Roosevelt did not order Marshall and Stark to refrain from warning Short and Kimmel in time to avert the Japanese attack. In the light of the fact that both Marshall and Stark knew by the night of the 6th that there was every probability that the Japanese might strike at Pearl Harbor the next

day, there seem to be only three possible explanations of why they did not warn Short and Kimmel: That they were idiots, that they were traitors, or that they had orders from Roosevelt not to do so. The last explanation appears the most plausible.

Report of the Joint Committee (Congress), Op. Cit. pp. 266A, 266S, "Additional Views of Mr. Keefe":

Throughout the long and arduous sessions of the committee in the preparation of the committee report, I continuously insisted that whatever 'yard stick' was agreed upon as a basis for determining responsibilities in Hawaii should be applied to the high command at Washington. This indicates in a general way my fundamental objection to the committee report. I feel that facts have been martialed, perhaps unintentionally, with the idea of conferring blame upon Hawaii and minimizing the blame that should properly be assessed at Washington.

A careful reading of the committee report would indicate that the analysis of orders and dispatches is so made as to permit criticism of our commanders in Hawaii while at the same time proposing a construction which would minimize the possibility of criticism of those in charge at Washington.

. . . The committee report, I feel, does not with exactitude apply the same yardstick in measuring responsibilities at Washington as has been applied to the Hawaiian commanders. I cannot suppress the feeling that the committee report endeavors to throw as soft a light as possible on the Washington scene . . . .

The affidavits and testimony at the further investigations contain many instances where witnesses gave testimony materially different from that which they had previously sworn to before the Army Board and the Naval Court. These changes were especially marked in testimony of certain key witnesses on the subject of the dissemination and evaluation of the intercepted messages in Washington. Again, before this Committee these same witnesses further changed their testimony from that sworn to twice previously, or pleaded lapses of memory.

The record of the high military and civilian officials of the War and Navy Departments in dealing with the Pearl Harbor disaster from beginning to end does them no credit. It will have a permanent bad effect on the morale and integrity of the armed services. The Administration had ample opportunity to record and preserve all the facts about Pearl Harbor, even if their public disclosure needed to wait upon the war's end. This was not done. The policy adopted was to place the public responsibility for the disaster on the commanders in the field, to be left there for all time. The policy failed only because suppression created public suspicion, and the Congress was alert.

About The Apologists for Washington

A most revealing characteristic running through the writings and arguments of the apologists for President Roosevelt is a common disregard for salient facts and avoidance of logic and obvious realities. I sent a copy of Theobald's *The Final Secret of Pearl Harbor* to the outraged parent whose objections inspired this account. His letter to me in answer grandly ignored the entire subject of the Magic messages and proceeded to a diatribe against Admirals Theobald and Kimmel whose "ultra-conservativism" and "disgrace" renders them incapable of an "honest or objective account of any democrat." An admirer of Admiral Halsey, he was mystified to find him lending his aid to such disreputable personalities by writing a foreword to the volume. Undaunted, however, he cites the words of Halsey to substantiate his contention that there was no reason to expect an attack on Pearl Harbor. His ability to see only what he wished to see is demonstrated by the following from his letter to me:

> Halsey, who was the most honest and forthright of the three has this to say in his forward: 'All our intelligence pointed to an attack by Japan against the Philippines or the southern areas of Malaya or the Dutch East Indies. While Pearl Harbor was considered and not ruled out, the mass of the evidence made available to us pointed in another direction.'

The outraged parent, lover of honesty, forthrightness, and objectivity in his accounts about Pearl Harbor, neglected to quote the three sentences of Halsey which preceded those he quoted and the sentence which followed immediately thereafter. I include them here in the interest of forthrightness:

> At that time I was one of the three senior commanders of the Pacific Fleet, serving under Admiral Kimmel. I am sure he kept me informed of all the intelligence he possessed. Certainly I did not know then of any of the pertinent Magic Messages' . . . .Had we known of Japan's minute and continued interest in the exact location and movement of our ships in Pearl Harbor, as indicated in the 'Magic Messages', it is only logical that we would have concentrated our thought on meeting the practical certainty of an attack on Pearl Harbor.

The Congressman appealed to by the outraged parent quoted above sent along a paper which purported to be an objective analysis of the available evidence relating to the Pearl Harbor story. I was privileged to photostat parts of it and to take copious notes on it in general. It was dated June 13, 1960, and was prepared by a "Joseph G. Whelan, Analyst in Soviet and East European Affairs, Foreign Affairs Division," evidently connected with the Legislative Reference Service of the Library of Congress. Quoting as sources exclusively from apologists for "The Establishment's Official Version," he cites Feis, Langer and

Gleason, Millis, and Trefonsse. He omits any mention of such authorities as Barnes, Beard, Theobald, Halsey, Kimmel, Morgenstern, and Tansill, and not one word does he quote from a single "Magic" message. On p. 11 he blandly observes: "There is no evidence available to indicate that General Marshall knew an attack on Pearl Harbor was imminent . . . . No evidence exists, as the Pearl Harbor Investigation indicated, that there was information suggesting a possible strike at Pearl Harbor, except for the Grew message a year earlier." And on p. 2 he says: "There is no historical evidence to support the thesis that President Roosevelt knew precisely when the Japanese would strike or where."

I suggest that even a most cursory reading of the "bomb plot" messages and the "one o'clock" message from the Magic interceptions, together with the knowledge that Marshall and Roosevelt were recipients of every single Magic message on the day it was decoded would indicate Mr. Whelan to be somewhat less than "forthright" in his gratuitous conclusions. The labored denial of Magic specifically to Pearl Harbor is directly symptomatic of a preoccupation with that naval base as a probable target.

And on p. 5, Mr. Whelan reports with approval that:

> During the Pearl Harbor Congressional Investigation Rear Admiral T.S. Wilkinson, former director of Naval Intelligence, was asked: 'Did you have any information, written or oral, prior to the actual attack, which specified Hawaii as a point of attack?' To which the Admiral replied, 'Not the slightest.'

At the time of the Magic interceptions, the then Captain Wilkinson was one of the seven men on the Navy department's distribution list for Magic who received every message on the day it was decoded. I submit that, his conclusions relative to Wilkinson's reply before the Committee—"Not the slightest": (1) he was a thoroughly incompetent person to occupy the sensitive post as director of Naval Intelligence, or (2) he was a victim of amnesia at the time of his testimony, or (3) he perjured himself before the Committee.

Summary on Saturday And Why The Lost Weekend

Theobald, Op. Cit., pp. 95-97:

> The recipients of Magic in Washington had known for over a week that the Japanese reply to the American note of November 26 would be a declaration of war. The 14-part message was that answer, hence definitely a declaration of war. Japan had started her three previous wars—with China in 1894, with Russia 1904, and her attack upon German-held Tsingtao in 1914—with surprise attacks synchronized almost to the minute with the deliveries of her declarations of war.
>
> The next day was Sunday, the day of the week upon which Japan was expected to deliver her surprise attack if she should ever decide to initiate a

war with the United States. A Japanese amphibious force was known to be in position to make a dawn attack upon the Kra Peninsula on the next day. During the earlier days of the week, the Japanese code-destruction messages made the imminence of war a certainty. The receipt of the Pilot Message made it practically certain that Japan would start the war on the next day, Sunday, December 7, 1941.

By mid-afternoon on that Saturday, official Washington had followed Japan's every diplomatic move for days, as she prepared for her proverbial method of initiating wars. It also then knew that magic was soon to provide information of the two items needed to complete the routine—the context of the declaration of war, and the time of its delivery.

Furthermore, due to fortuitous delays in the processing of four dispatches on the Tokyo-Honolulu circuit, the recipients of Magic were reminded on Thursday, again on Friday, and again on Saturday, the three days before the attack, that Tokyo's known interest in the exact location of U.S. ships in Pearl Harbor had not only continued, but had intensified. Was a nation, about to be subjected to an attempted (!) surprise attack as the first act of war, ever before so fortunate!

The Washington silence which followed the receipt of the Pilot Message was the most vital key to the true Pearl Harbor story. War within 24 hours, initiated by a surprise attack which, according to all the evidence, would be delivered upon the U.S. Fleet in Hawaii, stared General Marshall and Admiral Stark in the face from that moment onward, and they made no move during 21 of the 22 hours which intervened before the attack to inform Admiral Kimmel and General Short. Nothing but a positive Presidential order could have so muzzled them after the receipt of the Pilot Message. The later Japanese messages and the continuing absence of warning to the Hawaiian Commanders, discussed in the remainder of this chapter, merely add support and emphasis to this inescapable fact.

Beard, Op.Cit., pp. 279-281:

September 11, 1944, Forest A, Harness, Republican from Indiana, member of the Military Affairs Committee, delivered a long address in the House of Representatives on the subject of Pearl Harbor . . . .

In respect of an additional advanced notice of the Japanese attack, Mr. Harness spoke with assurance, though he furnished no documentary proof: 'There appears to be an abundance of evidence to show that 72 hours before the attack on Pearl Harbor, the Australian Government advised the American Government in Washington that an aircraft carrier task force of the Japanese Navy had been sighted by Australian reconnaissance headed toward Pearl Harbor; that our Government was again notified 48 hours before the attack that this Japanese task force was still in progress toward Hawaii, and the same notification was sent 24 hours before Pearl Harbor. None of this information was, I am informed, given to General Short.'

About The Failure To Give Adequate Warning To Hawaii

When he came to the explosive subject of the last warning message sent 'about noon' on December 7, which the Roberts Report vaguely mentioned, Mr. Harness declared categorically:

'The wire was sent by commercial radio instead of the usual more rapid direct military means. General Short will contend that this information was extremely significant because of the instructions to destroy the code which is only a last resort. General Short believes that if this message had been telephoned him at 1:30 A.M., he would have been sufficiently alerted by that information and would have been much better prepared when the attack occurred. This evidence will further show that at 9 P.M., December 6, 1941, the night before the attack,the Army dispatched 12 B-24 bombers from San Francisco to Honolulu for use in the general defense of the islands. These bombers were sent with their defense equipment completely inoperative, and arrived that way in Honolulu. All of the machine guns and small cannon were in their original wrappings and cosmoline, were not sighted in, and none of the ammunition was in position to be used. These planes arrived about half an hour after the attack started, and in the midst of it several of them were shot down and the crews killed. Fortunately the planes carried only skeleton crews. It is shown that the Army had been flying bombers from San Francisco to Honolulu in this same manner prior to this date, and General Short had vigorously protested against the flights being made without proper defense mechanism, but his protests were unheeded.'

Theobald, Op. Cit., pp. 118-119:

If the warning message had been sent to the Hawaiian Commanders, three hours before the attack, picture the Island of Oahu, commencing at 4:30 A.M.—telephone messages recalling personnel from their homes passing through centrals containing a goodly percentage of Japanese operators; roads to Pearl Harbor filled with Army guns, troop trucks, and other impedimenta; all roads crowded with officers and men returning to their stations; intensive activity at every Army post and Naval station; plane engines roaring at every Air station; ships raising steam and testing safety valves. The Japanese spies would have appreciated the meaning at once, and would have flashed the word to the Admiral in Command of the attacking forces. With all chance of surprise gone, the decision might well have been to cancel the attack.

Chapter III

Shifting Infamy's Blame; But the Eraser of History—Won't

Report of the Joint Committee (Congress), Op. Cit., "Additional Views of Mr. Keefe," pp. 266T-266U:

> With full knowledge of Japan's intentions prior to the attack, Washington had one plain duty to the American people. That duty was to inform them of their peril. This was not done. Washington had a further duty to make sure that our forces were ready to meet the attack by furnishing their commanders afield and afloat with all available information, or by evaluating that information and giving them appropriate clear and categoric instructions.

Assigning Responsibility

Those who find in various instances of poor coordination between the services the causes of Pearl Harbor are satisfied with a superficial explanation. The state of readiness of our armed forces in the field was a reflection of over-all policy adopted on the highest level in Washington. The President had delivered to him the Japanese intercepted messages and possessed much more information about Japanese plans and intentions than any field commander. He gave most minute directions to commanders in the field, even as to the scouting positions of individual ships, when he thought such directions necessary. A merger of the armed forces and unity of command in Hawaii in November and December, 1941, could not have eliminated the dangers in the policy of maneuvering Japan into striking the first blow. That policy would still have shaped the orders given, as well as the information sent to a single commander in the field.

Those who find American public opinion responsible for Pearl Harbor accept an entirely false theory. Enlightened public opinion is based on accurate public information. The American people, if kept well informed of their real diplomatic position, do not need an incident to unite them. If foreign policy and diplomatic representations are treated as the exclusive, secret information of the President and his advisers, public opinion will not be enlightened. The very nature of the consequent public alarm places the armed forces of the Nation in effective readiness and may even deter an enemy from executing its planned attack. The best deterrent to a predatory Japan in late 1941 was a thoroughly informed and obviously alerted America.

In this connection it will be noted that when the reports of the Army Board and the Navy Court of Inquiry were submitted to President Truman on August 30, 1945, he made the following statement:

'I have read it (the Pearl Harbor reports) very carefully, and I came to the conclusion that the whole thing is the result of the policy which the country itself pursued. The country was not ready for preparedness. Every time the President made an effort to get a preparedness program through the Congress, it was stifled. Whenever the President made a statement about the necessity of preparedness, he was vilified for doing it. I think the country is as much to blame as any individual in this final situation that developed in Pearl Harbor.'

An examination of the facts ought to compel any person to reject this conclusion. The record clearly demonstrates how the Army and Navy get the funds needed for national defense. The Army and Navy are required to submit their respective estimates each year to the Bureau of the Budget. This Bureau acting for the President conducts hearings and finally makes recommendations to the President as to the amounts to be recommended to the Congress for appropriation. The Congress is in effect the people of America. The record discloses that in the fiscal years 1934 to 1941, inclusive, the Army and Navy jointly asked for $26,580,145,093. This is the combined total of Army and Navy requests made to the Bureau of the Budget. In the same period the President recommended to the Congress that it appropriate to the combined services $23,818,319,897. The Congress actually made available to the Army and Navy in this period $24,943,987,823. Thus it is apparent that the President himself recommended to the Congress in the fiscal years 1934-1941, inclusive, that it appropriate for the Army and Navy $2,761,826,033 less than had been requested by the Army and Navy. The people's representatives in the Congress gave to the Army and Navy in the form of appropriations and authorizations for expenditure $1,256,667,926 more than the President had recommended in his budget messages to the Congress.

The mere recital of these undisputed figures should dispose of the contention that 'the country is as much to blame as any individual in this final situation that developed in Pearl Harbor.'

Campaign Memories

It is appropriate here that we again review the statements of President Roosevelt in late October and early November of 1940, cited near the beginning of this book:

While I am talking to you, mothers and fathers, I give you one more assurance. I have said this before, but I shall say it again and again and again. Your boys are not going to be sent into any foreign wars.

Your President says this nation is not going to war.

The first purpose of our foreign policy is to keep our country out of war.

A Japanese Views U.S. Heroes

Mitsuo Fuchida, "I Led the Attack on Pearl Harbor," *The Reader's Digest*, February, 1954, pp. 73-77, Condensed from United States Naval Institute Proceedings:

> As my group made its bomb run, American antiaircraft fire from shipboard and shore batteries suddenly came to life. Dark-gray bursts blossomed here and there until the sky was clouded with shattering near misses which made our plane tremble. I was startled by the rapidity of the counter-attack, which came less than five minutes after the first bomb had fallen. The Japanese reaction would not have been so quick—the Japanese character is suitable for offensives but does not adjust readily to the defensive ....
>
> During the attack many of our pilots noted the brave efforts of American fliers to get planes off the ground. Though greatly outnumbered, they flew straight in to engage our craft. Their effect was negligible, but their courage commanded admiration and respect.

The Newsreel Record

I was in one of the first infantry outfits sent to the Southwest Pacific area after the Pearl Harbor attack. I sat in a Melbourne theater and viewed the newsreel record of the devastating onslaught—the fires, the rolling smoke, the twisted metal, the capsized ships, the carnage. The narrator told the story. Those of you who were around remember the last heroic sentence: "At the end every single gun on every single ship was pointed toward the sky!"

I knew not at that time that the President who labeled it "a Day of Infamy" had known - and had not given warning. How many of those who had pointed their guns skyward would never see a sky again?!

Rewards For the "Faithful"

Morgenstern, Op. Cit. p. 399:

> One of the remarkable features of the Pearl Harbor story is that, almost without exception, those who played the administration's side in the controversy prospered, while everyone who showed a less accommodating spirit failed to win promotion and pay.
>
> Admiral Standley, member of the Roberts Commission, was retired as a rear admiral in 1936. Five and one-half years later, and five months after signing the report, he was advanced to admiral for 'eminent and conspicuous

service in the Spanish-American war.' Mr.Roosevelt discovered his heroic contributions forty-four years after they were made.

Gen. McCoy, a member of the Roberts Commission, subsequently was appointed chairman of the Far Eastern advisory commission.

Col. McNarney, a member of the commission, was shortly promoted to lieutenant general. After serving as chairman of the War Department reorganization committee in 1942, he was appointed Assistant Chief of Staff to General Marshall. At the end of the war he had been promoted four grades and installed as Commanding General of American Occupation Forces in Germany.

When a new classification of five-star generals of the Army was devised, Chief of Staff Marshall headed the list.

When five-star admirals of the fleet were created at the same time, Adm. King, who blamed the American people for Pearl Harbor, became one of them.

Adm. Ingersoll, deputy to Adm. Stark in naval operations, later was appointed commander of the Western Sea Frontier.

Col. Clarke, who carried the Marshall message to Gov. Dewey, was promoted to Brigadier General.

Adm. Stark, after serving as chief of naval operations, was given an assignment as commander of United States Naval Forces in Europe and was decorated with his second distinguished service medal by Roosevelt.

Gen. Gerow, who was castigated in three different Pearl Harbor reports for his conduct of the war plans division of the War Department, was, nevertheless, promoted from Brigadier General to Lieutenant General, placed in command of the 15th Army in Europe, and, at the end of the war, appointed Commandant of the Command and General Staff School at Fort Leavenworth.

Roosevelt, of course, got a fourth term.

Secretary of State Hull, whose diplomacy hurried the country into war, received the most ironic award. The Nobel Peace Prize and the large cash award that goes with it were conferred upon him in 1945.

Cols. Bratton and Sadtler and Capt. Safford, in comparison with these gentlemen, did not get ahead in the world

Cover Up Attempts

Morgenstern, Ibid., pp. 199-200:

Again referring to the disappearance of the 'winds' message, the Army Board said,

'This original message has now disappeared from the Navy files and cannot be found. It was in existence just after Pearl Harbor and was collected with other messages for submission to the Roberts Commission. Copies were in existence in various places but they have all disappeared . . . . The radio station logs, showing the reception of the message, have been destroyed within the last year . . . .

President Truman, Secretary of War Stimson, and Secretary of the Navy Forrestal, before releasing the suppressed comments on the 'winds' signal, busied themselves trying to discredit the existence of this message and endeavoring to prevail upon witnesses who had previously testified to having seen it or handled it to change their stories. Stimson, after receiving the Army Board report and suppressing it in October, 1944, undertook three personal investigations to achieve this purpose.

He first commissioned Maj. Gen. Myron C. Cramer to prepare a precis of the most damaging evidence against himself and the Roosevelt administration. He then directed Maj. Henry C. Clausen, a lawyer in civil life, to make a trip around the world, seeking out witnesses, even if he had to approach them in the middle of battle. Guided by Cramer's outline, Clausen would then 'refresh' their memory and submit affidavits for them to sign, altering their previous testimony on relevant points. No small part of the beclouding of the Pearl Harbor record is to be attributed to this mission.

Clausen (was) later promoted to lieutenant colonel . . . Chief of Staff Marshall, commenting on the irregularity of Clausen's activities, said he had never known of any other instance of a junior officer investigating actions or statements of superior officers.

Synthesis and Summary

I have presented an impressive array of documents relating to the attack on Pearl Harbor and events and moves leading up to it. This is not intended to be a definitive history, just as 2+2=4 is not an exhaustive survey of the field of mathematics. It is axiomatic, however, that one could have little understanding of advanced mathematics were he unaware of the simple equation quoted above; I likewise maintain that the basic documents of the Pearl Harbor story are at least *among* those included here and that one who is unfamiliar with them or who ignores them is not entitled to consideration as an authority on the subject. Apologists for Washington's role in the tragedy (such as those cited by Mr. Whelan for the Library of Congress, above) are distinguished by their failure even to mention all or most of the documents included herein—particularly the texts of the Magic intercepts.

Whatever else one may say, the question persists—what do you do about these facts? Like a wasp on the tip of a tightrope walker's nose, they demand attention. I submit that those Washington officials responsible for our defense were wrong when they ignored the "ships in harbor" and other significant

Magic messages—mistakenly or through intent. Today's historians should not make the same mistake.

We have followed the career of President Franklin Delano Roosevelt from his earlier extreme isolation to where the depression depths of 1938 and his election set-backs of the same year brought him concern over his prospects for a third term in 1940. Early in our writing we included a listing of progressive steps toward war taken by the President as 1940 approached and passed. Important strides were the Rainbow War Plans and the Presidential orders to the fleet to patrol the Atlantic supply lanes, to convoy Britain-bound supply ships, to trail German ships, broadcasting their positions for the benefit of British attackers, and, finally, to shoot on sight at any German naval vessels encountered.

After the Grew message of January 27, 1941, reporting on Japanese plans to attack Pearl Harbor in event of war with the United States, we observed the concentration of the Pacific fleet at Pearl Harbor by the President—over such strenuous objections by Adm. Richardson that the latter was removed from his command in Hawaii by the chief executive. Soon the President was ordering detachments of naval vessels on provocative sorties into Far Eastern waters while he speculated on the possibility of their being sunk and commented, "I just want to keep them popping up here and there and keep the Japs guessing."

The Library of Congress dates the breaking of the Japanese Purple Code as "sometime before July 1941." Other sources indicate that the time was probably as early as late 1940. We have seen that the Purple machines had been fabricated at least by early 1941, and the last machine sent out from the Navy Department (to Corregidor) was on its way in April. The singular preoccupation of Washington with Pearl Harbor as a place apart from other American outposts is intriguing, to say the least. It alone was singled out to be omitted when Purple machines were allocated—though we did supply the British with at least one. The Magic messages, supplied in volume to London, were scrupulously denied to Hawaii except that a few non-vital intercepts were transmitted on occasion to Adm. Kimmel. In his book, *Admiral Kimmel's Story*, he speculates that as an officer of his rank it would be presumed that he would be aware of the existence of Magic, and the provision of a few messages were to lull him into a false sense of security on the supposition that he was being provided with all the relevant intercepts.

Now that the bait was set, we have reviewed the August and November 26 ultimatums to Tokyo, the latter of such a chip-on-the-shoulder nature that Secretary Hull immediately informed Army and Navy leaders that the next step in Japanese-American relations was in their hands. And, rather pointedly, the latter message was dispatched on the day following the War Cabinet meeting recorded in Stimson's diary at which the president had discussed the question of "how we should maneuver them (the Japanese) into the position of firing the first shot."

We have been able to read the texts of the translations of the "bomb plot," code destruction, and "1:00 P.M." messages, and to see the President's reaction ("This means war!") to the first 13 parts of the 14 part message on Saturday evening, December 6, 1941. Then we learned of a most amazing turn of events. At the War Cabinet meeting on November 25th, President Roosevelt had foretold a "likely" surprise attack by the Japanese in the next few days. With all the "ships-in-harbor" Magic intercepts available and with the stage set for the attack, the two top commanders, Gen. Marshall and Adm. Stark—the immediate subordinates to the President as Commander-in-Chief and through whom warnings to Pearl Harbor would be channeled—both of these leaders who had received and read every Magic intercept up to that time, suddenly at this crucial time decided to ignore the most crucial of the messages and to make themselves unavailable for contact, one spending the evening enjoying the theatre and the other on that vital Sunday morning taking several hours for a leisurely horseback ride in the December air.

Cover Up And Investigation Obstacles

Then the efforts to cover up. The Roberts Commission, completely dominated by the Washington authorities, whitewashed the capitol principals and publicly cast the hapless Adm. Kimmel and Gen. Short to the wolves of Public denunciation. The latter two were never to be allowed courts martial with benefit of counsel and the ability to compel witnesses and subpoena evidence as well as to answer the charges leveled against them.

When both the Army Board and the Navy Court of Inquiry exonerated the Hawaiian commanders and laid responsibility on the Washington high command, Stimson initiated the strange investigation of Maj. Clausen to attempt to get witnesses to change their sworn testimony. Another chapter of this effort is recounted by Adm. Kimmel in his book, *Admiral Kimmel's Story*, p. 127 (this volume was sent to me by Mr. Henry Regnery, the publisher):

> On March 31, 1945, I read in the New York *Herald Tribune* a five-line dispatch which indicated a bill had been introduced in the Senate to prevent the disclosure of any coded matter except by permission of the head of a government department or by the President. I wrote that day to Mr. Rugg, my chief counsel, and asked that he investigate. It took several days for him to obtain a copy of the bill and to notify Senator Ferguson that its passage would close the door to any investigation of Pearl Harbor.

While I was in Washington on April 12, 1945, I received a message from Rugg in Boston stating this bill had been introduced by the chairman of the Senate military affairs committee, Senator Elmer Thomas of Utah, on March 30, 1945, reported to the Senate on March 31, and passed by the Senate on April 5.

When Senator Ferguson returned from a Caribbean trip he found the passage by the Senate an accomplished fact. I was desperate because if the House passed the bill, that was the end of all disclosures about Pearl Harbor.

So I gave all the facts about the bill to the *Washington Post* together with my views of the effects of such a law. I also telephoned several members of the House of Representatives.

The next morning the *Post* and the *Times Herald* gave the matter such publicity that when the bill came before the House committee they delayed action sufficiently to make a thorough investigation. When through administrative pressure a couple of months later the bill was brought to the floor of the House, it was defeated by a vote of that body.

Had this bill been made a law this account and Admiral Theobald's recent book would never have been written. Had I not read the obscure paragraph in the *Herald Tribune* the House would have passed the bill as the Senate did.

This bill and the unprecedented haste with which it was passed by the Senate is another indication of the administration's determination to suppress all knowledge of the Washington background to Pearl Harbor.

In the Report of the Joint Congressional Committee, cited often and at length above, the minority (pp. 497-502) recounts the unusual obstructions placed in the way of the investigation. A paragraph at the outset is revealing as to the bias of the Roberts Commission:

It is extremely unfortunate that the Roberts Commission Report was so hasty, inconclusive, and incomplete. Some witnesses were examined under oath; others were not. Much testimony was not even recorded. The Commission knew that Japanese messages had been intercepted and were available, prior to the attack, to the high command in Washington. The Commission did not inquire about what information these intercepts contained, who received them, or what was done about them, although the failure of Washington to inform the commanders in Hawaii of this vital intelligence bears directly on the question of whether those commanders performed their full duties. Mr. Justice Roberts testified before this Committee:

'I would not have bothered to read it (the intercepted Japanese traffic) if it had been shown to us (Tr., Vol. 47, p. 8836).'

The report continues (I have reviewed the following Presidential order previously):

Even before the Committee commenced its work, it was confronted with an order issued on August 28, 1945, and signed by President Truman, which severely limited the power of the Committee to gain access to the full facts. The order is as follows (Tr., Vol. 1, p. 26):

August 28, 1945
Memorandum for-The Secretary of State.
The Secretary of War.
The Secretary of the Navy.
The Attorney General.
The Joint Chiefs of Staff.
The Director of the Budget.
The Director of the Office of War Information
Appropriate departments of the Government and the Joint Chiefs of Staff are hereby directed to take such steps as are necessary to prevent release to the public, except with the specific approval of the President in each case, of ----

Information regarding the past or present status, technique or procedures, degree of success attained, or any specific results of any crypt analytic unit acting under the authority of the United States Government, or any Department thereof.
Harry S. Truman.
Restricted.

Later modification, as explained in the continuing report, left control of the secrecy of all records in the hands of the committee majority party members:

> Decisions were made by the majority ruling out evidence as 'not material to the investigation' without members of the Committee ever seeing the material about which the decision was made.

The minority includes testimony and data to show that prior investigations under neither Democratic nor Republican majorities or administrations had placed such restrictions on minority members of committees. Senator Burton K. Wheeler, Democrat from Montana, testified to the Senate as to the fact that as a minority member of a committee he had been refused files by a Republican Attorney General; whereupon, Coolidge, the Republican President, removed the Attorney General and appointed another who did cooperate. The report continues:

> Some of the effects of majority decision as well as gaps in the data and testimony due to other causes illustrate the great difficulty surrounding the work of the Committee.
>
> Secretary Stimson declined to appear on the ground that his health did not permit him to undergo the strain. Access to his diary was denied by majority vote.

To accommodate Secretary Stimson because of his illness, Senator Ferguson on March 6, 1946, submitted 176 questions as part of the official record for Secretary Stimson to answer as if propounded in open hearing of the committee (Tr., Vol. 70, p. 14437ff).

Secretary Stimson did not answer any of these questions, and the Committee made no effort to insist upon his answering these questions, which were highly pertinent to the inquiry . . . .

Secretary Hull made three appearances, in the course of which he gave his official version of the matters before the Committee and was briefly examined by the counsel, but minority members of the Committee were not permitted to cross-examine him. When his answers to written interrogatories from Committee members proved unresponsive, there was no way to secure further information from him.

The diary of former Ambassador Joseph C. Grew was likewise denied to the Committee. The assertion of its confidential character was somewhat belied by its submission for examination to certain individuals with a view to its commercial publication.

The denial to the Committee of the Stimson and Grew diaries was particularly obstructive because these principals placed excerpts of the diaries in the record and withheld the rest. This was contrary to the prime rule in American law that if part of a document is put into the record by a witness in his own behalf, the court is entitled to demand the whole of the document. Concerning each of these diaries the Committee, by majority vote, refused to issue subpenas for their production.

Many messages, probably several hundreds, between Winston Churchill and Franklin D. Roosevelt received prior to December 7, 1941, were not available to the Committee, although there is good reason to believe that they bore on the gathering crisis. Other messages between Mr. Churchill and the British Embassy and American authorities were made available to the Committee, but our Government replies or action taken were not so available . . . .

President Roosevelt's secretary, Miss Grace Tully, was permitted to determine for herself and the Committee and the country what portions of the official correspondence of the late President had any relevancy to Pearl Harbor. This could hardly be a satisfactory substitute for the responsibility placed upon this Committee.

With the damaging evidence we do have available as to the role of the President and his Washington aides, one wonders what evidence of a more damaging nature exists which evoked such determined efforts by President Roosevelt and his partisans to keep the record obscure. Such an attempt to keep the public ignorant in the service of his personal political ambitions was not out of context nor inconsistent with Roosevelt's public record. I quote here a relevant editorial from the *Tampa Tribune* for June 22, 1961, on the release of the Teheran conference documents:

> Skeletons abound in the just-released papers of the 1943 Teheran conference between President Franklin D. Roosevelt, British Prime Minister Winston Churchill and Soviet Dictator Josef Stalin.
>
> No American can read this record with pride.
>
> It shows, for one thing, that Roosevelt in effect consented to Russian annexation of a large part of Poland's territory on condition the deal was not officially discussed before the 1944 election. The American President frankly admitted in this private conversation with Stalin that he did not wish to risk losing the 6 to 7 million votes of citizens of Polish extraction.

Since we do not have available his own explanations, we can only speculate as to President Roosevelt's possible motives for his actions at the time of and prior to Pearl Harbor. Speculation, however, has the benefit of an environment of known factors. We observe a basically isolationist President prior to 1938. In that year the "Recession" found the business index at its lowest point of the entire depression and unemployment growing again to alarming proportions. Spending by the Federal government had reached the saturation point. This was the year of the revolt over the President's court packing scheme; and the election reverses which accompanied his attempted purge of his own party's leaders who refused to go along were most unsettling to his ambitions for a third term two years later. Earlier we named several authorities who gave personal testimony as to Roosevelt's concern over the outlook in 1938. Defense spending we know was discussed by the President and his advisers as a possible stimulant to the lagging economy. Certainly isolation no longer characterized the administration.

It is probable that by late 1941 Roosevelt had rationalized his position to the point where he felt the United States to be in actual danger of invasion by Germany. In the Second World War experts on logistics computed that some eight tons of equipment and supplies had to be moved in for every man landed on an enemy beach. We did not consider it safe to attempt the invasion of erstwhile friendly Normandy across 23 to 40 miles of English Channel until we had spent two and a half years in the buildup of the forces in England and in the devastating bombings of Continental targets. Hitler never felt it advisable to attempt an invasion across the Channel into England. It would seem unlikely that a German invasion across 2000 miles of unfriendly Atlantic Ocean was imminent in 1941, particularly with Stalin's hordes desiring nothing more than for Hitler to commit several millions of his finest troops thousands of miles beyond the sea—leaving a royal Russian road to Berlin through the eastern back door. However, there were undoubtedly numerous sincere people who feared such an attack prior to Pearl Harbor.

I think that President Roosevelt without doubt rationalized that the losses from the Japanese attack would be negligible, and he and his service chiefs were undoubtedly appalled at the devastation and loss of life. We were not aware that any nation possessed aerial torpedoes that would be effective in waters as shallow as those at Pearl Harbor. It seems that the Japanese had employed wooden fins and other innovations to create torpedoes that were most astonishingly effective. Washington had advised Admiral Kimmel (*Admiral Kimmel's Story*, p. 19) against the employment of anti-torpedo baffles in the harbor.

Conclusion

The question arises, "Why worry about this—what difference does it make? Many of the principals are long since dead and gone. So who cares?" In the answer lies concentrated all that is basic in the writing and in the study of history. Man is differentiated from the lower animals in that he possesses the ability to learn from the past. Accurate history makes the future the beneficiary of the past. There will always be those who for selfish reasons will desire to render a "managed" history to present and rising generations. We see the end of truth as each successive master of the Soviet Union remolds and doctors the record to enhance himself and to deflate his predecessors. Perhaps one of the most telling inherent and decisive advantages that will in the long run bring the triumph of the free world over international Communism is our willingness to accept the truth in the records of the past and to profit from it. It is because knowledge of the truth alone can make our nation strong that it is imperative that the Pearl Harbor record be revealed as it really was; it is a secondary but important by-product if guilt or dereliction of duty be transferred to the rightful principals and if those unjustly pilloried in the past be exonerated.

Again I quote Dr. Harry Elmer Barnes:

> It would appear that Roosevelt partisans will never concede his responsibility for the failure to warn the Pearl Harbor commanders unless revisionist historians produce a full confession in his own handwriting, signed by a notary public, with the notary's commission attested by a county clerk. Such a document is not likely to be produced.

A resourceful district attorney crusading against the organized rackets in one of our major cities found it impossible to secure confessions from the personalities involved. Possessed, however, of a wealth of facts and evidence on the organization's activities, holdings, and police records, he charted them in detail on a huge map of the city. The unmistakable pattern developed on the map by a crushing weight of eloquent detail formed a damning case against the hitherto untouchable overlords of the city's racket empire.

I have attempted to utilize a similar technique, constructing a mosaic of documentary evidence in the form, so to speak, of a huge jig-saw puzzle. The picture formed by the mass of neatly fitting parts is, I believe, unmistakably clear. The reader should, for instance, read the "bomb plot" messages without reference to apologies and interpretations of the principals involved. Would you have been concerned for the safety of the base had you had a son on duty there? And taking the sum of all the documentation presented here, could Washington ever have hoped for more evidence and fore-warning!?

It should be remembered that we are not here laboring to establish the plausibility of one possible thesis as to responsibility in a clueless murder mystery. Rather we are surveying a vast realm of cogent evidence and copious documentation to ascertain which of two projected theses is more logically derived from and related to the facts of the case. The acceptance of the one must necessarily entail the rejection of the other.

In the light of the knowledge of incontrovertible facts which we possess, it is not with amazement that we greet statements by the Washington principals that they had "not an inkling" of prior indication of the impending attack on Pearl Harbor—that they were "completely surprised"; it is rather with tongue-in-cheek. Yes, perhaps President Roosevelt was bending all his efforts to avoid our entry into the war, and perhaps the attack was entirely unforeseen by him and his top Washington aides. And perhaps the Japanese had lost their way and didn't know where they were nor that their bombs were loaded! And, to end our fairy tale, perhaps the 2,326 Americans killed at Pearl Harbor all lived happily ever afterward!

Bibliography - Book I

I am indebted to the publishers of several volumes from which I have quoted at length for permission to use references. The Yale University Press gave permission to cite passages from Beard's *President Roosevelt and the Coming of the War 1941*. The Devin-Adair Company most graciously allowed the use of materials from Morgenstern's *Pearl Harbor* and Theobald's *The Final Secret of Pearl Harbor*—both most valuable sources. Mr. Henry Regnery, president of the Henry Regnery Company, not only gave me permission to quote from Tansill's *Back Door to War*, but he sent me a copy of *Admiral Kimmel's Story* which provides some valuable insights into certain facets of our study. Mr. Regnery also has proffered other aid, including indirectly bringing me into contact with some of the principals in the Pearl Harbor story. It was through him that I came into direct contact with Dr. Harry Elmer Barnes and received some significant materials from that eminent historian. The basic report from the Joint Congressional Committee was made available to me by Representative William C. Cramer, of Florida.

Bailey, Thomas A., *The Man in the Street*, New York, Macmillan, 1948.

This volume is relevant to a study of Pearl Harbor because of the passages in which Dr. Bailey candidly and with approval reports that President Roosevelt deceived and tricked the American people while maneuvering the nation into war. This frankly Machiavellian concept is interesting in that as presented, it reflects a like philosophy on the part of our wartime chief executive.

Barnes, Harry Elmer, *"The End of the Old America,"* Reprinted from Modern Age, A Conservative Review, Vol. 2, No. 2 (Spring 1958).

This is one of a series of articles by Dr. Barnes forming a critical review of Pres. Roosevelt's World War II foreign policies. It analyzes the works of several writers who are apologists for Roosevelt, pointing out their onesided choice of sources. I have found it useful for the cogency of some of the author's analytical conclusions about Washington actions and responsibilities as to Pearl Harbor and for the forceful logic with which he bridges the gaps in the record.

Beard, Charles A., *President Roosevelt and the Coming of the War 1941,* New Haven, Yale University Press, 1948.

The late Dr. Charles A. Beard, considered in some circles the dean of American historians, was one of the first to delve into the materials unearthed in the various Pearl Harbor inquiries and investigations. This volume is a logical followup to the author's earlier American Foreign Policy in the Making, 1932-1940. Long on documentation, it treats events in two facets: appearances (or what was revealed to the public at the time), and realities (or the behind the scenes machinations of the President and his aides). Beard does not deal in detail with the Magic intercepts, seemingly concentrating on the two-faced character of our foreign policy. This is particularly good as a source for documentation on moves by Roosevelt in the Atlantic and pre-Pearl Harbor Pacific which were designed to edge us into war.

Chamberlin, W.H., *America's Second Crusade,* Chicago, Henry Regnery Co., 1950.

This volume is a convenient source for quotations from speeches of President Roosevelt on the aims of his foreign policy. It also contains some interesting syntheses on the President's steps into war, and—while not relevant to this study—later policy decisions by Roosevelt (such as at

Yalta) in the course of the war. The author develops an interesting, if singular, thesis of the U.S. President's role in instigating the conflicts between the European democracies and Hitler's Germany which eventuated in the European phase of the Second World War.

Fuchida, Mitsuo, *"I Led the Attack on Pearl Harbor,"* Reader's Digest, February, 1954.

This account, condensed from United States Naval Institute Proceedings, is a graphic first-hand reportorial review of the Pearl Harbor attack from the Japanese flight commander. It is especially poignant in its description of the attempts of Americans to put up a defense in spite of the great odds against them.

Kimmel, Husband E., *Admiral Kimmel's Story,* Chicago, Henry Regnery Co., 1955.

This book is not so valuable for what information Washington had, but rather for what the Pearl Harbor commanders did not have. It gives a picture of the persecution heaped upon one of the principals as a result of his being made a scapegoat by the Administration. It also presents a background of some technical considerations in the defense of Hawaii and of the Washington orders as to strategy and tactics. We find here a first-hand account from a primary source of the indignities suffered by the Admiral in the course of the conduct of wartime investigations designed to remove blame from Washington and to shift it to the Pearl Harbor commanders.

Morgenstern, George, *Pearl Harbor,* New York, Devin-Adair, 1947.

Morgenstern has written and compiled the most comprehensive work of all the historical studies of Pearl Harbor and its background. It is painstakingly documented at great length from primary sources. Here are the details of the diplomatic negotiations between our government and Japan during the many months preceding the attack. The impact of the broken Japanese codes and the intercepted messages is well presented, and the details of the various attempts to cover up through subservient "investigations" are told, even to the elaborate attempts to weaken and hamper the Joint Congressional Committee. The Clausen "investigation" is reported more fully than I have found anywhere else. This is a product of great depth of scholarship.

Tansill, Charles Callan, *Back Door to War,* Chicago, Henry Regnery Co., 1952.

This is a large more general volume, but it contains valuable materials giving an insight into President Roosevelt's conduct of foreign policy prior to the Second World War and into his attitude toward foreign affairs and toward the representatives of other nations. I have quoted some excerpts detailing provocative acts by American naval vessels in the Atlantic long before our entry into the war. These policies, dictated by Roosevelt, were patently not those of neutrality, nor were they designed to keep war from our shores.

Theobald, Robert A., *The Final Secret of Pearl Harbor,* New York, Devin-Adair, 1954.

This is the most utilitarian small volume available on the subject of Pearl Harbor responsibilities. Very readable in style, it contains a foreword by Admiral Halsey, details of distribution of our fabricated machines to decipher the Japanese Purple coded messages, names of Magic's recipients in Washington, the provocative war's-eve diplomatic maneuvers of our leaders with Japan, texts of the Grew warning and most essential Japanese messages in the bomb plot series and after, and Admiral Theobald's cogent and pointed conclusions and interpretations which are difficult to answer.

U.S. Congress, *Report of the Joint Committee on the Investigation of the Pearl Harbor Attack,* Washington, United States Government Printing Office, 1946.

This is the official report of the Joint Congressional Committee which in 1945-1946 conducted the most extensive of all the investigations of the conditions, personalities, events, and factors surrounding the Japanese attack on Pearl Harbor. All studies by historians or journalists must return to this report as basic. Herein are found a survey of prewar diplomatic exchanges between the United States and Japan, prewar requests of the services for appropriations together with Presidential requests and actual Congressional appropriations, maps, texts of many of the Magic intercepts of the Japanese Purple code, testimonies of numerous principals under questioning, majority and minority conclusions, a detailing of the significant limitations placed upon the committee's activities—particularly the minority party members, and most significantly the "Additional Views of Mr. Keefe." The latter signed the majority report, but in these heavily documented twenty-four pages he provides some of the most eloquent and forceful support for the thesis of the minority.

There are resumes of the earlier hearings and investigations, but the allusions to and excerpts from those hearings as they arose before this committee are more valuable and meaningful than the resumes.

Because of its nature, this report through much of its length must be considered a primary source—or a comprehension of primary sources. Its major drawback is its lack of an adequate index. Perhaps someone will eventually take the time and trouble to rectify this inconvenience.

Waller, George M. (editor), *Pearl Harbor, Roosevelt and the Coming of the War,* Boston, D.C. Heath and Company, 1953.

This is a small book containing relevant excerpts from the works of a number of authorities dealing specifically with their viewpoints as to the responsibility of President Roosevelt for Pearl Harbor—particularly as to his role in fomenting the attack. It is characterized by references from advocates of both the revisionist and the Roosevelt-apologist angles. These passages are limited primarily to statements of viewpoint rather than to detailed documentation and are notable as revelations of the quality of reasoning and propensity for dealing with relevant facts. Authors quoted from the apologist school are Feis, Hull, Rauch, and Stimson and Bundy. Revisionists included are Beard, Chamberlin, and Tansill. This collection edited by George M. Waller is designed for tasting; those in search of a main course will need to look elsewhere.

Whelan, Joseph G., No Title, Library of Congress, Washington, June 13, 1960.

Joseph G. Whelan is identified as an "Analyst in Soviet and East European Affairs, Foreign Affairs Division" on this paper distributed by the Library of Congress in response to queries by Congressmen as to the facts on Pearl Harbor responsibilities. If this be the only source of information available to inquiring Washington solons, they are indeed condemned to almost unmitigated ignorance.

For his format Mr. Whelan ignores all the classic authorities of the so-called "revisionist" school such as Beard, Morgenstern, Tansill, Barnes, Theobald, and even the impressive Magic intercept documentation of the Joint Congressional Committee Report. He takes a somewhat obscure radio series, the "Dan Smoot Report," lifting topic sentences from their accompanying paragraphs of strengthening evidence to create straw men at which to tilt. Though the selected bon mots from Mr. Smoot must merit much respect from any serious student of the data available to researchers, Mr. Whelan has utilized exclusively Roosevelt apologist sources to "answer" him with statements which blandly ignore the incontestable facts and evidence—at times to a point of possible perjury.

I would recommend a reading of this paper together with a study of the "bomb plot" Magic intercepts to all analytical students of the Pearl Harbor story. It is a revealing insight into the degree and quality of objectivity of the Washington apologists.

Book II

A President Gambles (gambols), and We – and Our Friends – Lose

Chapter I

Vacant Victory

"That was the saddest moment – the moment of victory." – Polish Correspondent in Europe on the 40th anniversary of V E Day.

I was in the Philippines when the news came, winding up 43 seemingly interminable months in the Southwest Pacific with the Forty-First Infantry Division. "Japan has surrendered! The war is over!" For us who had lived intimately next door to death in the many months of jungle warfare it was an incredible sensation of relief and elation. It was a time of thankfulness and celebration – an explosion of emotions long pent-up. I am sure that we shared that ecstasy with armed forces – both victorious and vanquished – around the world. Civilian populations at home and in other nations went wild with joy.

But not everywhere. For millions upon untold millions the sounds of happiness elsewhere were met by silence, by fear, by anguish – and the stark specter of death. In Poland and East Germany; in Estonia, Latvia, and Lithuania; in Albania, Bulgaria, Czechoslovakia, Hungary, Romania, and Yugoslavia; in Manchuria and Korea, as well as for many millions of Russian citizens themselves, the end result of the Second World War was the permanent clamping down of the pulverizing power of Josef Stalin and the Soviet Union with their terror and tyranny, their desolation and desperation, the extinction of the last faint candle of hope.

Wallace, Wallechinsky, and Wallace, in their column "Significa" in the Parade magazine for July 17, 1983, afford us one glimpse into the callous realities of those days:

> The United States helped condemn 2 million refugees to imprisonment or death by forcing them to return to USSR after World War II.
>
> Most of these Soviet refugees had been POW's or slave laborers. Some were civilians who'd survived the Nazi concentration camps. Yet Josef Stalin, in their enforced absence, had declared it unpatriotic to be captured alive and labeled them all traitors. Their fate was sealed by the signing of a repatriation agreement at the Yalta Conference in 1945. U.S. diplomats hoped that consenting to return all displaced Soviets – by force, if necessary might help

> insure the safety of the 24,000 GIs stranded behind Soviet lines at War's end.
>
> Bloody riots began in the detention camps as Soviet refugees resisted attempts to put them aboard eastbound trains. Many committed suicide. Others attacked GI guards, hoping to provoke them into firing fatal shots.
>
> More than 2 million refugees eventually were handed over to the Soviets. Once on home soil, they were shot, exiled to forced-labor camps or imprisoned.

Parenthetically, Aleksandr Solzhenitsyn, in his authoritative *Gulag Archipelago, 1918-1956*, gives background for the estimate that the total number forcibly repatriated, including anti-Communist Russian troops on the Eastern Front and in detention camps, was between six and seven millions.

Communism – Psychoanalysis of an Institution

To attempt to understand world affairs in this age without a comprehension of the nature of Communism – Russian and international – may be likened to Noah's assembling all the animals just as the rains began, only to find that building the ark had slipped his mind. In the latter 1940's in New York's Columbus Circle I debated many times with the American spokesmen for the Moscow line. By that time the record of history shouted the saga of Soviet sins, and those who had joined the Party in a sincere but misguided reaction against the Depression and the free enterprise system had become disillusioned, scrambling as rats to leave a sinking ship. Only the dedicated remained.

I want to emphasize that fact. It is difficult to believe that even the most naive could have failed to face up to the truth. I am inclined to view with skepticism those prominent individuals who continued after the war to lend their names, their money, and their influence to the odious aims of Communism. There may have been some rare exceptions of innocence or mistaken identities, but I can have few tears for those who persisted in their camaraderie with subversion.

It was, however, on the campus at Columbia University that I got my most revealing insight into the Communist mind. I was arguing one day with one of their bright young minions as perhaps several score students listened. I said, "Communism is by nature dishonest." He said, "No it is not!" I replied, "Yes it is. Lenin's commission to Communists was: 'It is necessary to use any ruse, cunning, unlawful method, evasion, concealment of truth.' That is a commission to dishonesty!" He said, "Lenin never said that!" We went through a sequence of "He did" and "He didn't" till I finally said, "Let's go over to the Butler Library and check out the book." He agreed, and we proceeded to check out the little 1919 work of his idol. I turned to the page and gave the book to him to read. There it was – there was no denying that Lenin had said it. My adversary stood there for a moment before he closed the book and passed it back to me. I shall never forget his answer, and I always remember it when I hear sincere persons say, "Why don't we just sit down and talk to the Communists?" He looked me in the eye and said: "He did say that, but it is not a commission to dishonesty because I could not be honest with myself as a Communist if I were not willing to be dishonest in order to bring about the triumph of Communism!" Observation: For the individual Communist, the motivation is not dialectics, but a compulsive, sadistic desire for power.

Brass Tacks – The Only Way to Go

This world is real. It doesn't start with "Once upon a time" and end with "and they all lived happily ever after." Some of the players are very, very good; but some of them truly are horrid. To pattern actions on the assumption that only happy dreams come true is indeed to invite nightmares. All the wishful thinking in the world would not transform Hitler's Holocaust into a tea party.

I know of no better guide for tomorrow than to search yesterday. This is the rare jewel that the writing and the study of history offer to us—a jewel that is, alas, too often scorned. If it is known that the next-door neighbors have a record of cannibalism, it probably would not be a good idea to leave the baby with them while you go shopping. Fire extinguishers are purchased today because of the memory of past flames, and we lock our doors as a result of burglaries of yore.

Stage—Setting for a Fairy Tale

From November 28th to December 1, 1943, President Franklin D. Roosevelt met at Teheran with Joseph Stalin and Winston Churchill in the first Big Three meeting of the Second World War. Long since the United States had earned the title of the "arsenal" of those who were fighting in opposition to Hitler's lethal legions. For more than two years—even from before our entry into the war—the U.S.S.R. had been the beneficiary of our magnificent production machine. Tanks, planes, guns, ammunition, and countless types of war materiel had poured from American factories and been carried across the seas in thousands of American ships to Russian armed forces eager for our advanced technologies. A Russia, for example, whose fleetest plane at 297 miles per hour, the Stormovik dive bomber—could watch helplessly as Hitler's heavy bombers pulled away from them at 315.

In May, 1943, the Americans, British, and Free French had finished with victory an exhausting campaign against the tenacious German forces in North Africa. In July and August had come our invasion and conquest of Sicily, and the downfall of Mussolini and Italy's surrender followed on September 3rd. By the middle of November our forces had established themselves across the peninsula beyond Naples and were moving forward relentlessly against the powerful and deeply entrenched Nazi troops to the north. We had more than paid our dues.

Now, let us take note of a detail of which the President was well aware as he came to the Tehran Conference. He had been apprised at least three times of the treachery of Alger Hiss: (1) in September of 1939 by Assistant Secretary of State Adolph A. Berle (who learned of the details from a primary source, Whittaker Chambers, who was also implicating himself—this was at the beginning of the Hitler-Stalin Pact), (2) probably early in 1940 from William C. Bullitt, who had been our first ambassador to the Soviet Union, and (3) in early 1941 from columnist Walter Winchell. To all of these he voiced jocular disdain, and he proceeded to promote Hiss through the State Department until Hiss finally was his right-hand adviser at the tragic Yalta Conference in 1945. (The accounts of the reports on Hiss to the President are outlined in de Toledano and Lasky's *Seeds of Treason*, 1950. The records of the trial of Alger Hiss which found him guilty of perjury are also substantiation.) An embarrassment of sources primary. May we gently recall to mind the phrases of our preface in regard to those who disavow the perfidy of Hiss and unquestioningly believe that F.D.R. would never have been party to such a sordid affair: your reverie is illusion. It simply was not so. It was never so. It is myth, not history.

In addition there were then some compulsive facts that were fresh in the minds of most Americans, including Roosevelt. In the mid-1930's Stalin had mounted a campaign to collectivize the holdings of the small farmers in the Ukraine. The right to own land was a cherished value—a distinction that set one in a class long desired and only relatively recently achieved from the days of the tsars. It was understandable that there would be resistance; the brutality with which it was crushed was incredible. There are many primary sources on this, one of the most graphic being Victor Kravchenko's *I Chose Freedom*. Millions were murdered, and other millions were relegated to the living death of Stalin's slave labor camps. The latter also became the tyrant's depository for many others who disagreed or were purported to have disagreed—politically with the regime.

William C. Bullitt, our first ambassador to the Soviet Union, in Appendix I of his *The Great Globe Itsel*f, includes a detailed listing of some twenty-five solemn international treaties and agreements which had been broken by Stalin before he met President Roosevelt at Teheran in November of 1943. These broken pledges focused world attention on the attitude of the Soviet government as to moral agreements when it was to their advantage to break them—they could have rolled them up and sold them to the Scott Tissue Company.

Then, on August 23, 1939, Stalin had made his infamous pact with Hitler, setting the stage for both bullying aggressors. The Russian share of the pillage would subsequently be torn from Poland and Finland (for the latter of which Russia earned the distinction of being the only nation ever expelled from the League of Nations for aggression) and the tiny Baltic States of Estonia, Latvia, and Lithuania. This pact released Hitler for his attack on Poland and the initiating of World War II—on September 1, 1939. And just sixteen days following the German onslaught, Stalin also hit Poland in an assault from the east, subsequently annexing all of eastern Poland. Later in 1939 he attacked Finland, and early in 1940 he appropriated much of her territory. Three months later he turned his attention to the Baltic nations. He invaded and conquered Lithuania, confiscating it for the Soviet Union. He invaded and conquered Estonia, confiscating it for the Soviet Union. He invaded and conquered Latvia, confiscating it for the Soviet Union.

Red Americans (and We Don't Mean Indians) True—to The Line

Meanwhile, the American Communist Party was demonstrating a slavish adherence to the Moscow lines as they twisted and contorted to keep in step. Bullitt again provides in his Appendix II sixty pages of extensive quotes from the New York *Daily Worker* to bear this out dramatically. The source of the brief excerpts from that Communist periodical which I cite in the following paragraphs is the appendix from *The Great Globe Itself*—many of which I have also reviewed in the original.

On August 18, 1939, less than a week remained before the consummation of the Stalin-Hitler Pact. However, the mood of the *DW* editorial is a call to arms:

> . . . talk of American isolation while the bandit Hitler goes about his robberies in Poland becomes real assistance to the Nazis in the present drive . . . . We should never forget that the fascist dictators have already begun the second imperialist war, and that they are striving to expand the present conflicts into a world war directed against the leading democracies; the United States, France, Great Britain and the Soviet Union.

By August 24th news had come of the Stalin-Hitler pact. The *DW* headline shouted

> [Russo-German] Non-Aggression Pact Weapon for Peace, Open to All Nations, says Browder (Secretary, American Communist Party, 1930-1945) . . . . there is a great deal of newspaper comment to the effect that this represents a change of policy by the Soviet Union, that it is a blow against Poland, and so on. All that, of course, is nonsense.

Now came the pinch for the Party—they were caught (forgive me) Red-handed! They were aware that the American public would not condone a war on the side of Hitler and Stalin, and the Communists opposed our entry on the side of England and France in opposition to Russia. What to do!? We see the direct relationship to policies during the Vietnam War and at present. "War" became an evil word, and defense expenditures were a means to take food from the mouths of the poor. In his little book *While You Slept*, John T. Flynn notes:

> 'At that time there came into existence a notorious Communist front known as the American Peace Mobilization. It was organized on the day of the Hitler-Stalin Pact and dissolved when the pact ended. Its purpose was to keep America out of the war against Hitler and Stalin . . . . In June 1941 it began to picket the White House with [Frederick Vanderbilt] Field in the line. The day that Hitler struck at Stalin it called off its pickets and began to shout for war.' (House Committee on Un-American Activities, Appendix IX, p. 43).
>
> On the eve of Russia's attack on Poland, September 16, 1939, the DW editorial said: The Capitalist Press and Pravda's Editorial on Poland . . . this is an imperialist war in which all the wreckers of small nations, from Hitler to Chamberlain, are vying for the domination of the world.
>
> Mighty and unruffled, the USSR stands as the main bulwark of world peace, the defender of small nations, and the champion of human rights and progress.

In the meantime Hitler was enjoying himself in an unequal contest in Poland. Finally he had the opportunity to show off his blitzkrieg tactics on a smaller nation, near-helpless against the assault. Heavy bombers swarmed over their targets like angry wasps to be followed by the hundreds of tanks in tandem with fighters and dive bombers, crushing everything before them in a devastating onslaught.

Suddenly, on September 17th, Poland was struck from the east by the massive armed might of the Soviet Union, that stalwart "defender of small nations."

Without pausing for breath, the *Daily Worker* on the following day bore the editorial:

> For National Freedom and World Peace . . . the Polish people . . . were being stabbed in the back by the Chamberlain Munichmen . . . . In this situation the Soviet Government sent in the Red Army, as an army of liberation . . . .Truly the Soviet Union has scored another triumph for human freedom—destined for the brightest page of history. It is in accordance with her steadfast unshakable peace policy and with her policy of neutrality.

Again, on September 19th the *DW* reaffirmed its "peace" policy:

> Declaration of the National Committee, Communist Party, U.S.A. The war that has broken out in Europe is the Second Imperialist War . . . . This war, therefore, cannot be supported by the workers. It is not a war against fascism . . . not a war with any of the character of a just war, not a war that workers can or should support. It is a war between rival imperialisms for world domination. The workers must be against this war . . . we must . . . find the most effective means of keeping out of the war.

I would think that at this point all the naive but sincerely confused followers of the Communist line would have become nauseated and disillusioned and have awakened to the fact that something was rotten in—uh—Poland. The record shows that, indeed, to be true. It is difficult to credit the innocence of any who remained. But on December 6, 1939, in the *DW* we find a statement by William Z. Foster:

The Communist Party opposes the Administration's plan to spend three billion dollars next year to strengthen the navy, army, and air forces . . . . The . . . government is following the policy of territorial aggrandizement which leads straight toward war, with all the attendant misery, poverty, enslavement, and death for the workers and other toilers.

DW—February 6, 1940: Earl Browder:

> The best contribution our country could make to bleeding Europe . . . . [would be] by serving notice that America will send not a dollar, not a gun, not a boy, for the imperialist war. Let's tell Europe, once and for all, that this time the Yanks are not coming.

There was more of the same on May 11, 1940, in the Editorial:

> This Is Not Our War—Keep U.S. Out of It . . . .The imperialist bandits in each country—the Anglo-French and Hitler bandits—a handful of the population—are turning the world into a madhouse of murder . . . . Starve the war and feed America. Keep America out of the criminal war.

The *Daily Worker* maintained its anti-war pose on up to the threshold of the attack by Hitler on the Soviet Union. A parting glance at this stance comes for us in these phrases from a few weeks before the break (April 29th, 1941):

> The Imperialists have made the war; we, the people, must make the peace. Get out and keep out of the imperialist war—No convoys, no AEF—The Yanks are not coming . . . . Against the militarization of the United States under the false pretense of national defense.

Blasphemy in Red

One of the areas where Communists and their like have been most insidious has been in the prostitution of sacred instrumentalities for their ungodly ends. They have been skillful at maneuvering the naive in some cases to take positions on issues that are completely out of line with the beliefs of those whom they purport to represent. I am a devout Methodist and the son of a Methodist minister. I, together with a preponderance of "little people" in my denomination, have resented the fact, but felt helpless, when a little group from time to time have assumed such titles as the "National Methodist Commission" on something or other, and then have proceeded to make far-reaching pronouncements on social or defense issues with which most Methodists strongly disagree. I am sure that members of other denominations have objected to similar practices in which the perpetrators have appropriated good names to advance ends with which most members are not in sympathy. Such was the Methodist Federation for Social Service which prevailed for a number of years during and prior to the Second World War. Herein were collected a number of leaders who have been identified under oath before Congressional Committees as Communists, although most members were non-Communist and often were ignorant of Communist aims. There was a need, however, for leaders who were *anti*-Communist.

One of the Communists was Winifred Chappell who was active in the policy determinations of the Methodist Sunday evening youth groups called the Epworth League. She wrote some of the programs for those regular meetings which were contained in a publication entitled the Epworth Herald. Usually the youth started by singing several hymns, they had a prayer, took up a collection, and then one of the group would read the evening's lesson verbatim from the Epworth Herald. The following passage staggers belief, but it was written by Winifred Chappell for an evening lesson during that period of the Russo-German Nonaggression Pact when it was the Communist aim to keep the United States out of the war against Hitler and Stalin. This passage was reproduced in a hearing before a Congressional Committee as reported by *U.S. News and World Report* in its issue for August 7, 1953. Here for church young people are the words of Winifred Chappell:

> Young church fellows of draft age must decide something when war breaks out. In general these youths have four choices instead of two, as most of them think. First, they can conform, yield to the draft, play the game of the war makers, be cannon fodder, get shot or gassed or blinded or de-legged or de-armed, but if possible, beat the enemy to shoot, gas, blind, de-arm the fellows on the other side first.
>
> In the second place, they can be conscientious objectors and go to prison.

A few score did that during the World War. A few hundred or thousand will do it next time. That takes even more courage than to go over the top. It takes just as much physical courage. The CO's in some prisons during the World War were subjected to extremely cruel treatment. But now a third choice, hardly so much as even heard of during the World War, appears in this possibility—stay out of jail. Why thus separate yourself from the masses? Why thus let yourself be put out of the game? Accept the draft, take the drill, go into the camps and onto the battlefield or into the munitions factories and transportation field. But sabotage war preparations and war; be agitators or sabotage; down tools when the order is to make and load munitions; spoil war materials and machinery.

The fourth choice is merely a further development of the third. It calls for sabotage but with a deliberate, conscious, informed intent to get rid of the present economic system, of which war is a part, and to build a new world, the existence for which peace is a necessity. If you will make this choice, make it now and begin to meet before war breaks with others of like purpose and of iron will to carry out the purpose. This means knowing what selfish capitalism is like, not just in general, but in particular; not flinching even from knowing by name and specific deed the big profiteers who have betrayed the people, how they have profited from the starvation of children; how they have called upon police and militia, clubbed and gas-bombed and machine-gunned to put down the workers when they cried for bread.

I would assume that, following this, the group would stand to sing a final hymn (perhaps on the subject of love or peace), join in the League Benediction, and then they would all go in to sing in the choir for the evening service.

It Seems to Me that We Have Heard That Song Before!

Before we press on with our story I think it appropriate to stand back and survey the record of that period in our nation's history and to contemplate the inescapable reality that in our present-day situation these strains are all too nauseatingly familiar. Never is there a positive plan for a defense of America—or of the Western World—that does not meet with pious objections from the drop-of-the-hat opposition (often with pronouncements of the "church leaders" and "church groups" whom they count among their numbers). And when implementations of those plans occur, such as draft records or the placement of missiles for the defenses of European nations, there are those ready to spill –supposedly, their—blood on the records, or to mass by the thousands to lay their bodies in the paths of military trucks and in turn be carried limply away, drooping like dead weights against their patient bearers. Again leaders and their sympathizers are slavishly following a line that emits a definite flavor of vodka.

It was obvious from late 1939 to the summer of 1941 that American citizens were never going to favor a war effort in support of Stalin and Hitler against the democracies of England and France. Therefore the line was: peace; war is evil; and anyone not opposed to war is vicious and degraded and actuated by greed. The U.S.S.R. was a victim of circumstances but doing the best it could by "heroically" invading and "saving" small countries.

It is easy to be against war, and many sincere dupes were taken in by a well-orchestrated campaign of deception as to the true aims. Two years later when Hitler invaded the Soviet Union and the same war became a holy crusade (as we shall observe), it was confusing to many who had been programmed to believe that pacifism was the only moral stand.

Now we are once again engaged in a prime program of pacifistic promotion. Again at the touch of a button the patently choreographed demonstrations of scores of thousands can be activated for whatever purpose or for whatever event for which they may be desired.

As we look back across the years at the anti-defense clamor during the months of the Hitler-Stalin Pact, is there anyone who would maintain that the in-the-know American Communist leaders were honest and sincere? Can we—with logic—think that their dishonest counterparts are not actively present today?

Some Details of Baltic Tragedy

George F. Kennan, in his comprehensive volume, *Russia and the West Under Lenin and Stalin*, says of the period of the Stalin-Hitler Pact:

> The Russians took their customary reprisals against 'class enemies' and deported innocent people to the interior of Russia in such numbers and with such callous brutality that hundreds of thousands of them appear not to have survived the ordeal. For the three Baltic countries, this division eventually meant the end of national independence. In the case of the Estonians, in particular, it meant the deportation and permanent dispersal of a large portion of the population—the literal removal of much of a nation from its homeland. For the Finns, it meant a bloody and terrible war. (p. 333)

I Think that I Shall Never See—a New Twist to Joyce Kilmer

There was, then, the coldblooded incident of the Massacre in the Katyn Forest, authenticated by an International Red Cross investigation. George Kennan again provides an account of events that were well-known at the time:

> The Russians, at the time of their entry into eastern Poland in 1939, appear to have made it a policy to arrest and deport to Russia all Polish officers on whom they could lay hands. Three camps were originally established to house

> these prisoners. They had contained in all about 15,000 men . . . not one of these men had been heard of since April 1940, more than a year before the German attack on Russia . . . [In] 1943 . . . the Germans . . . announced the discovery, on occupied Russian territory, in a place called the Katyn Forest, of mass graves containing the bodies of thousands of Polish officers who had been taken prisoner by the Russians in 1939. The men had obviously been cruelly executed, one by one, at the edge of the great pits, the bodies being then pushed in . . . . The graves discovered by the Germans, it soon developed, contained the bodies of men from one of the three camps. The fate of the inmates of the other two camps remains a mystery down to this day. (Ibid. pp. 359-360)

A Change of Plan

But to return once again to our friends at the *Daily Worker*. The surrender of France (June 17, 1940) had been preceded by the epic achievement at Dunkirk where 335,000 British and French troops were snatched from the fire and slaughter of the beaches by a motley array of more than a thousand ships and boats. Spirited to England, they would live to fight another day. Then during 100 days and nights at the end of 1940 and beginning of 1941 the aerial Battle of Britain demonstrated to Hitler that merciless and incessant bombing would not soften up the British nor break their indomitable spirit. Indeed, the R.A.F. and R.C.A.F. Spitfires proved to be better than anything he had to throw against them. Hitler had never, of course, trusted Stalin, but he had hoped to buy off the Soviet dictator temporarily with the nonaggression pact while quickly dispatching England and France. Later—perhaps—Moscow.

Now that plan had gone awry. Probably he had hardly entertained the idea that it might fail, but now for "Plan B." Russia would have to be taken care of before he would feel free to turn west again. On June 22, 1941, Germany attacked the U.S.S.R.

The *Daily Worker* hardly missed a step in the "To the rear-March!" The following day a "Statement of the Communist Party" maintained "The American people . . . will see in the cause of the Soviet Union the cause of all advanced and progressive mankind . . . . For full support and cooperation with the Soviet Union in its struggle against Hitlerism!" June 30th evoked: "Defend America by giving full aid to the Soviet Union, Great Britain and all nations who fight against Hitler!" On July 1st: "The great might of America must be thrown against Hitler . . . aid to Britain must be increased . . . . The way to defend America is by helping the U.S.S.R. smash Hitler."

Of course, the National Council of American-Soviet Friendship came into being almost immediately, numbering among its members many of those who so recently had excoriated the evils of war. As a Methodist I was not surprised to find among its sponsors the name of Bishop G. Bromley Oxnam.

On September 21, 1941, the *DW* exclaimed: To 'wait for Hitler to attack us' is to give America's most ruthless enemy the maximum advantages, and guarantee him the victory. It is the counsel of treason . . . . Let the United States, inspired and aided by the Red Army's resistance, take its rightful place in the battle.

We entered the war on December 7, 1941, with the Japanese attack on Pearl Harbor. On January 13, 1942, the DW, struggling to keep a straight face, wrote: "As to the Communist Party: its record is an open book in its consistent stand for American national defense against the Axis aggressors."

If any doubt remained that American Communists' allegiance was only to Moscow, the DW, on October 15, 1943, attacked the "fantastic notion that it is possible to equate the puny, limited war effort of Great Britain and the United States with the achievements and the sacrifices of the Russians who have carried the whole brunt of the war."

Of course, the United States had had, in addition to its considerable productive and military contributions to the European war, a little matter of the conduct of virtually the entire war against Japan throughout the vast Pacific. And to ensure that that latter effort remained a U.S. monopoly, on October 30th the *DW* added " . . . it is to be hoped that our delegation is setting its face against the brazen attempts of American defeatists to force the USSR into the war against Japan."

OK. Now let's review the awesome list of those unforgettable sins of Russia's Communist government and of Americans whose allegiance was to the Soviet Union—transgressions that were well known to Franklin Delano Roosevelt when he went to Teheran:

(1) Stalin's cruel liquidation of millions of his own people during the 1930's—the Kulaks, or small farmers in the Ukraine, by murder, imprisonment and slave labor

(2) The record of imprisonment and cruelty and torture in dealing with any political opposition or disagreement

(3) The institution of slave labor itself—the sub-human without-hope existence for millions of Russia's own population

(4) The Hitler-Stalin Nonaggression Pact of August 23, 1939, and Stalin's subsequent record of cooperation with the architect of aggression and the Holocaust

(5) Stalin's subsequent invasion of Poland, in league with Hitler

(6) Stalin's invasion of Finland, for which he was thrown out of the League of Nations—a record shared by no other national leader

(7) The brutal invasions, uprooting, and mass deportations of the little Baltic states of Estonia, Latvia, and Lithuania

(8) The unspeakable massacre of 15,000 Polish officers in the Katyn Forest

(9) The long record of broken treaties which lay at Stalin's doorstep

(10) The record of traitorous espionage by Hiss and others

(11) The record of the American Communist Party which slavishly followed the twistings, turnings, and complete reversals of the Moscow line, often to absolute disloyalty.

In addition there was the record of vast lend-lease aid from our factories' rich cornucopia of production, starting months before we were ever in the war, and given with no strings attached whatsoever. Also, aside from our almost exclusive prosecution of the war against Japan, there was the equipping of our other European allies, our participation in the successful invasions of North Africa, of Sicily, and of Italy (with the resultant Italian surrender), and the massive continuing anti-German campaign in Italy which helped greatly in relieving pressure on Stalin's forces.

Chapter II

Fantasy Farce

F.D.R.'s "Great Design"—or Grand Design

To different intimates Roosevelt expounded on what he variously termed his "Great Design" or his "Grand Design" for World War II and after. Forrest Davis, of the *Saturday Evening Post,* was briefed at great length by the President soon after his return from Teheran. He wrote two articles which appeared in consecutive issues of the Post, May 13 and 20th, 1944 after the President, himself, had edited them. They were entitled "What Really Happened at Teheran." From them and from his public actions before and following, it was revealed what Roosevelt had in mind. Ambassador Bullitt, however, clarified the plan most succinctly on page 21 of *The Great Globe Itself*—a plan to bring about the "conversion" of Stalin. The student of history will find that all of the record to that time—the bits and pieces, however hard to believe—fit into this simple framework; and the subsequent revelations as they have unfolded in all their sorry and horrifying detail fall into place in the mosaic pattern:

> (1) To give Stalin without stint or limit everything he asked for the prosecution of the war, and to refrain from asking Stalin for anything in return. [Roosevelt had told Bullitt that Stalin "doesn't want anything but security for his country, and I think that if I give him everything I possibly can and ask nothing from him in return, noblesse oblige, he won't try to annex anything and will work with me for a world democracy and peace."] (2) To persuade Stalin to adhere to statements of general aims, like the Atlantic Charter [Ed.—which would cost him precisely the same amount as a declaration that he preferred good weather rather than foul]. (3) To let Stalin know that the influence of the White House was being used to encourage American public opinion to take a favorable view of the Soviet Government. (4) To meet Stalin face to face and persuade him into an acceptance of Christian ways and Democratic principles.

That is correct. You may have an impeccable credit rating and may never have been arrested; but you must display your driver's license and credit cards when you make a purchase by check in a store. Stalin, with the record we have summarized, could get anything he wanted with no questions asked! Industrial power was the sine qua non of the Second World War. Gone long since were the millenia in which an army's might was reckoned by the number of its horses. Planes, tanks, battleships, aircraft carriers, trucks, jeeps, artillery pieces, ammunition, bombs, and a myriad other items great and small—together with advanced technology—these decided the issues. President Roosevelt had at his disposal an American productive machine such as no other nation had ever dreamed of. But at Teheran John R. Deane in his book, *The Strange Alliance*, p. 43, observed:

> Stalin appeared to know just what he wanted at the conference. This was also true of Churchill, but not of Roosevelt . . . . His apparent indecision was probably the result of our obscure foreign policy.

The President (Kennan, *Russia and the West*, p. 358) "had (already) gone very far . . . in encouraging the Russians and the world public to believe that . . . (in 1942) a second front would be created within the year" in answer to Stalin's insistence that it be done to relieve German pressure on Russia. Churchill, remembering Dunkirk, and more realistic about such premature action, was reluctant. In the end it was he who had to go to Moscow to get Roosevelt's chestnuts out of the fire and break the news to Stalin. The "guilt" thus created was self-made by the President as a result of one of his famous whims—a guilt not shared by the people of the United States nor by the hundreds of millions in eastern Europe and in Asia and Southeast Asia who were to fall under the yoke of international Communism. Diane Shaver Clemens, writing with a deep pro-Soviet bias in her book, *Yalta*, indicated the sense of "shame" expressed by Secretary of War Stimson in that Stalin would not have much of an opinion of people who would let Russia fight most of the war. The implication was that we would not be welcomed when the time came to share the world with him.

No Guilt—and an Opportunity Not Seized

On the contrary, five months before our entry into the war we had made our initial offer and arrangements to send large quantities of supplies to Stalin's beleaguered forces. Again two months before we entered we committed ourselves to accede to the Russian dictator's urgent request for even more immense supplies, which were desperately needed. William C. Bullitt (Op. Cit., pp. 192-3 and pp. 11-13) goes on to deal with our conduct of the negotiations:

> When the Soviet Union was dependent for its life on Lend-Lease Aid, President Roosevelt, as a quid pro quo for Lend-Lease Aid, could have obtained a written guarantee from Stalin that the western limits of the Soviet Union should be those of August, 1939, and that the Soviet Government would assent to the creation of a European Federation. . . . . In return for the

offer of such aid (we) asked nothing. The vital interest of the United States in a free and independent Europe was not expressed . . . .

To argue that Stalin might not respect, or would not respect, such a guarantee was to misunderstand the object of obtaining such a guarantee. That object had a positive side as well as a negative. The negative was to prevent Soviet subjugation of eastern, central and southeastern Europe. The positive was to clear the way for a constructive attempt by the United States to create a peaceful, democratic Europe which should be sufficiently strong and stable to defend itself from future aggression . . . . If (Stalin) had given such a promise with the intention of breaking it ultimately, he would at least have had to behave as if he had no intention of breaking it so long as he and his country were dependent for their lives on aid from the United States . . . .

In 1941 and 1942 the President had the power to compel Great Britain and the Soviet Union to accept proposals designed to produce lasting peace. He might have enunciated, and forced written acceptance of, a program for peace in Europe and Asia even more clear and specific than the program contained in President Wilson's Fourteen Points, which had given the United States the moral leadership of the world. That leadership was conspicuously ours during the First World War, and conspicuously not ours, or anyone else's, during the Second World War.

According to the account of the Teheran Conference in the *Encyclopedia Americana,* "He (Stalin) conceded that without 'American machines the United Nations could never have won the war.'" This would not seem to be an attribution of guilt or shame.

Making Stalin Look Good

Roosevelt seems to have beguiled himself that all decisions were on his own initiative. At Teheran, according to Forrest Davis, he "avoided the slightest cause of offense to the Kremlin." One of his aims was to popularize the Soviet Government with Americans, and former Ambassador Joseph E. Davies, in the light of that aim, wrote the unbelievably laudatory *Mission To Moscow*, which was also made into a movie. It is difficult to imagine that the President could credit one who had been quoted by the *Daily Worker* on February 25, 1942: "Ambassador Davies declared, 'by the testimony of performance and in my opinion, the word of honor of the Soviet Government is as safe as the Bible.'" And three days later the *Daily Worker* quoted Davies again: " . . . the Russians like ourselves . . . have no territorial ambitions." In short, Roosevelt's requests from Stalin were only things to make Stalin and Communism look better to the American people.

Working Behind the Backs of Our Friends

The American people, of course, recognized England, the Free French, and

China as our friends and team members in the struggle which had been thrust upon the world. The dictators were the "other side," and only by a historical mishap did we find one of them, Stalin, on our side—after a period of collaboration with the opposition. President Roosevelt's secret, behind the scenes dealings, seemed to go directly counter to the popular will, according to accounts now available.

At the Teheran conference it developed that Roosevelt, rather than having living quarters in the American Embassy or in the British Embassy, was invited by Stalin to reside in the Soviet Embassy. John T. Flynn, in his book *The Roosevelt Myth*, gives one report of what went on behind the scenes (pp. 358-9).

> Later Roosevelt told his son Elliott *(As He Saw It)* that 'in between times Uncle Joe and I had a few words, too—just the two of us.' As Stalin's guest in the Russian embassy, Roosevelt was accessible for a secret talk or two without Churchill's knowledge. One of these dealt with the Chinese Communist issue. Roosevelt told Elliott we couldn't do much about that 'while Winnie was around.' He brought up the question of a common front against the British on the matter of Hongkong, Shanghai and Canton. Chiang, Roosevelt told Stalin, was worried about what Russia would do in Manchuria. [Editorial note: This was breaking a confidence with Chiang, with whom Roosevelt and Churchill had just met at Cairo.] Roosevelt and Stalin agreed that Manchuria would remain with China and that Stalin and he would back Chiang against the British. Referring to this, Roosevelt confided to Elliott that 'the biggest thing was in making clear to Stalin that the United States and Great Britain were not in one common block against the Soviet Union' . . . and he was later to make another deal between himself and Stalin against Chiang.

Also, from Forrest Davis's "What Really Happened at Teheran" we get:

> Mr. Roosevelt sees no material risk in delaying a policy toward Germany until military pressure can be more forcibly applied.
>
> Nor does he confine his wait-and-see tendency to the German problem. A desire to extemporize in harmony with developing events, and not against them, has motivated the President's reluctance to commit the future of France exclusively to General DeGaulle.

The soon-to-be-published wartime correspondence between Roosevelt and Churchill (Warren F. Kimball, editor, *Churchill and Roosevelt: The Complete Correspondence*) gives some excellent primary sources relative to what many would call this duplicity. The account by Edwin McDowell in the *New York Times* was quoted by the *Tampa Tribune* of July 12, 1984.

> The Correspondence . . . reveals tension and even bitterness between the American president and the British prime minister over such matters as independence for India, how to guarantee elections in Poland and strategy for

dealing with the Soviet Union . . . . Since the British-American agreement in 1972 to declassify diplomatic and military records of the war era, scholars have been aware that the alliance of the two nations in World War II was beset by disharmony . . . .

Roosevelt . . . irritated Churchill by trying to prod him into promising independence for India during the war rather than after.

'American public opinion cannot understand why, if the British government is willing to permit the component parts of India to secede from the British Empire after the war, it is not willing to permit them to enjoy what is tantamount to self-government during the war,' Roosevelt wrote Churchill on April 11, 1942.

The following day a draft response for Churchill was prepared in Britain, subject to Churchill's approval, saying, 'I cannot feel that the common cause would benefit by emphasizing the serious differences which would emerge between our two countries if it were known that against our own convictions we were conforming to United States public opinion in a matter which concerns the British Empire and is vital to our successful conduct of the war in the East.'

The draft was never sent and instead, the final version of the cable was toned down. But it maintained that independence for India should not be discussed during the war . . . .

Churchill thought better of another message originally intended for the president—a harsh, bitter letter drafted by the prime minister himself—opposing the proposed invasion of southern France instead of using those Allied forces in Italy and the Aegean.

'I think I have the right to some consideration from you, my friend, at a time when our joint ventures have dazzled the world with success,' he wrote on June 30, 1944.

But the redrafted letter, sent one day later, was couched in language considerably more conciliatory . . . .

The two men also differed strongly over Roosevelt's desire to oust the British-sponsored King of Greece and hold free elections.

But perhaps the major irritant stemmed from Roosevelt's tendency to treat the British as a junior partner. One example was FDR's proposal for a private meeting with Stalin, in the belief that the Soviet leader would be more frank in discussing the Balkans, Finland and Poland without Churchill around . . . .

By contrast, the correspondence reveals that Roosevelt was less concerned about postwar Russia than about postwar France and the reconstitution of the Polish government . . . .

The correspondence also shows, Kimball said, that Roosevelt had a remarkably consistent foreign policy. 'The widely accepted interpretation is that in foreign policy he flew by the seat of his pants and dealt with problems as they came up,' he noted, 'But he was absolutely consistent in his belief that colonialism was the major postwar problem. He saw nothing wrong with great-power "leadership," but he was staunchly opposed to formal colonialism.'

All right! We have seen Roosevelt planning secretly with Stalin, the dictator, behind Churchill's back. We have observed his steadfast desire to break up the British Empire, and his animosity toward DeGaulle personally and French colonialism as well as British. He has plotted with Stalin to betray Chinese interests and British interests in the Far East, even though the Russian dictator has refused to join the war against Japan and would continue to do so. And he has carefully avoided any offense to Stalin, the ruthless dictator, over his plans for Poland and Eastern Europe. It is objectionable to him for our friends to have colonies; Stalin's conquests do not bother him.

Teheran—A President's Shame

I am outlining facts of history. I am amazed that these facts are unknown to—or ignored by—those who purport to be critical observers of the era and of the men who were the decision makers at the time. However, the June 22, 1961, Tampa Tribune carried editorial comment on the Teheran Conference:

> Skeletons abound in the just-released papers of the 1943 Teheran conference between President Franklin D. Roosevelt, British Prime Minister Winston Churchill and Soviet Dictator Josef Stalin.
>
> No American can read this record with pride.
>
> It shows, for one thing, that Roosevelt in effect consented to Russian annexation of a large part of Poland's territory on condition the deal was not officially discussed before the 1944 election. The American President frankly admitted in this private conversation with Stalin that he did not wish to risk losing the 6 to 7 million votes of citizens of Polish extraction. [This portion of the Tribune's editorial I cited in the Pearl Harbor discussion.]
>
> At another point, Stalin coldbloodedly proposed that to guard against a return of German militarism 'at least 50,000 and perhaps 100,000 of the German commanding staff must be physically liquidated.'
>
> Roosevelt's reaction to this monstrous proposal, as reported by his aide, Charles E. Bohlen, was that 'the President jokingly said he would put the figure of the German commanding staff which should be executed at 49,000 or more.'
>
> Churchill, however, voiced a strong dissent. He said war criminals should stand trial for their offenses but he vigorously objected to 'executions for political reasons.' No mass executions were carried out—at least not outside the Russian zones of occupation.
>
> Then there was the conversation between Roosevelt and Stalin on the Baltic states of Estonia, Latvia and Lithuania which the Russians had gobbled up in

1940 and soon afterward lost to the German invaders. Roosevelt was quoted as telling Stalin—again 'jokingly'—that—'when the Soviet armies reoccupied the Baltic areas he did not intend to go to war with the Soviet Union over this point.'

> He did urge Stalin to hold free elections in the little captive states, and Stalin blandly, replied, 'There would be plenty of opportunities for such an expression of the will of the people.' The opportunities, of course, were to vote for the stooges chosen by the Kremlin or be shipped to Siberia. The Baltic states have virtually vanished from sight; the world is reminded of their plight now and then when some bold Estonian, Latvian or Lithuanian slips through the Iron Curtain and takes sanctuary abroad.

Relative to the betrayal of Poland, George Kennan (Op. Cit, p. 357), comments with some depth:

> But one does not get—at least I do not—the impression that Roosevelt had any substantive objections—any real political objections—to seeing these areas go to Russia, or indeed that he cared much about the issue for its own sake. One gets the impression that it seemed to him of little importance whether these areas were Polish or Russian. His anxiety was rather that he had a large body of voting constituents in this country of Polish or Baltic origin, and a further number who sympathized with the Poles, and he simply did not want this issue to become a factor in domestic politics which could make trouble for his wartime leadership of the country.

It would seem not to be an inconsistent pattern for the president who was evidently the prime mover in the uprooting and incarceration of thousands of American citizens during the war—without due process of law—the Japanese on the West Coast. They suffered, according to Paul Greenberg in the *Fort Worth Star-Telegram* (July 15, 1983): (1) Two to three years of imprisonment, (2) The loss of homes and farms, which had to be sold under pressure, or which were lost because taxes and mortgages and insurance payments couldn't be paid from camp, (3) The dislocation and anxiety, (4) The educations and careers disrupted, (5) The old folks who had to start their lives all over again from scratch, and (6) Violation of the civil rights of citizens of the United States. Few episodes in American history are so fraught with lawlessness and injustice as this.

Casablanca Revisited

The Casablanca conference had occurred upwards of a year before Teheran. I must return there briefly to take note of a monumental error—the demand for "unconditional surrender" of Germany and Japan. In my research I have found this mentioned time after time, but never have I found it treated with more clarity and succinctness than in a column by Ray Tucker which appeared in the *Tampa Tribune* December 6, 1954:

> Another advantage handed to the Russians in the current conflict was F.D.R.'s impulsive Casablanca insistence upon 'unconditional surrender,' which he took from U. S. Grant. Roosevelt forgot that the Union Commander was thinking only of armies in the field, not of going governments. Grant was talking in military rather than political terms, a great difference.
>
> As predicted at the time, this ultimatum forced the Germans and Japanese to fight on until their countries' economic, industrial and agricultural resources were destroyed utterly.
>
> It eliminated two buffer bulwarks against Russian aggression in Europe and in the Far East. It forced the United States to pour out billions to rehabilitate our erstwhile enemies, in order to check the Communist onslaught.
>
> Churchill was not responsible for this blunder, as it appears now. In fact, Roosevelt blurted these terms on the spur of the passionate moment, and without prior consultation with the Prime Minister.
>
> Churchill has demonstrated only recently how far more foresighted he was than F.D.R. with respect to Moscow's postwar plans and attitude. Suspecting Stalin, he ordered Field Marshall Montgomery to be ready to rearm the Germans so as to block any Red advance into Western Europe. He did not permit battlefield smoke to blind him.

As regards both this topic and the question of Poland, Samuel Koo of the Associated Press reported (*Tampa Times,* December 26, 1981):

> Vatican City. The Vatican says President Roosevelt rejected repeated warnings by Pope Pius XII about the Soviet Union's postwar aims in 'Catholic Poland' and other parts of Eastern Europe.
>
> The wartime Roman Catholic pontiff also questioned the wisdom of the Allies'policy of 'unconditional surrender,' thinking it was 'vindictive' and could cause the Germans to fight longer. But the United States made clear that the policy was 'beyond discussion' and showed little interest in enlisting papal mediation to bring the war to a negotiated end, according to Vatican documents made public this week.

The information is contained in a 787 page book based on the Vatican Archives. It is the last of 11 volumes in a Vatican 'white paper' on the war years and the role played by the Italian prelate who became pope in 1939 and died in 1958.

> The final volume, titled 'The Holy See and the World War,' covers the period from January 1944 to June 1945.
>
> The Rev. Robert A. Graham, a U.S. Jesuit who edited the series, told a news conference Thursday Pope Pius saw 'a great danger in the complacency

in the White House' about the role of the Soviet Union in the postwar Europe.

Disquieting to the pope was the insouciance with which the Allies, and in particular President Roosevelt, appeared to regard the prospect of half of Europe occupied indefinitely by the forces of the Soviet Union,' said Graham. ' . . . For despite assurances from the president, the Vatican had no sign of any change of heart in Moscow as regards freedom of religion.'

Graham cited a Vatican memorandum given to Roosevelt's personal representative, Myron C. Taylor, after a papal audience June 21, 1944. It said:

'The Holy See is looking with great concern at the war aims of the Soviet government. The intention of occupying the Baltic states, part of Poland and some Balkan countries . . . might seriously compromise the cause of peace.'

The Communist takeover of Poland launched a determined struggle by the Polish church and its primate, the late Cardinal Stefan Wyszinski, against the government's attempts to reduce the enormous influence on the Polish people. And in 1978, after 33 years of Communist rule, 93 percent of the 35 million Poles were baptized Roman Catholics, and 78 percent attended church regularly.

One point stressed by a number of critics of our policy of unconditional surrender is the fact that we thereby ignored the anti-Hitler and anti-Communist forces in Germany. I think that nowhere has this been better stated than by George Kennan (Op. Cit., p. 367):

> But there was not only Hitler, in Germany. There was also the non-Communist German resistance. It was composed of men who were very brave and very lonely, and were so much closer to us in feeling and in ideals than they were to either Hitler or Stalin that the difference between them and us paled, comparatively, into insignificance. These men succeeded, at the cost of great personal and political danger, in establishing contact with the Allies during the war. They received literally no encouragement from the Allied side. They were obliged to carry out their tragic effort to unseat Hitler, on July 20, 1944, not only with the total absence of Allied support at that particular moment, but with no assurance of Allied support in future, or even of more lenient peace terms, in the event they should succeed and take Germany out of the war. The unconditional surrender policy, which implied that Germany would be treated with equal severity whether or not Hitler was overthrown, simply cut the ground out from under any moderate German opposition.

Some apologists for Teheran have tried to make the point that we were in a weak position because there was danger that Stalin might make a separate peace with Hitler, leaving the western Allies in the predicament of carrying on without the Russian forces. This supposition ignores some obvious realities of the situation. First, Adolf and Josef by this time were well aware of each other, and neither entertained any illusions about the other. Stalin, knowing that Hitler had tried to destroy him, would not likely have co-operated by dropping out, thus enabling the Nazi dictator to conquer the powerful—er ah—"God given" democratic Allies so fortuitously granted to the U.S.S.R. in spite of her sins. And once those Allies had been conquered there was the virtual certainty that Hitler would turn again on Russia—now without any Allies. By experience Stalin knew how well he could trust Hitler's agreements. Also, the hurdle of Stalingrad had been passed, and the Red Armies were on the offensive—with our Lend Lease aid. The Soviet dictator's insatiable lust for expansion would never have let him retire from so promising a fray.

Back to Teheran

A preponderance of the foregoing has consisted of a portrait of Stalin and Communism in the years and months leading up to Teheran. Nobody was better informed on this picture than was Franklin D. Roosevelt. On the other side of the balances were these factors: (1) Neither the United States nor our other allies had been guilty of the immoral stance of co-operation with Hitler and the rape of small countries in eastern Europe—including the Katyn Forest Massacre. We had a monopoly of the moral perspective. (2) Our military contributions had been crucial (including North Africa, Sicily, the defeat of Italy, and a continental second front across the Italian peninsula), (3) These events portended the ever more massive part our forces were to play in the crushing of Hitler, and (4) Stalin desperately had needed and would continue to need the colossal beneficences of our Lend-Lease, coming from our advanced technology and stupendous productive capacity. Perhaps never before in the history of the world had a leader of a great nation had it so uniquely within his power to formulate plans for widespread freedom and lasting peace, and to compel the enemies of peace and freedom into compliance with those plans. Such aims are not self-enforcing, after all; someone needed to have such plans for the liberty and self-determination of the nations of Europe—and, indeed, of Asia—and the restriction of aggressors within circumscribed boundaries until strength might be built in co-operative regional alliances. The President calculatedly chose to renounce such singular advantages and to rely instead on his "charm" and individual one-on-one persuasiveness to reform Stalin.

The objective of "Christian ways and democratic principles" for the tyrant of the Kremlin fell by the wayside, however, in Roosevelt's appeal—not to benevolent unselfishness and the Golden Rule—but to the "It's us against them" syndrome. It was the allurement of "What's in it for me?" that the President dangled before the Russian dictator. According to Forrest Davis (Op. Cit.), he "conducted at Teheran a seminar, for Stalin's benefit, in the good-neighbor policy." The import of this was that after the war the United States would be predominant in the Western Hemisphere, and Russia would be the prevailing power in eastern and northern Europe (as well as Asia, of course). One can read Stalin's mind now—"Just what I had in mind—for starters!"

In short, for whatever reasons, President Roosevelt, and those among his advisers who catered to him, disregarded history—tragically.

Chapter III

Cavalier Catastrophe

Now About That Lend-Lease –

Let's look at that Lend-Lease more closely. Figures are available from many sources, but the Americana Encyclopedia notes that in the first year of aid to Russia we gave them 3,052 planes, 4,084 tanks, 30,031 vehicles of various kinds, and 831,000 long tons of miscellaneous supplies. Major Erwin Christian Lessner of the Austrian army is quoted as their specialist and authority:

> The military situation in Russia, during the fall and winter of 1941-1942, was extremely critical. It can be stated without exaggeration that the final German defeat in Russia would not have been possible without United States and British equipment to make up for a part of the Red Army's losses. The Soviet government, however, was reluctant to give publicity to Allied assistance.

During the war the United States exceeded the Russian war expenditures by more than $125 billion!

In all, our Lend-Lease to the U.S.S.R. totaled some $11,141,470,000. It consisted of items which weighed 16,529,791 long tons, and required 2660 ships to carry it all—mostly ours. There are numerous sources for the statistics on the individual commodities sent—the various encyclopedias, books such as Major General John R. Dean's *The Strange Alliance,* Felix Wittmer's *The Yalta Betrayal*, et. al. Some notable items—not by any means an entire listing—were:

Trucks	437,039	
Tires	17,000,000	
Field Telephone Units	415,426	
Field Telephone Wire	670,000	miles
Field Telegraph Wire	1,105,024	miles
Submachine Guns	135,633	

Anti-Aircraft Guns	8,218	
Jeeps	51,503	
Radio Stations	35,941	
Motorcycles	35,170	
Combat Planes	14,798	
PBN and PBY Patrol Planes	185	
Railroad Cars	11,155	
Locomotives	1,966	
Railroad Wheels and Axles	100,000	long tons
Rails	500,000	long tons
Marine Diesel Engines	8,000	
Tanks	7,056	
Self-Propelled Guns	707	
Ships: Merchant Ships	100	
Submarine Chasers	100	
Torpedo Boats	200	
Boots	15,000,000	pairs
Cotton and Woolen Cloth	150,000,000	yards
Foodstuffs	4,478,116	long tons
Petroleum Products	2,260,371	long tons
Chemical Products	600,000	long tons
Explosives	300,000	long tons
Machinery	over $1,000,000,000	worth
Medical Supplies	over $1,000,000,000	worth
Tractors	8,075	

It would seem that a list like that would have provided some significant leverage as quid pro quos for the future safety of our nation and the safety and peace of the world, and certainly for the protection of small, dependent countries. That that was not even considered was tragic, and in no way commendable on the part of the leader of the "free" world.

Now it's time for us to look at probably the single most positive alternative that President Roosevelt had in his dealings with Stalin. We have looked at—or hinted at—a number of negatives—things which should not have been done. This one should have been carried out.

I would like to quote a sentence from William C. Bullitt, (Op.Cit., p. 203): "Winston Churchill, because he had the courage to let his constructive imagination rise to the demands of even the darkest hours, emerged as the noblest and most practical statesman of the Second World War."

And from the Ray Tucker column referred to prior to this:

> Another Churchill proposal vetoed by F.D.R. was that the invasion of Hitler's Europe should be launched through the Balkans instead of France. The more experienced British statesman pointed out that this strategy would give the Allies possession of a line from the Adriatic to the North Sea, and thus keep Russia out of Central Europe and the Balkans.

This idea evidently was a source of great levity to the President and his confidants with whom he chortled, according to his son Elliott (*As He Saw It*, p. 117). I quote from Felix Wittmer's reference to this in *The Yalta Betrayal*, pp. 46-47:

> President Roosevelt evidently thought that the British idea of some action in the Balkans rather than in Southern France was extremely funny. 'Whenever the P.M. argued for our invasion through the Balkans,' the magnificent hunch player chuckled as he recalled the Teheran plenary sessions in the presence of son Elliott, 'it was quite obvious to everyone in the room what he really meant. That he was above all else anxious to knife up into Central Europe, in order to keep the Red Army out of Austria and Rumania, even Hungary, if possible. Stalin knew it, I knew it, everybody knew it . . . .Trouble is, the P.M. is thinking too much of the postwar, and where England will be. He's scared of letting the Russians get too strong.'

Wittmer recalls that the accepted plans for a secondary invasion of southern France forced Gen. Mark Clark to weaken his army in Italy which had been poised for an otherwise certain victory over Gen. Kesserling's badly mauled Nazi army there. The chances for a Balkan offensive were thus weakened.

Now, look at a contemporary map of Europe (see illustration) and visualize the receptions and attitudes the various peoples might have demonstrated in the

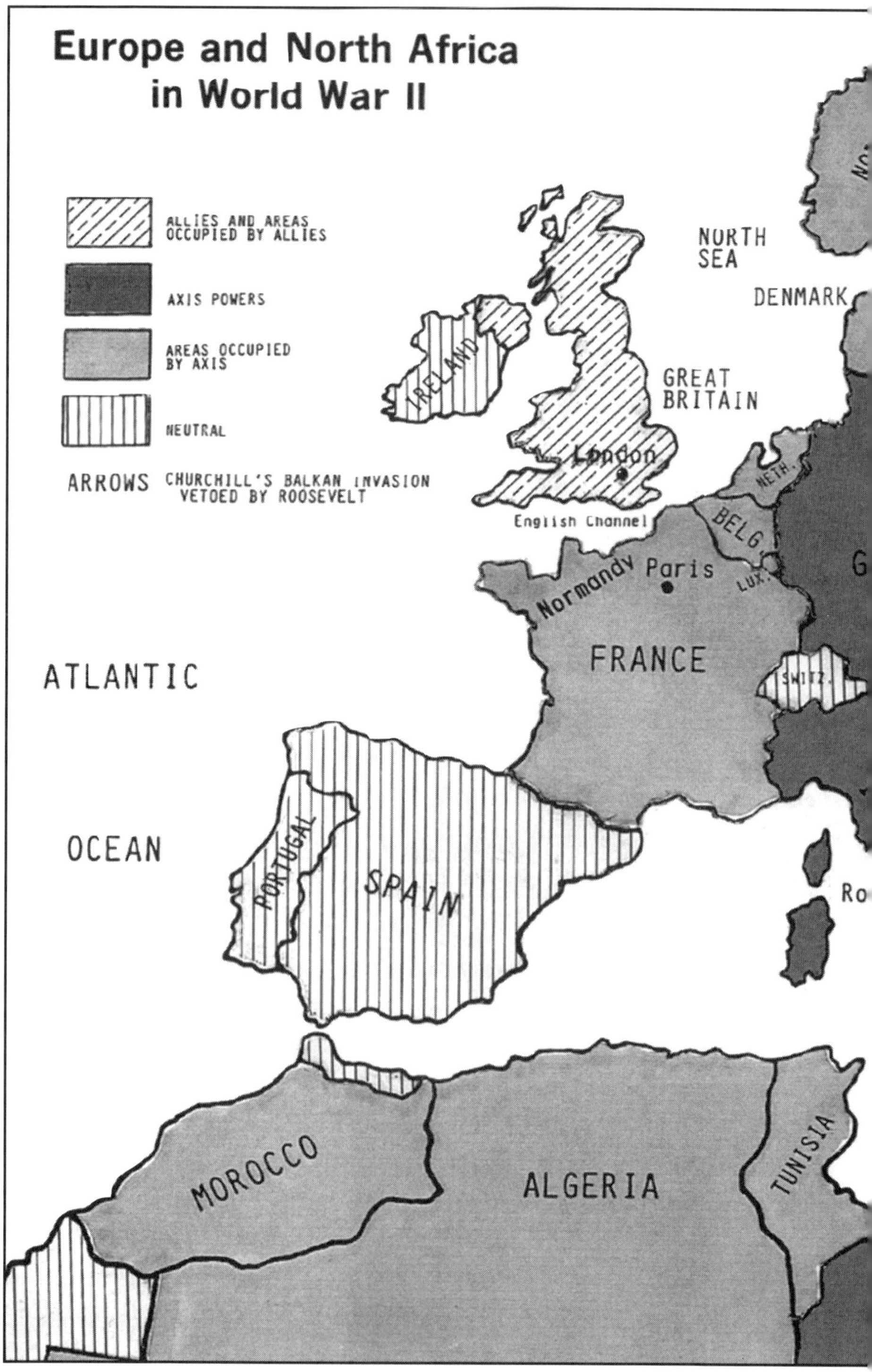
Europe and North Africa
in World War II
ALLIES AND AREAS OCCUPIED BY ALLIES
AXIS POWERS
AREAS OCCUPIED BY AXIS
NEUTRAL
ARROWS CHURCHILL'S BALKAN INVASION VETOED BY ROOSEVELT
NORTH SEA
DENMARK
IRELAND
GREAT BRITAIN
London
English Channel
NETH.
BELG.
LUX.
Normandy
Paris
FRANCE
SWITZ.
ATLANTIC
OCEAN
PORTUGAL
SPAIN
MOROCCO
ALGERIA
TUNISIA

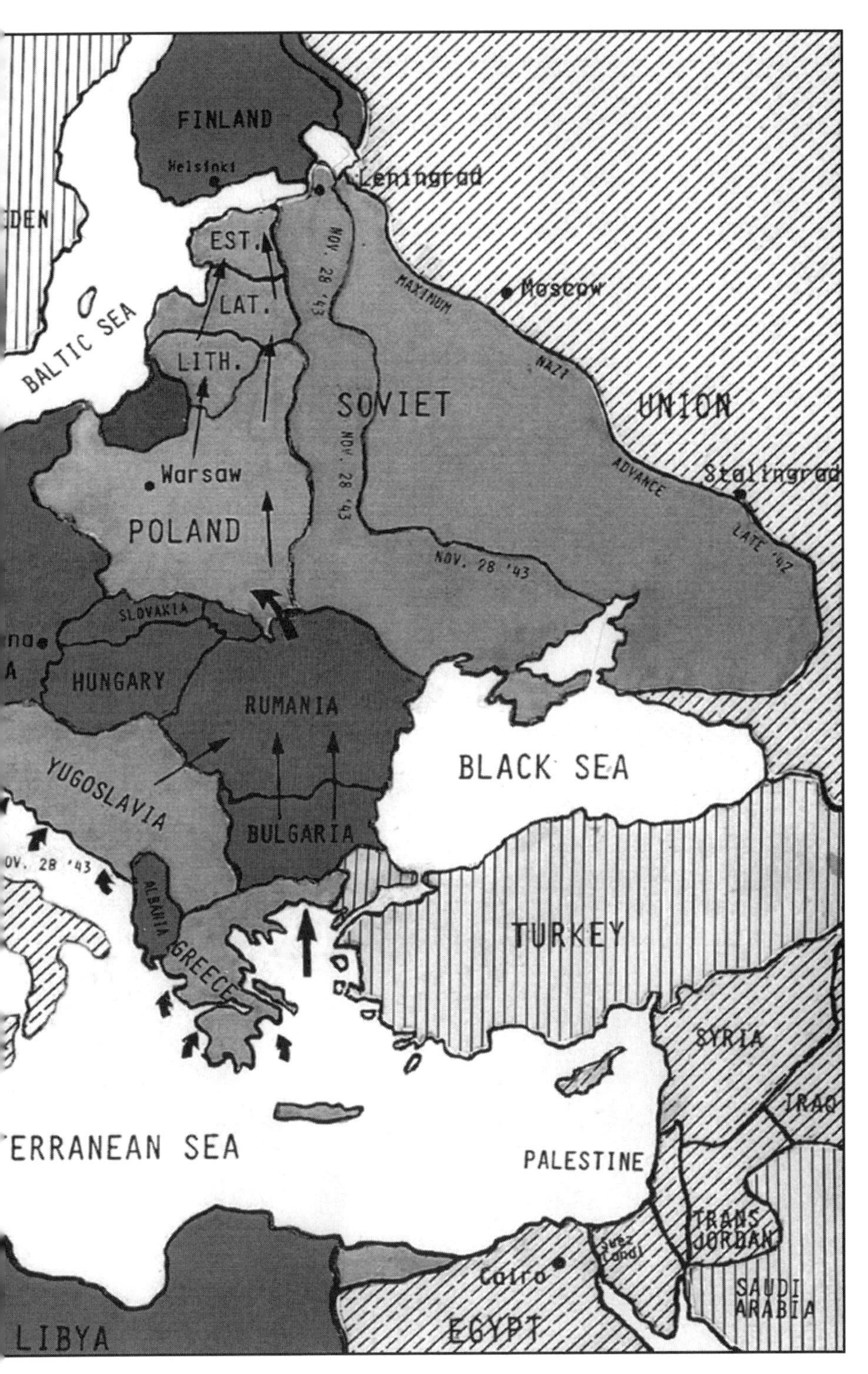

FINLAND
Helsinki
Leningrad
EST.
LAT.
LITH.
BALTIC SEA
Moscow
MAXIMUM
NAZI
ADVANCE
LATE '42
SOVIET
UNION
Stalingrad
NOV. 28 '43
NOV. 28 '43
NOV. 28 '43
Warsaw
POLAND
SLOVAKIA
HUNGARY
RUMANIA
YUGOSLAVIA
BULGARIA
BLACK SEA
ALBANIA
GREECE
TURKEY
SYRIA
ERRANEAN SEA
PALESTINE
TRANS JORDAN
Suez Canal
Cairo
EGYPT
SAUDI ARABIA
LIBYA

event of a projected second front across the Balkans and northward through the nations of eastern Europe.

Greece had been an early victim of German invasion in April, 1941. Mussolini had invaded Albania just two years earlier, in April of 1939, but when he sought to take over Greece in the fall of 1940 the ill-equipped but heroic Greek armies inflicted heavy losses on his forces and drove them back into Albania, pursuing them there. As Italian losses mounted in the ensuing winter months, it was not the winter weather that reddened the face of il Duce. The Nazis entered on their own and overwhelmed the Greeks and Allied forces. Greece surrendered on April 23, 1941. However, in both Albania and Greece, stubborn guerrilla forces remained active.

Yugoslavia had desired to remain neutral, but the German forces swept through in ten days, taking surrender five days before the fall of Greece. Belgrade, her proud ancient capital city on the Danube, with upwards of half a million inhabitants, had been declared an open city, but a great deal of it was bombed to ruins before it was occupied. Partisan guerrillas were energetically active from that time until 1945.

The Munich Agreement of 1938 had caused little Bulgaria to lose faith in the will of the Western democracies to resist Hitler's growing power. She was reluctantly pressured to support Germany in March, 1941. However, she did not send troops to the Eastern Front to aid the attack on Russia in June of 1941. When Russia declared war on Bulgaria September 5, 1944, a leftist regime came to power.

Rumania was bullied by Soviet and Hungarian troops in August, 1940. Two months later, without fighting, she became a "wretched satellite of Hitler" as German troops mastered the "tug-of-war" for her control and moved in to occupy and commandeer her valuable oil reserves. In August, 1944, her pro-German dictator, Marshal Antonescu, was overthrown, and Rumania officially became an Ally.

Hungary was forced to become a German ally in November, 1940. She co-operated in an attack on Yugoslavia in April, 1941. Hungary was dominated by Germany, and her population was intimidated by the Nazis. By February, 1945, Russia had completely moved into and taken over Hungary. According to the infamous Munich Agreement of September 29, 1938, Czechoslovakia was forced to surrender the Sudetenland to Hitler. In the following year Hitler dismembered Czechoslovakia, assuming dominance over Bohemia, Moravia, and Ruthenia, and recognizing the "independence" of Slovakia. Czechoslovakia was no more—except in battered spirit.

In March, of 1938, after fostering the growth to dominance of the Nazi party in Austria, Hitler poured his troops across the border and declared that Austria was a part of the Reich.

Earlier we outlined the march of Stalin through Estonia, Latvia, and Lithuania, and the concurrent bludgeoning of Poland by Hitler and Stalin together. The Katyn Forest Massacre of 15,000 Polish army officers was only a sample of the gruesome Soviet gifts to the Poles; the Nazi legacy during the war would be the slaughtering of some six million Poles, many of them Jews.

Finland, as we have related, was defeated by Russia in March, of 1940. In May the Germans began a secret infiltration. By June of 1941, when Hitler attacked Russia, there were at least ten German divisions standing ready on the Finnish-Russian border. Finland was captive to co-operation with Germany, as were Poland and the three little Baltic States.

As autumn fell across North Africa in 1942, the Axis powers held almost all of the areas except for the British grasp on most of Egypt and the Suez Canal. Fighting had been bitter, complicated by the collaboration of Vichy French officials and naval officers with the Nazis; and Morocco, Algeria, Tunisia, Libya, and much of the coastline of Egypt west of the Nile were in enemy hands. Early in 1943 the British Eighth Army, under General Montgomery, had begun to make remarkable progress, moving westward from Egypt across the coast of Libya to Tripoli. He was aided by the effects of a huge amphibious attack beginning November 7, 1942, in which vast American resources of men and materiel, as well as British, were landed at numerous strategic points all along the enemy-held coasts. By May 12th the struggle for Africa was over with the surrender of the German generals and their armies. In the North African campaign the Axis forces had lost more than 2500 tanks, 6200 guns, 70,000 trucks, and 8,000 aircraft.

In July and August had come the invasion and conquest of Sicily. Il Duce was ousted in Italy. Massive Allied units landed in force on Italian shores, and Italy surrendered. However, most of the peninsula was still in the grip of German armed forces who struggled tenaciously to retain it. Hard-fought landings were made in the Salerno area. On October 1, 1943, two months before the conference at Teheran, our troops took Naples. Eleven days earlier three Allied forces had joined to form a control line across Italy, amputating the foot from the boot. By mid-November the line had moved north of Naples on the way to Rome, where heavy rains and flooded streams slowed them down as much as did the enemy—but they were on their relentless way.

By 1943 the United States was producing more than 100,000 planes a year, and Germany was reeling under round-the-clock block-buster bombings from swarms of as many as 1200 planes in a single raid. Her war production was being systematically wiped out, and the Luftwaffe, with fewer and fewer aircraft, was forced to turn from the offense almost totally to defense. In February of 1944 alone possibly 60 per cent of the Nazi fighter plane production capability was destroyed, along with 80 per cent of the twin engine manufacturing plants. The Atlantic and the Mediterranean were dominated by our air power, and no part of the enemy's territory was safe from attack.

Let us review the picture: There were thirteen captive nations forming an unbroken line from the Balkans northward across eastern Europe whose populations (except for those few tied by treason to Hitler) would overwhelmingly have welcomed liberation by American and British forces—peoples who suffered persecution, slave labor, torture, and death at the hands of the Nazis—and many, also, so recently at Red hands.

North Africa had been swept clear of Nazis. Sicily and vast areas of Italy had been won, with land, naval, and air bases within easy fighter plane distances to use as a huge powerful spring-board to launch attacks into areas with deep hatred for the enemy forces that occupied them.

This was the plan that President Roosevelt thought was "extremely funny," and at whose author—Winston Churchill—he sneered for his having the effrontery to mistrust the intentions of Stalin, that great lover of his fellow man—to utilize a cannibalistic figure of speech.

Now, let us return to the map of Europe. Where do you imagine Stalin would have wanted us to make the second front? That is correct—exactly where we made it and where the Germans were expecting it to be! Right across the Channel from England into Normandy. Why would the Russian dictator desire that? The powerful German forces in France, and Germany itself, stood between us and all of the countries of eastern Europe which he coveted—some of them for the second time around—or more. It would be out of the question for us to go beyond Germany and liberate any of those nations; the surrender of Germany would, indeed end the war and leave them at Stalin's mercy.

Again the map. With Allied forces controlling North Africa, Sicily, and much of Italy; with the U.S. Air Force dominating Mediterranean skies; and with the Wehrmacht and Luftwaffe awaiting an attack on the beaches at Normandy, picture an invasion up through the Balkans and continuing northward through Central Europe, Poland, and the Baltic states, and possibly into Finland itself. It would not have been as easy a campaign, considering the terrain and distances, but it would surely have saved many lives through the shortening of the war. Our forces would have driven a wedge between Germany itself and her vast armies on the eastern front, cutting their vital supply and communications lines. And to whom do you imagine that those eastern European nations or the German armies in them would rather have surrendered—to our forces, or to the Russians of Katyn Forest repute? And at war's end it would have been we and our democratic Allies occupying all of those areas including East Germany. The Russians would have been allowed to move into those which they had possessed prior to the war. But we find that President Roosevelt had already arranged to give much of that territory to Stalin, and that was only a prologue to what he would surrender—needlessly—at Yalta.

Months before Yalta, however, Stalin would give another demonstration of his true brutal colors. I turn again to the words of George Kennan (Op. Cit., p. 365):

> Yet it was three months after the Normandy landings, at a time when the second front was already a successful reality, when Paris had already been liberated and Allied troops were at the gates of Germany, and when the liberation of Soviet territory itself—the Soviet territory of 1938, at any rate—was no longer at stake, that there took place the most arrogant and unmistakable demonstration of the Soviet determination to control eastern Europe in the postwar period: Stalin's reaction to the Warsaw uprising—a demonstration so revealing that no one in the West had the slightest excuse for ignoring its lessons. You will recall what happened on this occasion: how the members of the Polish underground, operated by the Polish government-in-exile, tried to seize the city from the retreating Germans; how the Soviet forces paused at the gates of Warsaw for many days, letting the Germans make short shrift of this resistance; and how, when the United States government asked permission to use the facilities of the American air bases in Russia with a view to dropping supplies by parachute to the beleaguered Poles, Stalin's answer was a snarling no. How could it have been more clearly demonstrated that Russia was claiming the future Poland as its own and proposed to make no concessions to the democratic forces in that country?

Meanwhile, Old Friends at the DW

We must remember to touch base with our friends back at the *Daily Worker*—flag-wavers all. In an editorial on January 25, 1944, on a fourth term for the President, they noted: "Roosevelt is a national asset . . . . The people want Tehran for America and for the world—and that means they want Roosevelt." And on the following May 28th they commented on the "dissolving" of the Communist Party to form the "Communist Political Association" for the 1944 election: " . . . the national unity which is required can only be attained in America at present on the basis of the capitalist 'free enterprise' system." That the organization might aptly have chosen the name "Chameleon" is demonstrated by the contrast with former stands in its editorial for November 27th, less than three weeks after the election:

> For Universal Military Training. 'We believe the great majority of Americans are convinced universal military training is essential today . . . such a step is inseparably connected with the kind of foreign policy the people voted for November 7 . . . we join in urging support for such a measure.

In the weeks and months following the Normandy invasion it is interesting that as the armed forces of the U.S.S.R. began to flood through the little countries of eastern Europe, pursuing the German armies that had occupied them, the Russians began to declare war on the governments of those small nations, establishing an adversarial relationship. On the eve of the American election and also the eve of the 27th anniversary of the Communists' overthrow of President Kerensky and the Duma, Stalin took note of the importance of Normandy (I. Spector, *An Introduction to Russian History*, p. 377):

> There can be no doubt that without the organization of the second front in Europe, which pinned down 75 divisions of the Germans, our troops would not have been able in so short a time to break down the resistance of the German troops and drive them from the confines of the Soviet Union.

There we had from Stalin's own mouth a statement to relieve the most guilt and shame-ridden of those American advisers who had felt that there was not enough that we could do for nor give to the Russian dictator in penance for the absence of a second front in France—and our supposedly niggardly efforts in the war in general. On the contrary, it would appear from Stalin's statement that the U.S.S.R., indeed, was in our debt for the rapid and virtually entire liberation of her land. It can hardly be conceived that conditions only eleven months before had been such as to merit humiliation other than that willfully self-imposed.

At this juncture it is particularly revealing to note the still unrelenting abjection and humiliation which characterize the words of one of our observers of the scene as late as the Yalta Conference, Diane Shaver Clemens in her book, *Yalta*. She continues to depict the American participants as plagued with shame and guilt, and indicates that Stalin could not have much of an opinion of people who would let Russia fight most of the war—that he would not be disposed to let them share the world with him. She speaks of the Soviet Union as forced on the "defensive" in the talks, implicitly wronged and misunderstood. They had to compromise "possibly" more than any others. She hints (p. 290) at the raising of "serious questions about American intentions." "On the other hand, the Soviet Union during the war," she says, "remained basically co-operative." Such a diagnosis is rare, but we can see our friends at the *Daily Worker* nodding in approval.

But back to the real world. We have observed the cold-blooded action of the Soviets at the time of the Warsaw uprising, and it was quite evident that their dealings with the Baltic states and eastern Europe in the fall of 1944 harked back to their brutal invasions during the days of the Hitler-Stalin Pact. To quote Kennan (Op .Cit., p. 366):

> What was at stake from September 1944 on was only the question of Russian postwar aims in eastern and central Europe; and on this subject we no longer had the right to entertain any illusions.
>
> Let us remember, in particular, that a considerable portion of American Lend-Lease aid, particularly industrial equipment, reached Russia after this date. It was after this date that both the Yalta and Potsdam conferences took place. It was after this date that we decided to associate ourselves with the Soviet armistice commissions in the Balkans. It was after this date that we entered into the Declaration on Liberated Europe, made the unreal and unwise deal over Poland, and exerted ourselves mightily to bring Russia into the United Nations. Would it not have been better to have paused at that time, to have had, then and there, the frank and unsparing political clarification with Stalin which the situation demanded?

Of course, Mr. Kennan knew well when he wrote, as he also knew well in 1944, that Stalin was as despicable as Hitler and could be trusted to do just as he was doing, had done, and would in the future do. And yet our policy continued—give, give, and give in and give in.

Adolph A. Berle, formerly an Assistant Secretary of State, has testified as to the two factions in the State Department in the autumn of 1944—the "trust the Russians" group, and those who, like him, were reading events and actions clearly and desired to utilize our power while there was still time to call the Soviet's hand. History tells, sadly, which faction won.

Chapter IV

Asia: Vanquishment for Victory; Europe: The "Promised" Land

The Yalta Conference, an inexcusable tragedy, occurred in the Crimea February 4-11, 1945. This was probably the darkest hour for civilization and freedom in the history of the world. In its discussion, Americana observes: "At the time, Germany's surrender within the ensuing six months seemed a virtual certainty, and Japan's defeat within a year probable." Japan, however, was actually on the verge of collapse, and President Roosevelt knew it. In a remarkable revelation of this, W.H. Chamberlin, in his America's Second Crusade (pp. 218-9) reports:

> Apologists for the Yalta concessions maintain that Japan in February 1945 presented the aspect of a formidable, unbeaten enemy . . . According to an account later published by Arthur Krock, of the *New York Times*, an air force general presented a report at Yalta pointing to the complete undermining of the Japanese capacity to resist. But the mistaken and misleading view that Japan still possessed powerful military and naval force prevailed.
>
> Acceptance of this view by Roosevelt was especially unwarranted because two days before he left for Yalta Roosevelt received from General MacArthur a forty-page message outlining five unofficial Japanese peace overtures which amounted to an acceptance of unconditional surrender, with the sole reservation that the emperor should be preserved. The other terms offered by the Japanese, who were responsible men in touch with Emperor Hirohito, may be summarized as follows:
>
> 1. Complete surrender of all Japanese forces.
> 2. Surrender of all arms and munitions.
> 3. Occupation of the Japanese homeland and island possessions by Allied Troops under American direction.
> 4. Japanese relinquishment of Manchuria, Korea, and Formosa, as well as all territory seized during the war.
> 5. Regulation of Japanese industry to halt present and future production of implements of war.
> 6. Turning over of any Japanese the United States might designate as war criminals.

> 7. Immediate release of all prisoners of war and internees in Japan and areas under Japanese control.
>
> MacArthur recommended negotiations on the basis of the Japanese overtures. But Roosevelt brushed off this suggestion with the remark: 'MacArthur is our greatest general and our poorest politician.'
>
> That the President, after receiving such a clear indication that Japan was on the verge of military collapse, should have felt it necessary to bribe Stalin into entering the Far Eastern war must surely be reckoned a major error of judgment, most charitably explained by Roosevelt's failing mental and physical powers.
>
> Captain Ellis M. Zacharias, Navy expert on Japan whose broadcasts in fluent Japanese hastened the surrender, asserts that intelligence reports indicating Japanese impending willingness to surrender were available at the time of the Yalta Conference . . . .
>
> [Note, p.219] The story of the Japanese peace overtures is told in a dispatch from Washington by Walter Trohan, correspondent of the *Chicago Tribune* and the *Washington Times-Herald*. It appeared in these two newspapers on August 19, 1945.

Now a brief reprise. We need to remember what Mr. Roosevelt had said his plans were: to give Stalin without stint or limit everything he requested and to ask for nothing in return. In his clandestine meetings with the Russian tyrant behind the backs of our long-time allies, he had gone beyond a policy of patiently waiting for Stalin to come up with such ideas on his own; the President himself gratuitously advanced concepts beyond the wildest dreams of the Communist leader. This was not a mere proffer of guns and bullets. As for Asia, who before the war had been the chief competitors of Russia for domination? Japan (going back in this century to the Russo-Japanese War), Great Britain (India, Burma, Pakistan, Ceylon, Malaya, Singapore, Hong Kong), France (French Indochina- including Cambodia, Laos, and Vietnam), and China (Manchuria, including ports and railways coveted by China, Russia, and Japan). Of course, Japan would be removed by the war, her armies on the Asiatic mainland (including Manchuria) defeated and expelled, and her grasp of other territories terminated. The Communist leader had the President's assurances that he would stand as a powerful opposition to the continuation or reinstituting of the colonialism of Britain and France in those areas of Asia listed after their names above. Stalin had also been assured of Roosevelt's support against Chiang Kai-shek. Mao Tse-tung was leader of the Chinese Communists. Several moves had undermined Chiang's position. He was having to fight Mao and the Japanese at the same time. Then he was ill-served by our dispatching Gen. Joseph W. Stilwell to be his military adviser. The thrust was to get Chiang to co-operate with Mao rather than for Mao to cooperate with Chiang. Finally, it was the U.S. decision to force unity between Chiang and the Communists by promises of aid and credits if they would comply. Smith Hempstone's newspaper column of April 11, 1975, observed that in the summer of 1937 Mao controlled only about 35,000 square miles of territory and some one and a half million people out of 450 million.

> While Chiang's Nationalists hurled themselves against the Japanese, the Communists carefully husbanded their forces for the civil war that they knew would follow an Allied victory. By the time Japan surrendered in August, 1945, the Communists had consolidated their position to the point that they controlled 225,000 square miles of territory with a population of 65 million.

During that truce the Communists expanded the counties they held from 57 to 310. And from V J Day there was a two year embargo on aid to China. We shall presently observe the reasons for this. Hempstone continued in the same article: "Between 1945 and 1949, when Chiang left for Taiwan, the Nationalists' position . . . simply disintegrated in the face of attacks by fresh, well-disciplined Communist troops."

More on this anon.

All right. Now why did Roosevelt refuse to heed the news of impending Japanese surrender? We have seen that the President had a plan, his "Great Design," which was infinitely more important to him than the realities of the situation—indeed, it ignored reality altogether. The shameful betrayals at Teheran of Poland and the Baltic States (the details to be cemented into place at the Yalta Conference as gangland executioners have at times used cement around the feet of enemies destined for swimming lessons) were possible because Stalin was already in the European war. [And, thinking purely in a postwar vein, wouldn't it have been nice to have been able to make the peace arrangements for Europe without having to take into account the U.S.S.R. and Stalinism?!] But Russia was <u>not</u> fighting against Japan and had thus far scrupulously avoided even the appearance of such an "evil." We <u>had</u> the opportunity then to make peace in Asia without Stalin's and Russia's being involved! But to carry through with his Great Design Roosevelt needed to get Stalin into the war in Asia so that he could give to the Soviet dictator all the vast concessions that were in store for him in that area of the world. The greatest single error in Asia was bringing Russia into the war; Roosevelt did it, and he <u>bribed</u> Stalin to come in at great expense to us and to China and to peace and freedom in Asia.

I cannot hold with those who plead that the President was forced by conditions to lure Stalin into the war against Japan—that the "Land of the Rising Sun" was still a formidable adversary which would necessitate an invasion at the sacrifice of possibly hundreds of thousands of American lives. The Japanese peace overtures and our photographic evidence of bombing devastation to cities and factories, as well as our general intelligence on the enemy's fighting potential gave a compelling picture of a "setting Sun." However, a *New York Times* dispatch (*Tampa Tribune*, August 2, 1985) reported that a research team made public

> . . . documents from United States archives showing that planners for the Joint Chiefs of Staff estimated in 1945 that an invasion of Japan would leave 40,000 American servicemen dead, 150,000 wounded and 3,500 missing in action. Other professional military estimates were in the same general range.

One consideration, however, was the unhappy error of the President himself—the prescription for "unconditional surrender." That was a dictum which might have constrained a fanatical enemy to fight till the last drop of blood had been spilt. Again, the peace overtures would belie that; but had that not been the case, a Presidential statement correcting the mistake would have served to bring the matter into proper focus. Roosevelt, of course, was aware already of the imminence of a discovery soon to be known to Hiroshima and Nagasaki!

The wily Stalin, however, played hard-to-get. Kennan (Op. Cit, p.381) recounts that in October of 1944 General John R. Deane, head of our military mission in Moscow,

> . . . in reviewing for Stalin the course of the Pacific War . . . stressed that plans for further operations would depend partly on what Russia was willing to do. Stalin, surprisingly, countered by asking whether we were really sure we wanted Russia to participate. Would we not prefer to finish off the Japanese alone? If so, this was all right with him . . . . Suffice it to note that it was a smart move on Stalin's part. It wiped out his previous [secret] statement of intention to enter the war anyway, without compensation, and it put us at once in the position of supplicants. The answer given was that of course we did want Russia to enter the Pacific War as soon as possible, and with all available strength. In particular, we wished the Russians to destroy the Japanese forces in Manchuria. This desire implied of course an initial Soviet occupation of the highly strategic Manchurian area which was formally part of China and in which Russia, as we knew had been politically interested for a half-century past.
>
> Stalin, in replying, said that the Soviet forces, in order to accomplish this mission, would have to carry out an outflanking movement which would take them around to the south through the vicinities of Peking and Kalgan, and that an occupation of the North Korean ports would also be necessary. He further observed that there were 'certain political aspects that would have to be taken into consideration' in connection with Russia's entry into the war. Please note

that these operations he mentioned would obviously place Russia in complete military control of Manchuria and its railways as well as of the Kwantung peninsula. By virtue of these proposed operations alone, to which we gave enthusiastic assent, Stalin would be placed in a position to do what he liked with these areas, whether he was promised any special rights there or not . . . .Two months later, in December 1944, our ambassador to Russia, Mr. Averell Harriman, sounded Stalin out, on the President's instructions, as to what he meant by the 'political aspects' which he had said would have to be taken into consideration. Stalin replied by naming most of those things that formed the basis of the subsequent Yalta agreement. With a sweep of the hand against a map he indicated the southern part of the Kwantung peninsula. He wanted a lease on the Manchurian railways. He desired that southern Sakhalin and the Kurile Islands should be ceded to Russia . . . .[At] Yalta . . . Stalin upped the ante slightly, demanding Port Arthur . . . and insisting on language which recognized Russia's preeminent interest in Dairen and in the Manchurian railways.

According to the *Americana* account:

After the expiration of the Russo-Japanese Neutrality Pact on April 25, 1945, the Japanese made several futile attempts to negotiate with the U.S.S.R. and to obtain Russian mediation for peace with the western allies . . . . The fighting contribution of the Russians to Japan's collapse was not very great.

However, Stalin had another request for Roosevelt to arrange for at Yalta. Details are available from many sources, but John T. Flynn, on p. 149 of his book *While You Slept*, gives a succinct statement of this:

The United States would have to provide fuel, transport and equipment for 1,250,000 men, 3000 tanks, 5000 planes, and various other requirements. This would give Stalin an army of 1,250,000 Russian soldiers on the borders of Manchuria.

The first Atomic bomb was dropped on Hiroshima on August 6, 1945; the Nagasaki bombing was on August 9th. On August 10th Japan announced its approval of the Potsdam surrender arrangements, and President Truman announced our acceptance of those terms on the 14th. In the midst of this on the 8th Russia declared war on Japan. The Americana comments: "Japan's surrender did not stop the Russian advance or the capture of Japanese forces." And this huge "Ivan-Come-lately" Communist army which we had equipped and provided with transport (*While You Slept*, p.170) "took Manchuria [and] enabled the Japanese to deliver their arms to the Chinese Communists and for the first time set them up in business as a powerful war machine." We have observed already that our government placed an embargo on aid to the Nationalists beginning with V J Day. How does one say in Chinese: "With friends like that . . . .?"

The other possible competitor of Stalin for control in Asia was France, in French Indochina—principally Laos, Cambodia, and Vietnam. France had been influential in parts of these areas since the early nineteenth century, but they were recognized as French protectorates and colonies since about the time of the American Civil War and Reconstruction period. They had been administered with considerable dignity and often with surprising rights to self-government. There was a stamp of the French language and culture and Christianity (predominantly Catholic) intermingled with the native, and there was brisk two-way commerce. Throughout the area rivers provide the most feasible method of travel, but the French were responsible for the building of thousands of miles of railroads. In Vietnam alone they were responsible for the construction of nearly twenty thousand miles of highways where almost none had been before, and school systems produced a degree of literacy of some 75% of the population. In World War II all of this was swept under the domination of the conquering armies of Japan.

President Roosevelt, as we have seen, had made no secret of his antipathy to British and French colonialism—and, as a matter of fact, to British and French postwar desires of any kind. He had a rather deep-seated animosity toward the Free-French leader who came into more and more prominence, both militarily and politically, as the war years advanced—General Charles De Gaulle. Bernard Ledwidge's authoritative book, *De Gaulle,* (p.196) observes the President "had a rooted antipathy to his character and aims." On pp. 175-176 he called De Gaulle "an egoist." On p. 142 Ledwidge records a pet disparagement by Roosevelt: "Therefore, 'The Bride' became a favorite description of De Gaulle with the President." On pp. 148-149—In May, 1943: "What really irked Roosevelt was that since Casablanca, De Gaulle had won majority support in North Africa, as well as widespread sympathy in Britain and the United States, for a Fighting French takeover of the administration." He was fearful of De Gaulle's growing popularity, and that the President's slights and ill-treatment of the French leader would be used against him by his opponents in the election of 1944. On p. 117 the author comments on Roosevelt's prejudice against De Gaulle as a postwar leader of France who would, of course, seek to reinstitute the prewar colonialism of his nation. And when De Gaulle was left out of the deliberations at Yalta: "The British and Russians both told him informally that his exclusion was Roosevelt's doing and not theirs, and the Americans did not seek to deny it." (p.193)

Of course, when the French sought American aid in early 1945 as preliminary to re-establishing their place in Indochina, the President refused it; he wanted to keep them out.

The Yalta gains of Russia (and the Roosevelt concessions) were, in general, a continuation of the long-since established pattern of the President's "Great Design." This was particularly true in regard to Europe because all the nations to be considered there were already involved in the war and had been so before the entry of the United States; the President had to be more "creative" about concessions in Asia because Russia had not been involved in the war against Japan, and she would never have been even when he died. It must be remembered that it was America's industrial might and technology which placed Roosevelt in his position of dominance so far as decision making was concerned. In short, he could "throw this weight around." George Kennan masterfully summarizes the critique of the President's machinations and intrigue (p. 355, Op. Cit.):

> I have in mind here what seems to have been an inexcusable body of ignorance about the nature of the Russian Communist movement, about the history of its diplomacy, about what had happened in the purges, and about what had been going on in Poland and the Baltic States. I also have in mind F.D.R.'s evident conviction that Stalin, while perhaps a somewhat difficult customer, was only, after all, a person like any other person; that the reason we hadn't been able to get along with him in the past was that we had never really had anyone with the proper personality and proper qualities of sympathy and imagination to deal with him, that he had been snubbed all along by the arrogant conservatives of the Western capitals; and that if only he could be exposed to the persuasive charm of someone like F.D.R. himself, ideological preconceptions would meet and Russia's co-operation with the West could be easily arranged. For these assumptions, there were no grounds whatsoever; and they were of a puerility that was unworthy of a statesman of F.D.R.'s stature.

William C. Bullitt (Op .Cit., pp. 20-26) gives a similar summation.

What was it that was given to Stalin at Yalta from the European theatre? We have observed the forcible repatriation of millions of anti-Communist refugees and troops to Russia. The *Americana* notes in general that: "The Yalta Conference firmly established Russian zones of influence in eastern and central Europe," but in detail it adds: "Russia claimed part of East Prussia, including the big city of Konigsberg, for itself. This claim was not contested." This, of course, had been a part of Germany. Eastern Poland went the same way, up to the Curzon Line—one third of the country, as proposed by Roosevelt, himself (James F. Byrnes, *Speaking Frankly*, p.29). Poland was to have its boundaries extended westward across East Germany to the Oder River; and Stalin had our assurances that we would not stand in the way of a government for Poland dominated by him—if indeed there were many objectors remaining after the ill-fated Warsaw uprisings described earlier. The Baltic States of Estonia, Latvia, and Lithuania had been swallowed already by the U.S.S.R., and Communists controlled Albania. Yugoslavia was turned over to the Communist Tito who would ruthlessly slay the greatest hero of his nation, General Mihajiovic, to keep him and his great popular following from impeding Communist domination. Romania's government was in league with the Soviets; and Czechoslovakia, invaded months before by Stalin's forces, would soon belong to him. The Russian dictator also received Roosevelt's promise that in the United Nations organization he could have three votes to only one for the U.S., Britain, and France—and all other nations.

Bullitt (Op. Cit., p.45) comments cogently:

> It is as true today as in 1832 that Russia can only hold Poland by uncivilizing it. And the same is true of Estonia, Latvia, Lithuania, Rumania, Hungary, Bulgaria, Yugoslavia, Austria, Czechoslovakia, and Germany. The relentless eye of the dictator in the Kremlin can distinguish only serfs and enemies; and the neighbors of Russia, if they do not wish to be the one, must reconcile themselves to being considered the other.

In the West the IOU's from Teheran, Yalta, and the other great conferences already were being exacted as the Russian armies overwhelmed the same small foes whom they had conquered several years earlier while Stalin still had his "nonaggression" pact with Hitler—and more. Demaree Bess, writing in the *Saturday Evening Post* (March 20, 1943, "What Does Russia Want?") more than eight months before the Teheran Conference, spoke prophetically of Russian aims:

> Since they have made their desires so clear in negotiations with the Germans and later with the British, nobody has any right to be surprised if the Russians move again into all the territories they occupied in 1939 and 1940 and incorporate them into the Soviet Union.

Two months after Yalta General Patton, whose troops had advanced beyond Germany,and whose sometimes two hundred mile a day pace was straining the abilities of quartermaster suppliers, was ordered to stop in his tracks. (That sentence of mine also came perilously close to outrunning the verb!) On the threshold of the capture of Prague, the capital of Czechoslovakia, he and his men were ordered to pull back out of the country because the Red armies were scheduled to have the honor of "liberating" Czechoslovakia. Patton's remark on the occasion was, "Oh, for pity sakes!" or words to that effect. General Eisenhower stopped his victorious armies on the banks of the Elbe River—so that the Russians could take Berlin.

Many authors have pointed out that the tragic forfeitures of Roosevelt to Stalin in Asia came as a complete surprise to Truman when he found himself suddenly projected into the Presidency—a fait accompli. (Truman also had had the atomic bomb secret kept from him.) I do not plan to deal in detail with that here except to observe that the peace proposals of the Japanese, which Roosevelt ignored at Yalta, would certainly have obviated the use of the bomb. Revelations that the Japanese had made plans to be used in case of a U.S. invasion are irrelevant. We all have gone through fire drills which most of us feel we will never have to use. If we had had no A-bomb and had insisted on making an invasion in spite of the peace overtures, we could not realistically have expected the Japanese not to have had plans for that eventuality and just to have "rolled over and played dead."

William C. Bullitt (Op. Cit. pp. 150-151) aptly describes the situation brought on by the death of Roosevelt:

> President Truman inherited an American foreign policy in bankruptcy. President Roosevelt had gambled on his ability to convert Stalin from the aim of imposing Communist dictatorship throughout the earth to the aim of establishing a world collaboration of independent states. He had lost his gamble . . . . By the autumn of 1945 it was clear, except for those who did not wish to see, that the Soviet Union had replaced Germany as the embodiment of totalitarian imperialism, and that the foreign policy of the United States had been based on wishful thinking.

As an aside relative to the willingness of German armies (or conquered East European nations) to surrender eagerly to forces of democratic nations as opposed to the alternative of fighting on to the bitter end against Stalin's Communist forces of Katyn Forest massacre fame, I recount some noteworthy events. I am thinking again of Churchill's plan—rejected by Roosevelt and Stalin—of an invasion up through the Balkans and Eastern Europe. Defeated armies are, per se, defeated. Nash Stublen, a staff writer for the *Tampa Tribune*, writing at the 40th anniversary of the German surrender, tells of his personal experiences when that time came:

> Three days later on April 30, I was on duty at my gun emplacement on the bluff overlooking the Elbe when I spotted a white flag on the other side. I radioed to my company headquarters what I saw.
>
> It was an advance party of a German V-2 rocket division that had outrun the Russians to surrender to the Americans. On the same day, Hitler had married his long-time mistress, Eva Braun, and they both had committed suicide.
>
> After the surrender was officially executed, an engineering battalion made arrangements to bring the 10,000 man division across the Elbe on May 1 and 2. Disappointed that I couldn't take part, a fellow soldier, who spoke fluent German, and I found a rowboat and crossed the river. We sneaked up the road on which the German convoy was traveling. In German, my cohort shouted, 'throw out your weapons.'

More than 25 did from German Lugars to what looked like a six-shooter from the Wild West days. When one German threw out an unarmed hand grenade, we decided it was time to take leave.

We placed the guns in a towbag and headed back across the river in the boat, which almost sank from the new weight.

Smith, Muzzey, and Lloyd's *World History,* pp. 804-805, continues:

In the next few days, as the rest of the Nazi stronghold crumbled under the blows of the Allies, German divisions began to give up en masse. On May 3 a million troops surrendered in Italy and west Austria. Two days later 500,000, in the Netherlands, Denmark, and northern Germany, surrendered to Field Marshall Montgomery, and another 500,000 to General Devers in the south. The situation was now so confused that Admiral Doenitz declared that further fighting was senseless.

We are tragically familiar with the story of Russia's crushing of liberty in all the territories of all the nations they occupied in eastern and central Europe. At no time did they permit democratic elections with true freedom of choice. Eibling, King, and Harlow's *History of Our United States*, pp. 572-573, tells of two sordid episodes in Berlin:

Although Berlin lay within the Russian Zone, the four conquering powers had agreed that the city should be divided into zones and governed by representatives of the four powers. The Russian zone came to be known as East Berlin and the other three zones as West Berlin.

In 1948, in an effort to drive the Western powers out of Berlin, the Communist bosses set up a blockade. No food, fuel, or raw materials could come into the city by surface transportation. This meant that Russia deprived a city, the size of Chicago, of all connections by land or water with the free world.

Britain and the United States promptly met the challenge. Giant planes loaded with supplies, took off for Berlin from bases in West Germany. They flew more than two and a quarter million tons of food, coal, and supplies of all kinds into the city by air. In about ten months the Russians saw that they were getting nowhere and agreed to end the blockade. The Communists had lost an important battle in the Cold War, and they, as well as the whole free world, knew it.

West Berlin irritated the Communists. Here was a prosperous community in the midst of a shabby-appearing satellite, East Germany. West Germany was a haven for East Germans wishing to flee to the freedom of the West. Many escaped each year until August 13, 1961. That day the Soviets began building a huge wall along the East Berlin border to check the flight of as many as 2,000 East Berliners a day. It was built of steel and concrete, topped with barbed wire and broken glass. The wall was lighted at night and guarded by sentries and vicious dogs.

> In spite of Communist efforts to stop them, men still risked their lives in attempts to escape. Those who were caught trying were shot. In 1962 a young German was shot and left to bleed to death in sight of friends who watched from free Berlin. Even the help of the Red Cross was refused.

And the same book (p. 567) tells more under the coming of Khrushchev to power:

> Khrushchev showed that he would use brute force to keep himself in power when, in 1956, he ordered Soviet troops to shoot down non-Communist Hungarians. It was he who ordered the Berlin Wall built. During 1962 alone his guards shot down more than forty persons who tried to escape to West Germany.

These things were not done in secret; I am relating events well known to followers of the news. The *World Almanac* gives the story from Czechoslovakia:

> In February, 1948, the [minority] Communists seized power in advance of scheduled elections. In May 1948 a new constitution was approved. Benes refused to sign it. On May 30 the voters were offered a one-slate ballot and the Communists won full control . . . . A harsh Stalinist period followed; with complete and violent suppression of all opposition.
>
> In Jan. 1968 a liberalization movement spread explosively through Czechoslovakia. Antonin Novotny, long the Stalinist boss of the nation, was deposed as party leader and succeeded by Alexander Dubcek, a Slovak, who declared he intended to make communism democratic. On Mar. 22 Novotny resigned as president and was succeeded by Gen. Ludvik Svoboda. On April 6, Premier Joseph Lenart resigned and was succeeded by Oldrich Cernik, whose new cabinet was pledged to carry out democratization and economic reforms.
>
> In July 1968 the USSR and 4 Warsaw Pact nations demanded an end to liberalization. On Aug. 20, the Russian, Polish, East German, Hungarian, and Bulgarian armies invaded Czechoslovakia.
>
> Despite demonstrations and riots by students and workers, press censorship was imposed, liberal leaders were ousted from office and promises of loyalty to Soviet policies were made by some old-line Communist Party leaders.
>
> On April 17, 1969, Dubcek resigned as leader of the Communist Party and was succeeded by Gustav Husak. In Jan. 1970, Premier Cernik was ousted. Censorship was tightened and the Communist Party expelled a third of its members. In 1972, more than 40 liberals were jailed on subversion charges. In 1973, amnesty was offered to some of the 40,000 who fled the country after the 1968 invasion, but repressive policies continued to remain in force.
>
> More than 700 leading Czechoslovak intellectuals and former party leaders signed a human rights manifesto in 1977, called Charter 77, prompting a renewed crackdown by the regime.

The Associated Press, September 9, 1983, carried a more recent glimpse:

A well known Czechoslovak cyclist and his family sailed across the borders of their Communist homeland in a hot-air balloon patched together with raincoats and asked for political asylum in Austria, police said Thursday.

Police said Robert Hutyra brought his bicycle with him in the perilous escape.

Hutyra, 38, his 36-year-old wife and their two children, a boy and a girl, ended their precarious, 50-minute escape shortly before midnight Wednesday. They touched down in the northeastern border village of Drasenhofen, a police official said. Mistelback is about 18 miles from Drasenhofen.

'They got out and walked into town, where police were notified,' the official said in a telephone interview. He said the family then asked for political asylum.

The night flight had been planned for two years, the official quoted Hutyra as saying.

Authorities would not release the names of the other family members.

The Hutyras 'built their balloon at home and started in the dead of night just on the other side of the border' where they abandoned their car . . . . The balloon was made of raincoats sewn together and was kept aloft with lit propane from a canister fastened underneath [the official] said . . . .

The duty policeman at Drasenhofen said the family stood on a platform surrounded by a steel railing . . . . Hutyra told police that 'Czech border guards saw the (propane) flame about two and a half kilometers (1.6 miles) above them and fired flares but apparently couldn't make the thing out' . . . .

In a similar escape nearly four years ago, two East German couples and their four children rode their homemade balloon across the border to northern Bavaria in West Germany.

Chapter V

China Again, in Depth—and Treachery

Now let us return to China and the Far East—China, which holds the keys to most of the Asian conquests of the Communists which followed the fateful flaws of Yalta. On August 15, 1945, while the Russian hordes were sweeping through the already surrendered Japanese forces in Manchuria (They must have "fought" longer after the surrender than they had before it), the *Daily Worker* editorial proclaimed:

> Prevent Civil War in China—Not a single American gun, soldier, plane or other war equipment must be placed at the disposal of the fascist clique in Chungking . . . . The State Department should be bombarded with messages demanding the recall of Ambassador Hurley and Gen. Wedemeyer, and the immediate cleansing of the people in the State Department responsible for this suicidal policy.

And Diane Shaver Clemens (*Yalta*, p. 245) echoes a similar line:

> As we have seen, the extent of Soviet claims in the Far East was continually being adjusted to American plans and ideas. Roosevelt hoped to expel the 'imperialists'—Britain, France, and Japan—from China and Korea, and possibly from Indochina and Hong Kong, and to substitute American economic hegemony. The president realized that the United States alone could not fill the vacuum left by the collapse of Japan and the debilitation of France and Britain. To fill the gap, he sought to promote the Soviet Union as America's junior partner in Asia. After the war, the United States would control China and occupy Japan; the Soviet Union would receive territorial concessions from Japan and a share in Manchuria and Korea. The British were to be left out entirely.

But, alas, there were powerful voices—oral and written—who pushed for the same ends espoused by the *Daily Worker*, and who—amazingly—maintained reputations of respectability. Some of these ladies and gentlemen were gathered together in the Institute of Pacific Relations with some known Communists, including the millionaire Frederick Vanderbilt Field. There seem to have been no falling-outs among them over programs, and they seemed to have an untoward influence on the policies of the State Department. Not the least of these was one Owen Lattimore who purported to be an "expert" on Asia. If you have read all that I have written in this treatise thus far (and Mr. Lattimore was aware of all these facts) it may be somewhat nettlesome for you to see what he had to say in his book, *Solution In Asia*, p. 139:

> . . . the Soviet Union stands for . . . strategic security, economic prosperity . . . free education, equality of opportunity, and democracy: a powerful combination.
>
> The fact that the Soviet Union also stands for democracy is not to be overlooked. It stands for democracy because it stands for all the other things. Here in America we are in the habit of taking a narrow view of foreign claimants to the status of democracy. If China, or Russia, or some other alien people does not measure up to the standards of the particular American modification of Anglo-Saxon democracy, we say that it is not democratic. We are going to find ourselves boxing with shadows instead of maneuvering in politics if we stick to this habit.

On page 150 Lattimore continues:

> Russia, to maintain her present comparative advantages, would have to keep up the trend toward increased personal liberty and economic prosperity which has contributed so largely to those advantages."

On 190-191:

> When Japan begins to show an ability to make progress politically, we must expect the leadership to be left of center and at least liberal enough to be friendly with Russia.

And of China he says (p.197)

> As soon as democratic processes have indisputably begun to work, we should advocate (and if asked to, assist in carrying out) a reorganization of the National Army and the disbandment of superfluous troops.

William F. Buckley, in his column in the *Tampa Tribune* April 30, 1969, quotes from a blurb on the jacket of one of Lattimore's books: He shows that all the Asiatic people are more interested in actual democratic practices such as the one they can see in action across the Russian border, than they are in fine theories of Anglo-Saxon democracies which come coupled with ruthless imperialism . . . . He inclines to support American newspapermen who report that the only real democracy in China is found in Communist areas.

Now, it happens that "the standards of the particular American modification of Anglo-Saxon democracy" include the concepts of liberty, freedom of choice (as between two or more political parties), of sovereignty's residing with the people, and of reverence for the dignity of the individual. Those are not just American standards—they are the highest fulfillment of the vision that began with ancient Greece, was enriched by the Christian ideal of human worth, and yes—includes those eight long centuries of the slow and magnificent development of the Anglo-Saxon heritage of the Rule of Law. We have made some "particular American modifications," too, of which we are justly proud. Many nations have been inspired to follow these ideals in whole or in part; but I cannot swallow the line that Owen Lattimore or any other thinking person could confuse these things with either Hitler's Nazism or Stalin's GULAG administration of slave labor and the massacre in the Katyn Forest.

Some there were who went along, however. John T. Flynn's little book, *While You Slept*, in chapters 8 and 9 displays a tirelessly and exactingly researched study of books on China published during the crucial period in which decisions were being made by the United States which would seal the fate of that most populous nation in the world and the most strategically located for the spreading of Communism to Indochina and Korea. Mr. Flynn begins (on p.66):

> I give below a list of some 30 books on the general political situation in China published between 1943 and 1949—the crucial years in the crucifixion of China. This list was made up from the *United States Publishers Catalogue* and checked against the *Book Review Digest* . . .
>
> There were 30 such books. Of these, 23 were pro-Communist; only seven were anti-Communist books. By pro-Communist I mean books which gave the weight of their evidence and special pleading to the Chinese Communists. I give here a list of the titles and authors, and a mere note to indicate the character of the book.

Then he listed the 23 pro-Communist books and the seven anti-Communist books. After an analysis of the leading book review digests whose stands could make or break a writer's endeavors, he finished with:

> Then there are the *Nation* and the *New Republic* and the *Saturday Review of Literature*. The reason these last three are important is because they have a large circulation in college and literary circles. The reviews in these publications are usually watched carefully by the booksellers . . . I should think we might well dismiss this whole subject [of the 30 books on China—more than three to one on the pro-Communist side] with the following simple statement:
>
> Every one of the 23 pro-Communist books, where reviewed, received glowing approval in the literary reviews I have named—that is, in the *New York Times*, the *Herald-Tribune*, the *Nation*, the *New Republic* and the *Saturday Review of Literature*. And every one of the anti-Communist books

was either roundly condemned or ignored in these same reviews.

Flynn takes the mystery out of this development with the revelation that pro-Communist reviewers had a monopoly—a "closed shop" as it were on the job, and most of them were reviewing each other's books. He continues:

> The extent to which the authors of the pro-Communist books engaged in puffing each other's books and in blasting the works of the anti-Communist authors in these five journals is very revealing. Here is the number of reviews each wrote:
>
> | | |
> |---|---|
> | Lattimore and wife | 13 |
> | Snow and wife | 10 |
> | Smedley | 6 |
> | Gayn | 4 |
> | Fairbank | 4 |
> | Jacoby and White | 4 |
> | Harrison Forman | 1 |
> | Foster Rhea Dulles | 1 |
> | Rosinger | 1 |
>
> In other words, these authors wrote 12 books out of the 23 pro-Communist volumes. Then they turned in 44 reviews of the books listed. Of the seven anti-Communist books, some of the writers of the pro-Communist books, by which I mean the Lattimores and the Snows and their like, got a crack at every one of them. That is, of the anti-Communist books, John K. Fairbank, Agnes Smedley and Harrison Forman got a shot at one book each, Edgar Snow at two, Annalee Jacoby at two and Owen Lattimore at three.
>
> Some of these pink and Red propagandists were not content to usurp, by whatever strange means was at their disposal, the last inch of space in books and magazines. They were not content to promote with rosy reviews the books that sang the praises of the Chinese Reds and the crimes of their opponents. They lost no opportunity of making publication difficult for anti-Red books and of killing them when they were issued.

Here is a notable phenomenon. We find a remarkable duplication between the names of some of the writers listed, the leaders of the Institute of Pacific Relations, and the leaders of the *Amerasia* magazine of spying fame. George E, Sokolsky's column, which was carried in the *Tampa Times* April 7, 1950, tells the story and lists some of our friends:

> The original officers of the 'Amerasia' magazine were: Editorial Board: Frederick V. Field, Chairman; Philip J.Jaffe, Managing Editor; Lillian Peffer, Assistant Editor; Harriet Levine, Secretary; T.A. Bisson; Ch'ao-ting Chit; Kenneth W. Colegrove; Owen Lattimore; William W. Lockwood; Cyrus H. Peake; David H. Popper; William T. Stone. (From issue of August 1938, Vol.11, No.6)

Sokolsky relates the story of a raid on the "Amerasia" offices which occurred after top secret information showed up in an article in the magazine.

> Five persons entered the premises at midnight of March 11 [1945], one a mechanic. The reason for the late hour was that the office was in use all day Sunday until 5 . . . . [Its] premises seemed very busy. In it was located a large photo-copy room with an unusual amount of equipment. Such equipment could not have been needed to produce this small magazine . . . . On the library table was an envelope containing secret documents . . . . In that envelope were found six documents, hastily copied on a typewriter from original Navy documents, all marked 'Top Secret' . . . .
>
> In Philip Jaffe's office were found a bellows-type suitcase and two briefcases, suitable for carrying documents. The suitcase was marked 'P.J.J.' Scores of secret documents were found in these three receptacles. They were from the State Department, Naval Intelligence, Army Intelligence, and the O.S.S. Some were original documents; some typewritten copies, with four or five carbon copies. There were also photostats of State Department documents.
>
> The raiders actually took some of the documents as samples. All the O.S.S. documents were stamped with a declaration to the effect that possession of such articles by an unauthorized person constituted a violation of the Espionage Act. One of the photostats, from the State Department, showed the complete distribution of all groups in the Chinese Army, the places where located, under whose command, naming units division by division and showing their strength.
>
> Four agents saw all the documents and are therefore witnesses to the transaction. They have never been called in any investigation, although five years have passed and the statute of limitations has been permitted to run.

John T. Flynn (*While You Slept*, pp.38-39) quotes Dean Acheson, the U.S. Secretary of State, at a November 14, 1945, meeting in Madison Square Garden to honor the Red Dean of Canterbury: "There is the fact, for example, that never in the past has there been any place on the globe where the vital interests of the American and Russian people have clashed or even been antagonistic . . . " And State Department policy relative to China was (I quote Flynn, p. 40) " . . . the Communists were not Communists and . . . they were more democratic than the Nationalists and . . . they were not dominated by Moscow." It's a great pity that Lattimore "failed" to impress upon State Department policy makers how transfixed the Chinese Communists were with the "democratic practices" they could "see in action across the Russian border!"

To quote Flynn again (p.33), he describes the results of a 1947 investigation of the State Department—facts well known at the time:

> At one time—in 1947—following an investigation which the (State) Department, under Congressional pressure, was forced to conduct into its own

affairs, 203 of its staff were dismissed in one haul. Of these, some 91 were dismissed because they were homosexuals—a rather heavy contingent—and the balance—112, because they were security risks.

Now, a few words are in order here to elucidate terminology for the neophyte. (I'm proud of that sentence—William F. Buckley, move over!) There are two basic classifications of personnel who are (or should be) denied the right to handle secret government documents; this is for the protection of the citizenry and the government. Any questions should be resolved in favor of those being protected. The two classifications are "security risk" and "loyalty risk."

Security risk: It is obvious that Top Secret documents should not be passed to kindergarten or elementary school children to take home at the end of the day. A known unprincipled or dishonest person might not be averse to selling out to the highest bidder. Some people are—or may be—mentally unbalanced, or they may be individuals of notably poor judgment. The right to handle secret government documents is <u>not</u> one of those found in the first ten amendments to the Constitution. A blabber-mouth certainly should not be entrusted with secret documents. It goes without saying that an alcoholic or a drug addict would be in a category not to be considered for security clearance. Which brings us to the one you were worrying about—the homosexual. I can hear the chorus now shouting, "Discrimination!" It so happens, however, that quite a few of the classic spy cases in history have involved homosexuals. A current British case (news accounts from the wire services) had seven of them as its stars. Why should this be? It has been only relatively recently that such individuals have been demanding recognition and their "rights." It is probably true still that most of them would prefer to have that facet of their personalities remain undisclosed. For this reason the homosexual is inordinately vulnerable to blackmail when trapped into affairs with operatives of other nations. We are dealing with conditions as they are in reality rather than as we would wish for them to be. Thus we have basic groups under the label security risk.

Loyalty risk: A loyalty risk is a person whose loyalty is, or may be, to a nation other than our own. Any Communist would be a loyalty risk, per se—as would certainly be the case with any person who has already been involved in passing secret documents to representatives of unfriendly powers. Any loyalty risk is obviously also a security risk; but it is possible that security risks may be loyal to our country—until the testing time comes.

To return now to the George Sokolsky column quoted above which gave the details of the "Amerasia" treachery. I quote again: "Four agents saw all the documents and are therefore witnesses to the transaction. They have never been called in any investigation, although five years have passed and the statute of limitations has been permitted to run." May I point out this salient detail: Nobody ever sued Mr. Sokolsky for libel—nor anyone else who was repeating the unsavory details. Nobody! No member of the "Amerasia" staff, no member of the Congress, no functionary of the State Department—nobody! Furthermore, we find the unprincipled principals weeping and "beating their breasts" in public gatherings to protest their innocence and patriotism; we find many leaders of both houses of the Congress protesting their innocence and patriotism; we find the functionaries of the State Department protesting their innocence and patriotism; and we find the vast majority of the media protesting their innocence and patriotism. And all of these were quick to pillory and to hurl their anathemas at any lonely leader who took issue with the prevailing dogma. Congressional investigations were held to stigmatize—not the traitors and their protectors—but those who courageously tried to stand in opposition to the miscreants. Yes, the "Amerasia Americans" were deemed to be loyal, patriotic, and great leaders; and those who took issue with them were unwise and reprehensible. But it simply wasn't so. It never had been so. It was myth, not history.

As a footnote to the aforementioned carefully researched analysis by John T. Flynn of the pro-Communist monopoly on books and China during and following World War II, I would like to recall to mind a few relevant sentences from Buckley and Bozell's *McCarthy and His Enemies*. In reference to a publication called the *Far Eastern Survey* they note: "The influence of the *Survey* is not to be measured by its circulation, which was small, but by its unchallenged domination—in company with *Pacific Affairs* (IPR) and *Amerasia* (an offshoot of the IPR)—of the field . . . . Not one article during the entire 1943-46 period suggested the possibility that China's communists were sure-enough Communists. "In analyzing a magazine that has no editorial page, the most indicative index of editorial bias is the book-review section. During the years in question, the Far Eastern Survey's pro-Communist batting average in that area was a cool 1.000."

Now, I submit that this China story I have recounted is not a pretty one for the United States—nor proud. I have long felt shame for what those Americans who shared responsibility did to help bring on the tragic consequences for China, for our nation, and for our world. Someone can check me out on this—I do not remember the source—but long ago the report came to my attention that in the entire first two years after Pearl Harbor the grand total of all arms and military supplies sent from the U.S. to China was enough to keep one American division in the field for one week. Well, that's the view from here.

I have had the good fortune to be introduced to a book that gives the view from there. A former missionary to China, Mrs. Elizabeth Andrews, lent me a copy of *A Different Kind of War*, by Vice Admiral Milton E. Miles, U.S.N. The book's jacket tells how the author was sent under secret orders shortly after Pearl Harbor to set up the "United States Naval Group, China, commonly known as the 'Rice Paddy Navy.'" His assignment was

> to establish weather stations and a system of coast watchers to support the Pacific Fleet and, ultimately, a possible invasion of the Chinese coast. Starting with only himself and with the good will his cooperative spirit evoked from the Chinese government, by the end of the war Miles commanded more than 2500 American volunteers from all the services and between 50,000 and 100,000 Chinese—fishermen, pirates, police and regular guerrilla forces. Not only did his men forecast the weather for all of Asia and report on Japanese fleet movements along the enemy-held coast, this ragged but highly efficient organization also accounted for some 71,000 enemy dead and untold damage to the Japanese supply lines.

The amazing achievements of Admiral Miles were in no small measure a result of his deep friendship and strong alliance with the powerful commander of China's far-flung intelligence network, General Tai Li. The victim of many malicious slanders from the Communists, as well as Western vilifiers, worked with Miles with telling effectiveness in the setting up of SACO (the Sino-American Cooperative Organization)

> for the training, equipping, and operating of guerrilla troops against the Japanese occupation forces. Wildly and often hilariously extemporized as they were, the exploits of SACO belong among the annals of American heroism.
>
> The high-level SACO agreement did not stop some American military commanders from opposing Miles' operations in China and working to undermine his efforts. Miles tells how professional jealousy and distrust of Tai Li led U.S. Army, State Department, and O.S.S. leaders to duplicate his efforts and to thwart him by cutting off much-needed supplies . . . .
>
> *A Different Kind of War* . . . is also a convincing demonstration that Americans can fight a guerrilla war in Asia—and win it.

One nagging impediment with which Miles had to deal was presented by the "old China hands"—those whose prejudices from past generations of "white supremacy" brought them to look upon the Chinese as inferiors—a servant class. As events unfolded these people worked against a strong central government for fear it might come to oppose their erstwhile status as a dominant group. Thus their efforts tended by indirection—and sometimes by direction—to advance the Communist cause.

General Stilwell was the Army's Commanding General for the China-Burma-India Theater. From the ranks of the State Department came one John Paton Davies to be the General's "political adviser." He proved to be prejudiced against the legal government of our Chinese allies, which placed him on the side of the Communists, of course. He subsequently misrepresented Stilwell's views in a report to the State Department as being opposed to cooperation with the Chinese Nationalists. This, Miles had reason to believe, was the view of Davies, but passed in over Stilwell's appropriated signature. This would seem consistent with the report in Buckley and Bozell's *McCarthy and His Enemies,* (p. 208) that

> the McCarran Committee had found that Davies had 'testified falsely before the subcommittee in denying that he recommended the Central Intelligence Agency employ, utilize and rely upon certain individuals having Communist associations and connections.'

Supplies of any kind were difficult for Miles to come by all the war long. In early 1943 after a year in China, he had still only five hundred tommy guns in the whole country—and he had been supplied only 225 clips for them (p. 125). He had no weapons for sabotage and almost no explosives. On p. 128 he noted

> It was two years before we received as much in a month as six planes could have delivered in a single trip over the Hump, and it was not until the very last weeks of the war that we had even <u>one</u> plane for use in moving stuff within China itself.

And on p. 341 he observed:

> China actually received no Lend Lease material whatever until June 1944. And what arrived then? Sixty mountain guns—320 anti-tank guns— and five hundred bazookas.
>
> From July 1943 to October 1945," reported Miles on p.570, "the Army Transport Service had carried just under four thousand tons over the Hump for us. China National Airways Corporation—CNAC—had carried another 350 tons. In the last months of the war we had sent several convoys over the Burma Road and these—counting the weight of the trucks, the gas they used, and goods they hauled—brought us almost as much in three or four months as we received by air in the same number of years. That made our total 3 1/2 years' supply about nine thousand tons—less than the U.S. Army, China Theater, was receiving by air <u>in three days</u> as the war approached its end.'

It seemed that personages from the States had had their minds made up for them about General Tai Li before they left home, and the prejudices of Washington powers relative to Miles's Navy group had been firmly implanted.

Joseph Alsop sounded off about the unit's "uselessness and duplication," and he inveighed against the "infamous" General Tai, enraging Miles's men by claiming publicly (pp. 319-320) that they went to great lengths to escape the shame of being associated with him.

In an appearance before the Joint Chiefs of Staff in early 1945, General Albert C. Wedemeyer, who had replaced General Stilwell as commander of Americans in the China Theater, castigated General Tai as an "unsavory character" (pp. 452-453) and reported that the Generalissimo, Chiang Kai-shek, desired Wedemeyer to assume direct command of SACO's operations—a change that the Generalissimo had not even entertained. The source of the diatribes against General Tai was the Yenan Chinese Communists, according to Miles, and their supporters in Washington. (p.482)

> They hated him even worse than they did the Generalissimo because, in the 1920's, Tai Li had joined them for a few months in order to learn what made them tick. Chou En-lai and he had actually been classmates at school but later it had been Tai Li who had reported that the Chinese Communist Party was Russian-controlled. Knowing this and having himself become a strong anti-Communist, Tai Li missed few opportunities to point out that Chou and his party would be traitors to China. Furthermore, he had been largely responsible for chasing them out of Kiangsi Province, and had constantly worked for the development of a strong and honest central government that would not be easy to overthrow.

Miles was charitable in his attitude toward General Stilwell whom he regarded as a "dedicated" soldier whose difficulties in Burma caused him to lose perspective as to the threat in China from Japanese—and from the Communists. He saw Chiang Kai-shek as competing with him for vitally needed supplies, and he developed and nurtured a profound animosity toward him which led to overtures to the "Communist-trained troops at Yenan [p. 332]. Admittedly, they were bitter enemies of Chiang Kai-shek and the Nationalist government, but Stilwell nevertheless sent them a military mission with promises of aid."

He coveted the position of field commander

> of all troops in China . . . . But at that psychologically important instant General Stilwell unfortunately received additional backing . . . . A telegram arrived from President Roosevelt restating all the things Stilwell believed to be necessary to his control of the situation. And the language that was used, when translated into Chinese, sounded both peremptory and patronizing. Coming as it did, after the reversal of the Cairo agreement, it was a double slap at the head of the government of China.

Stilwell was advised by John Stewart Service (p. 333) that the Nationalists were "more interested in fighting Communists than Japanese." Service said the

Communists "should be more useful than the Kuomintang's 'traitorous' and 'demoralized armies.' He also expressed the opinion that any new government would be better than the one China now had." Service was true to form. Later we find this report (Buckley and Bozell, Op. Cit. p.148):

> The Tydings . . . Committee's [Congress] own record makes it clear that no matter what Service report might be 'singled out' one was likely to find pro-Communist bias . . . uncontestedly . . . . Service had urged that America should transfer its support to the Chinese Communists.

It would appear that when it came to the acquiring of State Department advisers, our side was out of luck, and the Communists were undefeated, untied, and unscoredon.

Admiral Miles was certainly a splendid primary source as to the fighting and other wartime efforts that were ongoing within China, and his book is a rich source of such accounts—often described with rollicking humor. On pp. 234-5 he recounts:

> Ultimately there were more than a thousand of us [Americans], working intimately with a hundred thousand [Chinese] guerrillas, with two or three hundred thousand plainclothesmen . . . . Regularly we sent in reports of what they accomplished to the Intelligence Section of China-Burma-India Staff with the accounts of damage and casualties checked by Americans.

None of this ever reached print, but grandly fabricated tales of the Yenan Communist "accomplishments" were regularly being glorified in American newspapers. I was able to gather from several sections (notably pp.453 and 477) incomplete totals of SACO exploits in three provinces from February to August of 1945: nearly 2,000 actions, nearly 30,000 Japanese killed, nearly 10,000 wounded, over 271 captured, and more than 25,000 Chinese puppet troops of the Japanese taken into custody. (I have quoted previously far more complete totals from the jacket of the book.)

On p. 347 Miles reports:

> During five months from April 1944 through August, these units had also accounted for one steamer, thirty sampans, eleven trucks, one locomotive, and twenty-three railroad cars. During the month of September alone, however, they accounted for thirty bridges, twenty-nine steamers, six warehouses, three gasoline and ammunition depots, ten trucks, nine locomotives destroyed and one damaged, forty-three freight and passenger cars destroyed and ten damaged. Most Japanese wounded were evacuated by their comrades, and their numbers given here are consequently only partial.

SACO was also rescuing quite a few American airmen who had been downed, and they had an elaborate network for reporting the weather throughout the Far

East, which was of immeasurable value to the Navy and Air Forces.

An amusing (?) sidelight to this (p. 376) had to do with Petrosky, a young American officer who had led a brilliant winter patrol in the heroic accomplishment of deeds such as have been outlined above. His superior in SACO recommended him for the Navy Cross. Army red tape and downgrading intervened.

> The medal came through as the Bronze Star; which was fine with Petrosky. But unfortunately, when the two of them went on to Kunming, they landed just in time to see a commotion and they went to see what it was. A young lieutenant was being handed a Bronze Star. And for what? For 'meritoriously conducting a motor pool.' 'I couldn't look at Petrosky,' Joe told me later. 'I just spat on the ground and walked away.'

A mission from the U.S. Army to ascertain the needs of the Communists for supplies turned out to be "delighted" with everything the Reds let them see (pp. 342-3), but the weather wasn't ever right for them to go out and observe them in action. The same mission never demonstrated any desire to check out the guerrillas of SACO who worked no matter what the caprices and vagaries of the weather.

> In the last months of the war communications from an American officer (p.486) with Chinese Intelligence told of Communist troops' being equipped with Russian heavy and light machine guns and Russian rifles and ammunition. They also possessed more than eighty Thompson submachine guns removed from slain loyal Chinese Nationalist troops, and there was proof of Communist attempts to kill Americans evidently unsuccessful. On pp. 341-342, Miles recalls:
>
> None of our SACO people ever saw any anti-Japanese action by the so-called Yenen Reds . . . . General Chennault, whose planes undoubtedly saw more of what was going on in China than anyone except the Chinese themselves, reported that, beginning in the spring of 1944, the Reds had not sabotaged a single Japanese troop train. In October 1944 I myself turned in several reports from several different sources that the Chinese Communists were actually supporting the Japanese and that the reverse was also true. In fact . . . the Japanese . . . agreed to turn over to the Yenan Communists certain northern China areas they were no longer strong enough to hold.
>
> After the Japanese were defeated, Miles says on p.403, enormous quantities of Japanese munitions and supplies fell into the hands of the Yenan Reds, and when our Chinese friends had used up the little ammunition they still retained, General Marshall forbade their having more.
>
> Brave General Liao of the Fifth Column [a SACO unit] was later killed by these very Chinese Communists, and General Gao, from SACO's Camp Four, was captured by them and was savagely flayed alive!

This is what had happened in decisions relating to China in the "Great" Conferences. Roosevelt and Churchill met with the Generalissimo and Madame Chiang Kai-shek at Cairo from November 22 to 26, 1943. Promises were made of a joint Chinese-American-British offensive in the Bay of Bengal in March of 1944. Only a week later, as the President's "Great Design" began to unfold at Teheran, the promises to China's leaders were broken as the emphasis turned to European needs where the desires of Stalin—and Churchill—were paramount. This was a complete double-cross, and devastating effects immediately began to make themselves felt in the Orient. As Miles put it (p.327): "Great Britain and the United States, without even asking to be released from the agreement they had entered into with Chiang Kai-shek, threw China by the board." This paragraph is a historical parenthesis—a look back at the decisive determinations which nearly two years before the war's end cast their malignant shadows before them. The Yalta Conference, as we have seen, sprung the trap door of the scaffold upon which China and Southeast Asia had already been placed.

In the waning weeks of the war our U.S. Army—or the part of it which had impact on the developing power structure for postwar China—was weighted in influence heavily toward the Communists, who were to be referred to as "our allies"—and (Miles, p. 483) as "bandits" rather than "Communists." And "we had continuing proof that, as the Japanese moved out of this area or that, they turned towns they had held over to these Communists who they knew would continue the fight against the Chinese Nationalist government."

And on p. 484 Miles gives specific detailed accounts of several such movements where not a shot was fired—all duly reported with no effect.

There were rumors of a mysterious U.S. air drop of four hundred Thompson submachine guns which neither Miles's SACO guerrillas nor General Tai's troops had received.

> Finally, however [Miles, p. 487], we heard that sometime during the spring of 1945, numbers of both Thompson submachine guns and carbines had been dropped to Communist plainclothesmen in Pootung, a suburb of Shanghai.

And on p. 505 Miles relates:

> The fact is that at the very same time G-5 was refusing us medical supplies lest they might be of some help to the Chinese who were so successfully fighting our mutual enemy on the coast, eleven tons of American medical supplies were being flown to the Yenan Communists!

On p. 193 Miles reports that

> both our Embassy and the O.S.S. objected strongly to much that we were

> doing for the Chinese, arguing that we should provide them with nothing that might prove useful to them once the war had been concluded.

And on p. 586 Miles tells how Chinese Army morale received a deep blow when they were issued American guns for which there was no ammunition. "These weapons were all recalled and stacked in warehouses." The Chinese soldiers had

> liked those wonderful new weapons, but now they were once more given the old worn guns they had used so long against the Japanese . . . . The American guns, incidentally, were still in the warehouses—unused—when they were later captured by the Communists.

Meanwhile Wedemeyer's staff was creative in its efforts to harass Admiral Miles and SACO, demanding intricate records and repetitive reports (pp.453-4) of each man issued a weapon, thumb prints, receipts, his qualifications to utilize it, and his ability to take care of it. This was, you must be aware, under combat conditions. On p. 456 Miles comments:

> The army cut our manpower, stopped our supplies, started competition, made repeated investigations, and delayed everything . . . . I was . . . forced to spend far more hours struggling through Army roadblocks than fighting the Japanese.

And he learned that it was General Wedemeyer, himself, who had refused to release SACO's achievements for publication out of misplaced fear that SACO would show up the record of the Army. This was quite evidently the reason for stringent limitation orders on virtually every SACO activity (pp. 458-9)—orders which were modified only after vehement objections.

General Claire L. Chennault, of "Flying Tiger" renown, testified to similar difficulties in a letter written to Admiral Miles in 1958 (p. 259): "I always found the Chinese friendly and cooperative . . . . But Washington gave me trouble night and day throughout the whole war!" And Miles added, "And much the same was true in my case. My biggest problems were with my own countrymen."

When time was of the essence, it was General Wedemeyer's lack of understanding as to the nature and aims of the Communists in China which placed untimely insurmountable obstacles in the way of any Nationalist attempt to position themselves to the north in invaluable Manchuria as the retiring Japanese hold on its vital railways, cities, and ports left those luscious prizes open for plucking by the Yenan Reds. It was the General's view (Miles, p.491) that the Nationalists and Communists were similar to the Democrats and Republicans in our own country, and they would patch up their differences in a spirit of friendship.

> Here was error in thinking that the general later courageously recognized. The Communists were not just another party. They were committed to complete rule . . . . General Wedemeyer, in his book <u>Wedemeyer Reports</u>, has said that it took him some time to realize the truth about the Communists, and that he had State Department advisors who were partisans of these enemies of ours.

As for the fatal delay, the general insisted the Chinese must be clothed before they left in "warm winter clothing" for which they would perforce have to wait till it was flown in from Alaska (though the Chinese manufactured warm padded cotton uniforms which they already had, and which passed the test of China's most frigid weather with flying colors).

> And (Miles, p. 566) these Chinese troops must also be inoculated before they left—not on the way or after they arrived. This was over the objection of Chiang Kai-shek to whom it was obvious "that the vacuum created by the departure of the Japanese from weakened Manchuria and northern China would draw Russia in . . . . The Russians, of course, were entirely willing to be drawn in.
>
> They hurried, in fact, to support the Chinese Communists.
>
> So Manchuria was lost—and in a matter of days!

As for General Marshall (subsequently to be Truman's Secretary of State), Admiral Miles sets forth a completely one-sided record of warm support for the Chinese Communists and bitter opposition to the Nationalists. The catalogue of his depredations against our friends in China was and would be a tragic and unbroken documentation of dastardly disservice, unrelieved by any subsequent Wedemeyer—like confession of contrition and error.

We have already taken note of the fact that while the Yenan Reds were being allowed to acquire great quantities of Japanese arms, the troops of Chiang Kai-shek, held in the south by American orders—were forbidden by Marshall to be resupplied with ammunition when their own meager supplies were exhausted.

In the spring of 1945 General Chennault was cut down by the removal of half of his command (Miles,pp.457-8).

> Chennault himself wrote that, in order to get him shoved out, General Marshall put pressure on Wedemeyer . . . .
>
> Generalissimo Chiang Kai-shek trusted 'the Flying Tiger' more than any other foreigner in China . . . . I was glad to take the time to recommend Chennault for a Navy Distinguished Service Medal. I prepared several pages of enumerated instances of coastal successes in which he had effectively cooperated with the Navy. My recommendation also had concurrence from the Navy—from Admirals King, Nimitz, Spruance, and others—but the medal was never presented. I understood that it was held up by objections that came from General Marshall personally.

On pp. 567-8, Miles emphasizes again the "favored status" which our government's policy—as well as, of course, Russian—gave to the Yenan Reds. It was not just smiles of blessing; it was vast amounts of heavy armament from Japanese stores, and some from Soviet stores, as well as lighter armaments. It is true that some American weapons were supplied to some Nationalist divisions, but artillery was limited to only one battalion per division. General Marshall, in China now, insisted that the Reds be looked upon as friends and that the Nationalists be forced to take them into the government. By December of 1945, shortly after the Japanese surrender, Marshall's plans were (Miles, pp.572-3) an insistence that the Reds be given positions in the Cabinet.

> General Marshall, as President Truman's personal representative in China, held the rank of ambassador and was supported by a group of advisers from the State Department practically all of whom were anti-Chiang Kai-shek. 'Even the interpreters are "loaded," the boys in my group wrote me, meaning, by that expression, that they were pro-Communist or that they leaned in that direction . . . . Mao Tse-tung, the outstanding leader of the Chinese Communists, spent long evenings with Marshall, and other Communists also saw him, but resident Americans, regardless of their experience and ability, were seldom permitted to do so.

It was in March of 1946 that Miles's great friend and co-warrior, General Tai Li, was killed in an airplane crash in China. Miles was chosen by the Secretary of the Navy to represent the United States at the funeral and to carry a letter from the Secretary to the family, together with the Legion of Merit which had been awarded to Tai Li. Admiral Miles (p.579) continues:

> . . . while a letter of condolence was being prepared for the generalissimo, General Marshall, recently back from China, walked into Secretary Forrestal's office and said that he understood that they were sending me out to attend Tai Li's funeral. They admitted, of course, that that was the case, whereupon General Marshall said that if I went he would ask President Truman to cancel his own orders. If any aid or comfort whatever, he said, were to be given to Tai Li or his successor it would prejudice the delicate negotiations he was promoting between the Communists and the Nationalists because Tai Li was known to be the foremost Chinese anti-Communist.

Admiral Miles did send some personal letters to Tai Li's family by another officer who was flying to China, and the medal also was dispatched. Miles concludes the account of the incident (p.580), showing the incredible depths to which Marshall's "anti-anti-Chinese Communist" prejudice extended:

> In Shanghai Admiral Cooke, who carried the medal, and Captain Beyerly started for the Nanking funeral service. They were met at the airport by representatives of General Marshall's staff, who said that Admiral Cooke could not attend the funeral service, nor could he present the medal.

I submit that if our government's opposition to the Communists had displayed even a modicum of the pertinacious perseverance demonstrated in this instance by one who was to have so powerful a say in the determination of the outcome, China might be an Oriental democracy today.

And so, in spite of President Roosevelt's working so assiduously to expel the evil colonialists, Britain and France, from Asia—including Indochina; despite his conniving with Stalin behind the back of the Chinese leader, Chiang Kai-shek; despite his refusal to accept the abject peace proposals of the Japanese at the time of the Yalta Conference—but rather insisting on bribing Stalin to come into the war against Japan with vast territorial concessions and arming of a Russian force of one and a quarter million men to invade Manchuria; despite the fact that his actions had created monstrous power vacuums in Asia by removing all of our friends—vacuums into which Communism relentlessly moved; despite the fact that our *Amerasia*-influenced foreign policy boycotted aid to the Nationalist Chinese before and after VJ Day; and despite the powerful domination of Congress and public opinion by Top Secret document snitchers and their friends in the political book writing and book reviewing fields—despite all this the Communists won in China and Southeast Asia; and Chiang Kai-shek was exiled to Formosa.

The cogently prophetic words of Walter Lippman pose an imperative background here. Writing in 1943 in *U.S. Foreign Policy* he observed:

> Manifestly the peace of the Pacific has turned and will turn upon China. All the international wars of the Pacific, including the war we are now waging, have turned upon China; and the future of China will for good or evil determine the future in the whole great basin of the Pacific.

True!

An old lady, famed for the fact that she could always find something good to say about anyone, was challenged by an acquaintance with: "I'll bet I know somebody you can't say anything good about—you can't say anything good about the Devil!" The lady's reply was, "Well, he's always on the job!" Of course, that description would also be appropriate for roaches—as a group.

It is appropriate for the Communists—and their fellow travelers—as well.

I was reminded forcefully of that several years ago in a vivid personal experience. Chiang Kai-shek had been driven out of China finally in 1949 and had fled with his remaining troops to Taiwan. Three decades had lingered by. Chiang was now dead, but not before he had established a strong economy, with industries such as textiles, clothing, electronics, processed foods, chemicals, and plastics where there had been almost no industries during a half century of

Japanese rule. There was a solid production of agricultural products, beef, pork, fish, as well as crude oil and steel and electric power. There were upwards of five million each of television and radio sets, and a literacy rate of nearly 90%. Communists coveted Taiwan.

On January 24 and February 2, 1979, I was "privileged" to hear at my own church in Tampa (First United Methodist) and a week later at the Trinity United Methodist Church, Ewing Carroll, Jr., who for more than ten years had been a missionary to the Hong Kong circuit of the We-Li District of the United Methodist Church in Hong Kong. He characterized Chiang Kai-shek as "corrupt and oppressive." I mentioned the fact that Chiang and Madame Chiang were members of the Southern Methodist Church. Carroll said he had "heard that rumor," but (on January 24th) said he "worshipped in a Baptist church on Taiwan." A week later he told the other church that Chiang "worshipped in a private chapel." He described Mao, the Communist, as a "great man," and reported that the current Chinese dictator was "loved" and "cheered" whenever he appeared in public. I remembered that Hitler's listeners were not noted for their booing!

Carroll's answers to listeners' questions had no pattern of authority—no "sources"—but, without consistency of fact and data, lauded the Communists and damned the Nationalists. When I asked him question after question to reveal his bias, he just replied with blank unsupported statements that I was "just wrong." Most hearers accepted his misleading statements.

He said that "Americans err who think that God got on the boat with the last missionary to leave when the Communists took over." He was asked, "Are there churches there now?" Carroll's answer: "What is a church?" Christians were able to "get rid of their church buildings"—the Communists "took them off of their hands" but "paid them for them." Now they have "cottage prayer meetings like John Wesley!"

"The Communists have eradicated prostitution for a billion people;" Taiwan is "just a huge brothel." Three per cent of Chinese are Communists; the rest "believe in Socialism." Under Communism age is revered; workers retire at 80% of their last income. [World Almanac, 1982 per capita income: China $588, Taiwan $3000.]

The Nationalists "invaded Taiwan, killing hundreds of thousands." [Not a word about the Red's killing of Christians when they took over.] "Fourteen million Taiwanese hate the Nationalists." "Three million Taiwanese Christians are imprisoned." "Two million Bibles in the Taiwanese language are kept in warehouses because the government will not allow them to be given out."

I said, "But Communism is inherently atheistic . . . ." Carroll interrupted: "Communism is not atheistic; Marx was just reacting to the evil state of the church in his own country." Oh? Anyone remotely conversant with Communist ideology is aware that atheism is a basic cornerstone. Max Eastman, the preeminent authority on Marx, puts it in a nutshell: "Marx was an implacable enemy of religion."

What is laid bare by this incident? We have a "missionary" lobbying—and very loose with the truth—lobbying in my own large protestant denomination to swing American influence toward an aggressive Communist Chinese takeover of the Nationalist stronghold of Taiwan. Roaches and Communists—and the Devil—are "always on the job!"

Chapter VI

F. D.R. "on the Couch"

Perhaps at this point it would be appropriate to appropriate from the lexicon of the great Shakespeare a familiar line: "Meanwhile, another part of the forest." Let us indulge ourselves in an aside as it were—an intermission if you will—to ask ourselves about this man, Franklin Delano Roosevelt, and perhaps come up with some answers that accommodate or square with the actions we have observed.

Let me interject here that I have no empathy with those who have read the Japanese spy messages dividing up the waters of Pearl Harbor and seen President Roosevelt's name on the list who read them eight weeks before the attack, and who have seen the detailed evidence of his intense personal interest in subsequent (and prior) messages about Tokyo plans—and who maintain that the President still was an innocent and ignorant bystander. And there are those incomprehensible ones who, in the words of Jeremiah, "having eyes, see not." Among those, of course, were the majority of the Joint Congressional Committee, as well as the great fraternity of textbook authors and professors who tenaciously hold to their "faith" in a dream of childhood.

The facts are inexorable: Roosevelt secretly worked hard for many months to maneuver the United States into the Second World War—finally successfully—while publicly avowing the politically popular promises that his aims were diametrically the opposite of what history proves them to have been.

As to the Union of Soviet Socialist Republics, Joseph Stalin had set up there one of the most ruthless, tyrannous despotisms that had ever cursed the earth. It had destroyed its own citizens, killing them and committing them to slave labor by multiple millions. And in a period of many months in a nefarious alliance with Hitler, Stalin had invaded, ravaged, and conquered the small nations of Eastern Europe. Then when Hitler had turned on him, there was revealed the odious story of the Katyn Forest Massacre. Meanwhile the slavish following of the Moscow line by American Communists was made nauseatingly clear, as well as their participation in long-lived traitorous spying and the theft of top-secret documents in collusion with Soviet diplomatic personnel. All of this was well-known to President Roosevelt.

The President was also well aware (as was any American high school graduate who had managed to stay awake in his history classes) of our warm, close friendship with the great democracies, England and France. We had had, as well, a deep community of interest with the Nationalist government of China; and the average United States citizen was in no doubt about which side he favored as it concerned the Nationalists and their Communist foes.

It does not require a deep political insight to ascertain what would have been the outcome of the 1940 Presidential election had Roosevelt announced that he was striving to get the United States into the war. And further, that if he should be successful, he planned to utilize all the great power of the Presidency and of the United States to advance the aims of the U.S.S.R. as opposed to the aims of our friends, Great Britain, France, and the Nationalist Chinese—except, naturally, the cooperative effort to defeat the Axis Powers (which, of course, was imperative in order that those Soviet aims might be realized).

Psychoanalyzing A President

Let's look at President Roosevelt, the man. It is difficult to find a confirmed student of Roosevelt who looks upon him as possessing a deep and abiding philosophy which pervaded his beliefs and motivated his actions as, for example, Patrick Henry with his ringing, "Give me liberty, or give me death!" or Abraham Lincoln's stirring phrases at Gettysburg:

> . . . that we here highly resolve that these dead shall not have died in vain—that this nation, under God, shall have a new birth of freedom—and that government of the people, by the people, for the people, shall not perish from the earth.

He was, it seems, actuated by political expediency. Certainly no friend of his, John T. Flynn nevertheless (p.78 *The Roosevelt Myth*) has given a pretty accurate picture:

> The test was the value of the theories as vote-getters. To put the matter in a word, he was in every sense purely an opportunist.

Flynn (p.103) quotes Vice President John Nance Garner (*John N. Garner's Story*) as saying "he was a hard man to have an agreement with—he would deviate from the understanding." This was a trait that resulted in Garner's not being along when the third term was initiated. Faithful advisor Raymond Moley had left a year earlier, and he wrote his best-selling book, *After Seven Years*. We will revisit this subject anon.

We have occasion to observe Roosevelt's superficiality. He bandied about frivolously phrases which possessed great and lasting import to the lives of thousands—millions yea, hundreds of millions of people. His glib use of the term "unconditional surrender" we have noted. The imminent disaster and tragedy of the ill-considered Morgenthau Plan for postwar Germany would have seen the wrecking of its mines and the destruction of its factories and industries which were the life blood—not only of Germany, but for much of the entirety of Europe. The area would have been reduced to primarily pastoral and agricultural. Roosevelt said of his agreement with the plan "that he had evidently done so without much thought" (Quoted from Henry L. Stimson by Cordell Hull, *Memoirs of Cordell Hull*, Macmillan, 1948). Fortunately other leaders used more thought.

We remember the great good humor of the President in agreeing with Stalin upon the execution of "49,000 or more" of the German commanding staff—over the outspoken objections of Churchill.

Many and varied have been the labels applied to those who have been identified as leaders in American history—Federalists, Antifederalists, Strict Constructionists, Free Traders, Protectionists, the Great Compromiser, Radicals, Conservatives, Expansionists, Democrats, Republicans, Socialists, Populists, Suffragettes, Feminists, War Hawks, Doves, et al. It would appear that the most apt appellation for our only four-time president was that he was a "Rooseveltist." Please bear with me, those who are more or less infuriated by such a characterization.

In the Presidential Election of 1932 the incumbent President Hoover met with stinging repudiation at the hands of Depression-impelled voters and the Democratic candidate Franklin D. Roosevelt. In fact, more than two years before Hoover had entered upon the presidency, the nation's intoxication with the high-flying Florida land boom received a devastating sobering up —first with the inevitable effects of vast overextension (like a giant chain letter fashioned from fanciful fat real estate deals), then with the disastrous hurricane of September 18, 1926, which ravaged southern Florida, leaving four hundred dead, thousands injured, and scores of thousands homeless. And less than eight months after his inauguration the Stock Market Crash resoundingly heralded the fall of the walls of prosperity as had Joshua's trumpet blasts presaged the toppling of the walls of ancient Jericho. In 1930 the Democratic Party wrested control of the House from the Republicans, and a group of recalcitrant members of Hoover's party in the Senate effectively sabotaged effective cooperation from the Congress at a time when teamwork was sorely needed.

The Twentieth Amendment would not be passed until 1933, moving future beginnings of Congressional terms and Presidential inaugurations ahead from March to January. Hoover was overwhelmed by Roosevelt in the election at the beginning of November in 1932. He would not be able to escape from the Presidency until four months later —a third of a year. Meanwhile, panic strode like wildfire across the land, and laughed at the hapless and helpless lame-duck President.

A bit here about a "run" on a bank. A bank is not a storage place for cash. Most of its volume of transactions is carried on through credit instruments, of which checks, mortgages, and notes play a vital part —as well as stocks and bonds. There must be cash enough on hand to care for the everyday transactions of the bank's customers, but the vast majority of its capital is in the form of loans and investments from which it earns returns for its stockholders and depositors and for the costs of being in business. Runs on banks are a rarity now, to a great extent because most accounts now are under the protection of the Federal Deposit Insurance Corporation —but not before Hoover left office.

A run was a psychological phenomenon in which unreasoning mass fear to the point of desperation swept through a bank's depositors, and they rushed en masse to withdraw their funds in cash before the banks failed. And the banks—failed. If the man in front of you in the line has just been told the bank is out of cash, you are not apt to feel like making a deposit. The bank might have been in good working order with its loans and investments carrying on and profiting, but if its clientele had lost confidence in it and in its ability to carry on daily business, it failed. Some banks paid off their depositors and stockholders at ninety cents or one hundred cents on the dollar-but many months, or even years later.

People were uncertain —were terrified —about the future changes. As time rolled into February and the first days of March, more than three hundred millions of dollars in gold was withdrawn from American banks. Hundreds yea, thousands of banks were failing, taking with them multiple millions in individuals' and families' life savings at the depth of the depression.

At the beginning of February, hoping to prevent the collapse of the banking system and the misery and despair that would bring, Hoover proposed to the Federal Reserve Board a one day closing of all banks during which they would prepare statements of their assets to officially separate those banks which possessed strength from those that were insolvent. The government would declare the solvency of those that were so, and would guarantee their solvency during the crisis to forestall the runs. An apportioning of deposit accounts in ratio to size of deposits where assets were not 100 per cent viable would be done in a fair manner to protect against further losses. This was a revolutionary proposition, but conditions demanded radical measures. The Attorney-General, however, held that the President possessed no such power. In the extreme emergency, nevertheless, if he could be assured of a Congressional resolution in support (from a Congress dominated by the opposing party) and the approval of the incoming President, it might be carried out. It does not take much imagination to perceive the chaos that would have resulted had Hoover given such an order and had the Congress and the threshold President come out in opposition.

President Hoover, in a personally handwritten letter to Roosevelt in mid-February, explained the banking crisis in detail and appealed for a statement of assurance to calm the mind of the public —and one which, coming from FDR, would have ensured Congressional support. The legal basis for the bank closings and the stopping of the withdrawals of gold and currency was to be a World War I law, the Trading With the Enemy Act.

On February 25th Hoover was informed that those around Roosevelt expected the imminent collapse of the banking system, which they welcomed as a political godsend for Roosevelt and the Democratic Party. And the banks kept failing, taking the savings of the people. Twelve days had elapsed since a messenger from the President had personally put Hoover's letter into Roosevelt's hands.

On March 3rd Hoover phoned Roosevelt to discuss the banking problem. Roosevelt informed Hoover his advisers had recommended against closing banks.

As sources for this discussion I have used contemporary news accounts and a number of historical reference texts. Most detail comes from Raymond Moley's *After Seven Years*, Frederick Lewis Allen's *Only Yesterday*, and John T. Flynn's *The Roosevelt Myth.*

We remember well that following his inaugural address, President Roosevelt issued a proclamation of a banking holiday, basing it on the Trading With the Enemy Act. The draft for the official declaration was —the one that Hoover's advisers had prepared for him, and which circumstances—and Roosevelt—had prevented his using. The new President was the hero of the day, and he and those around him accepted the plaudits of the country. Meanwhile, the discredited ex-President retired with the blame for the losses in thousands of recently-failed banks which he had fought a compassionate, sympathetic, battle to save. Roosevelt had displayed notably that he had no aversion to profiting at others' expense—that such result was indeed the outcome of conscious plan.

In this connection I requote here a sentence from the *Tampa Tribune* editorial cited above commenting on the Teheran Conference revelations. (I also quoted from George F. Kennan's *Russia And The West* to the very same effect.):

> It shows . . . that Roosevelt in effect consented to Russian annexation of a large part of Poland's territory on condition the deal was not officially discussed before the 1944 election. The American President frankly admitted in the private conversation with Stalin that he did not wish to risk losing the 6 to 7 million votes of citizens of Polish extraction.

In the analysis of the tragedy of Pearl Harbor, of the machinations preceding it in Roosevelt's endeavors to entrap the nation into the war, and of the subsequent massive program of intrigue to cover up his deeds, we have had a chance to observe the depths of deceit to which the President was willing to go. In his report to the nation about the incident with the destroyer *Greer* he made no pretense at honesty; and all the while during the 1940 third term election campaign and after, he was alleging that his entire aim was the keeping of our nation out of war. After following the Japanese messages planning for the attack on Pearl Harbor and refusing to allow any of that material to be transmitted to Admiral Kimmel and General Short, and knowing the exact time of the attack 22 hours beforehand and refusing to permit any viable warning, he allowed Kimmel and Short to be saddled with the opprobrium—the blame and the shame—and to be drummed out of the service in disgrace.

Curtis B. Dall in his book *FDR, My Exploited Father-In-Law*, p.167, tells of an interview he had with Admiral Kimmel:

> 'Of all that crew then in Washington,' the Admiral said, 'Secretary Knox appeared to me to be the man most motivated by the factor of honesty.'
>
> 'What about FDR,' I asked. The Admiral paused and looked outside for a moment, then he continued, ' . . . I say that he would not hesitate for a moment to take advantage of anyone, including his own mother, if necessary, should it tend to advance him politically.'

I quoted earlier from the *Fort Worth Star-Telegram* the particulars of the inexcusable and unconstitutional uprooting and incarceration of many thousands of American citizens of Japanese ancestry after Pearl Harbor.

This is a commentary on the type of man that Roosevelt was—a powerful man who did not hesitate to take great risks at the tragic expense of many millions of other human beings—so long as the outcome redounded to his own personal benefit. How else could these events possibly be interpreted? And this is history—not myth.

Our Friends—OOPS!—Too Bad!

We have recounted how solicitous the President was for the success of Stalin and his strong arm Soviet seekers for insuperability, together with their Communist Comrades in China. We have noted how he conspired behind

Chiang's back to turn over Manchuria and her railways and ports to the bitter enemies of the Nationalists in Russia and in China itself.

We have brought out the never-flagging support by the President for all of the Soviet aims in Europe and Asia—wartime and postwar; but we have seen his virulent anti-colonialism where England and France were concerned. He needled Churchill in an endeavor to squeeze Great Britain into granting independence to India while the war was on, and he tried to embarrass the British leader by demanding that the British-sponsored Greek king be deposed and elections held right in the middle of the war. He proposed that he and Stalin form a common bloc against the British on the control of Hong Kong, Shanghai, and Canton; and he worked insistently to oust England from any claim or influence in Burma, Pakistan, Celon, Maylaya, and Singapore.

Forrest Davis, in those Roosevelt-edited accounts about Teheran referred to earlier, notes that in keeping the example set by his thrifty Dutch and Scottish ancestors,

> The President had looked up the cost to Britain of maintaining its flag in the Caribbean and offshore islands. It came to something like $20,000,000 a year. That, said the President, was too big a bill for prestige.
>
> Economically, he added, the islands were a headache, and he was not in the habit of buying headaches. This led to an entertaining disputation [to FDR]. Newfoundland was mentioned, the prime minister observing Britain never would relinquish Newfoundland willingly, it being the oldest crown colony. Mr. Roosevelt challenged the designation. Nettled, Mr. Churchill replied, 'I never heard a more preposterous statement: of course, Newfoundland is a crown colony. I ought to know; it's a part of my government'
>
> Mr. Roosevelt declined to give ground. 'It's not a crown colony,' he countered: 'It's a crown colony in bankruptcy. There's a difference.'

And to report a short quote from the *Tampa Tribune* editorial on the release of the Teheran Conference papers (as reported by the President's aide, Charles E. Bohlen):

> Then there was the conversation between Roosevelt and Stalin on the Baltic states of Estonia, Latvia and Lithuania which the Russians had gobbled up in 1940 and soon afterward lost to the German invaders. Roosevelt was quoted as telling Stalin—again 'jokingly'—that 'when the Soviet Armies reoccupied the Baltic areas he did not intend to go to war with the Soviet Union over this point.'

Forrest Davis, again (Op. Cit.), substantiates this presidential ploy, noting that Roosevelt never mentioned the Soviet dictator's record of recent aggressions in those victimized little nations; he indicated that he fully expected it to happen again. There was no chiding Stalin about the ghastly massacres in the

Katyn Forest, no expressed fulminations about the insidious ubiquitous Communist spies in our government, no indignation as to the Russian collaboration with Hitler and his fellow Nazis while France and other nations were being conquered. No, the President was trying to impress Stalin that we could be trusted—"to convince Russia of . . . the good faith of this country."

We have noted that the President was "less concerned about postwar Russia than about postwar France." On this Forrest Davis reports Roosevelt's "reluctance to commit the future of France exclusively to General DeGaulle." We have observed the President's bitter jealousy of the leader of the "Fighting French"—jealousy of his leadership and successes and his immense popularity in North Africa, Britain, and the United States. He feared that knowledge of his attempts to undermine the French General would cost him votes in the 1944 Election—and he resented that. He referred to DeGaulle as an "egoist," and his favorite epithet which he relished hurling in decriptions of him became "the Bride." He was responsible for the exclusion of DeGaulle from the Yalta deliberations; he was deeply prejudiced against the idea of DeGaulle as a postwar leader, and he was unalterably opposed, early in 1945, to any resumption of the prewar French leadership in Indochina. Of course, in all these cases—China, England, France—when the aegis of our friends was removed, vacuums were created. And Communism—as does nature—abhors a vacuum.

We shall presently see in more elaborate detail some of the President's designs relative to those friends.

Why?!

Let us hold up to the light all the possible diagnoses we can construct for what President Roosevelt did with his "Great Design," and why. For clarity I shall repeat here the steps in Roosevelt's plan as it appeared early in this treatise:

1. To give Stalin without stint or limit everything he asked for the prosecution of the war, and to refrain from asking Stalin for anything in return.
2. To persuade Stalin to adhere to statements of general aims, like the Atlantic Charter.
3. To let Stalin know that the influence of the White House was being used to encourage American public opinion to take a favorable view of the Soviet Government.
4. To meet Stalin face to face and persuade him into an acceptance of Christian ways and democratic principles.

The possible evaluations or constructions relative to Roosevelt's plan as I can see them are:

1. FDR was unintelligent.
2. FDR was ill.
3. FDR was constrained to do what he did by vast circumstances beyond his control, and did the best he could under those conditions.
4. FDR was naive.
5. FDR was dominated by Stalin.
6. FDR was a Communist.
7. FDR was correct and wise in his "Great Design" plans.
8. FDR was actuated by motives which grew out of his particular individualism and are traceable to the patterns of personality he had manifested long before and continued to manifest all during the course of the war.

(I have not included one choice which I am sure some readers may entertain as an explanation—that Roosevelt was deranged. This is not a credible alternative because FDR was closely observed by too many confidants and witnesses for it to have gone unreported.) Let us analyze each construction in depth.

1. FDR was unintelligent. This is untenable because, if for nothing else, his four elections to the Presidency displayed him as a master politician; and he had a way of accomplishing his purposes and concealing his methods (when he so desired) that was probably unmatched in American history.

2. FDR was ill. Roosevelt at the age of 39 was stricken with infantile paralysis which rendered him thereafter crippled in his legs and unable to walk without the use of braces and canes. He labored to make himself otherwise physically fit; a part of his regimen being a strenuous program of exercise and swimming, much of it at his home at Warm Springs, Georgia. He became very active in affairs of the Democratic Party in the state of New York and nationally. He was twice elected Governor of New York and, of course, four times President of the United States. Throughout his years in the Presidency he kept a hands-on policy in affairs of government, particularly when it came to matters of politics and those considerations which had to do with his own personal aims as he had outlined them, whether publicly or in secret. His adept maneuverings to bring us into war and the elaborate and minute details of his activities in carrying out his "Great Design" were not the program of an invalid. It must be remembered, too, that the first overt steps in his appeasement policy toward Stalin came nearly four years prior to the Yalta Conference when he offered vast quantities of aid in military supplies to the Soviet dictator—nearly five months before our entry into the war at Pearl Harbor. And his artful manipulations in the implementation of his blueprint toward "Uncle Joe"—as he called him—were not the workings of a sick man in the common understandings of the word. I think that any thoughts about illness as an explanation are erased when we recall

at Teheran that the President's incisive mind did not fail to remember and to avert the negative effects of millions of potential adverse U.S. Polish votes by providing for secrecy for decisions about Soviet postwar mastery of Polish borders until after the 1944 Presidential Election. [I recognize that that last sentence is long and somewhat convoluted—but I said it, and I'm glad!]

3. FDR was constrained to do what he did by vast circumstances beyond his control, and did the best he could under those conditions. The protagonists for this contention have formidable obstacles indeed in endeavoring to lay a respectable foundation for this argument. First, we had no debt whatsoever to Stalin. On the contrary, during nearly two years at the beginning of the war, Stalin had actively cooperated with Hitler in his infamous nonaggression pact, invading the smaller Eastern European nations of Poland and Finland and the little Baltic nations of Lithuania, Estonia, and Latvia. The heinous Russian massacre of Polish officers in the Katyn Forest had been laid bare to the world. We had not the most infinitesimal reason to trust Stalin. On the other hand, our vast industrial capacity was fueling the war efforts of both England and Russia with desperately needed lend-lease supplies. Also, virtually the entire load of the war against Japan was being borne by the United States. The victorious campaign in North Africa had been spearheaded by United States forces, as had the crusade in Sicily. Italy had surrendered in early September of 1943, and our and other allied troops were battling their way up the Italian Peninsula against the powerful entrenched armies of Germany. In addition, the armed might of Hitler's legions had driven deep into the heartland of Russia and still, even in September of 1943, three months before the Teheran Conference, held positions hundreds of miles within the Soviet borders. Had he been able to trade places with President Roosevelt with all the leverages of strength he possessed, I think there is no doubt that Churchill would have welcomed such a grand opportunity.

4. FDR was naive. Don't be naive! The American Heritage Dictionary includes here the terms: artless, lacking critical ability or analytical insight, innocent, guileless. Roosevelt was, on the other hand, shrewd—without peer when it came to discerning "what was in it for him" politically. The words "shrewd" and "naive" are mutually exclusive. One cannot be "shrewdly naive."

5. FDR was dominated by Stalin. In this sense of the term, "domination" arises from qualities of personality—persuasiveness to the point of being overpowering on the one hand, and on the other hand an attitude of subordination. It is true that Stalin was used to being in the ascendancy, but it was not persuasiveness to which he owed that position—it was FEAR! On his part subordinance or inferiority would seem to be postures far removed from the psychology of the President. He fancied <u>himself</u> to be dominating Stalin.

6. FDR was a Communist. We have observed that where personal philosophy was concerned, FDR was a "Rooseveltist." It is true that he shared with the Communists what seemed to be an insatiable desire for power. The Communists, however, sought—and seek—power as a means to bring about a group ascendancy. With the President the aim seems to have been always a personal one. There is no doubt, I think, that Roosevelt never entertained the slightest conception that any actions or plans of his were anything but thoroughly loyal and in the interests of our nation. We are all to a great extent the prisoners of our own thoughts. As Hayek expressed it:

> We all think that our personal order of values is not merely personal but that in a free discussion among rational people we would convince the others that ours is the right one.

In this particular, since the parts that the President was fitting into his "design" were "of necessity" mostly being kept secret, the entirety of where it was leading our nation and the world never became the subject of public discussion—pro and con –; and he never had to defend the concepts. And those concepts never received the benefit of liberation from the constraints of the mind of their originator.

7. FDR was correct and wise in his "Great Design" plans. Obviously the "Great Design" was a tragic failure for President Roosevelt, for our nation, for all those nations who were depending on our leadership to accomplish a just and lasting peace, for all those peoples who were kept under or who came under the tyranny of Communist controls, for all those lovers of or seekers for freedom everywhere, and for the world as a whole. Hundreds of millions of people who are now under the heel of despotic rule—or who have lost their lives there in the more than two score years since World War II—or whose lot it has been to perish in wars resulting from Communist greed for ever-more conquests of territory—all these were placed on the altar of a plan that had not the faintest iota of a chance of success. All of these terrible losses must be owned as the awful responsibility of President Franklin Delano Roosevelt of the United States of America.

The considerations that should have been weighed against such a course—or courses—were those vast certain sacrifices—territorial and human—that I have referred to in the previous paragraph. The side for freedom was left with no leverage—as though parents of a child held hostage by a kidnapper sent their only remaining son as a messenger with a million dollars in gold, even before requesting negotiations.

The chances for success rested on the threads of life of two old men—Roosevelt (who was dead before the end of the war) and Stalin (who survived less than a decade).

If converted, Stalin would certainly not have remained as leader. The qualities of ruthlessness and bloodthirst that had brought him to the pinnacle of an evil totalitarian empire were the qualities that kept him there as others, lusting for the lash-hand, lurked in the offing looking for the slightest sign of weakness—as jackals contemplating a feast. The "golden rule" had not brought such a tyrant to power, and would not keep him there.

All past history showed the improbability of success: the Communist writings of Marx, Lenin, and Stalin; the Russo-German Nonaggression Pact of 1939-41 with Stalin's record of brutality therein; Russian enslavement of her satellites and of her own people (strangulation of freedoms, purges, slave labor); the record of failed international pacts and agreements; the Soviet record of dishonesty, opportunism, and atheism; the never-wavering following of the Communist "line."

The most eloquent consideration, however, lay in the comparative chances for success of other plans. A synthesis of various proposals, such as those which follow cried for consideration.

Russia had been invaded by the vast might of the armed forces of Hitler. She desperately needed our aid. In return for its offer we could reasonably have asked or stipulated:

a. That Russia leave all other countries alone at the end of the war—get her public promise (We have earlier quoted William C. Bullitt to the effect that, as long as Russia was dependent for her life on our military supplies and aid, Stalin would have had to act as though he intended to keep such promises. And meanwhile our constructive plans for the Eastern European nations—the Balkan and Baltic states, and for China and Southeast Asia, would have progressed too far for Russia to interfere effectively—we had reason to hope—before she no longer needed our aid.)

b. That Russia stay out of the war against Japan, including the ensuing occupation areas—instead of (as we did do) "bribing" Russia to come into the war with supplies and territorial concessions.

c. That, as Churchill had strongly advocated, the major second front on the continent of Europe be up through the Balkans, thus separating Russia from the rest of Europe and cutting the German supply lines between Germany and her forces on the Russian Front (I have discussed this at length earlier.)

d. United States leadership and protection in forming a democratic federation of Western Europe, starting before war's end—thus presenting to the U.S.S.R. a fait accompli.

e. Restrictions of Russian occupation forces, if possible, to Russia itself

f. That the Russian government allow it to be observed that their citizens were being made aware of U.S. lend-lease aid.

g. That U.S. and British planes be assured use of Russian airfields in the carrying out of wartime objectives, which, of course, were benefiting the Soviet Union, as well.

These proposals cannot be deprecated as twenty twenty vision more than four decades after the conclusion of the war—"easy to possess perfect hindsight from this vantage point." For virtually every condition for these elements of "hindsight" was starkly in place at the time Roosevelt (with Churchill) met Stalin at Teheran. These were not selfish aims. The freedom of our people and of all peoples was a legitimate objective.

NOT ONE of these ideas was even considered by President Roosevelt! He still insisted on giving to Stalin "without stint or limit" and making no constructive proposals whatsoever for the freedom side. Never in the history of the world had one human leader had so much power in his grasp to utilize as leverage for the betterment of all mankind—and he squandered the opportunity.

8. FDR was actuated by motives which grew out of his particular individualism and which are traceable to the patterns of personality he had manifested long before and continued to manifest all during the course of the war. We have observed Roosevelt's shallow superficiality that prompted him—"without much thought" to toss glib phrases trippingly on the tongue with scant thought for their tragic trauma to teeming multitudes affected thereby. Remember the Morgenthau Plan for postwar Germany, the flippant flinging of the phrase "unconditional surrender" as an ultimatum which caused enemy peoples to fight to the bitter end; the lighthearted Teheran toast with Stalin to the postwar execution of "49,000 or more" of the German General staff. How wrong could Sherman be! War is not Hell—it's a game!

Selfishness and a lack of compassion were characteristics immoderately manifested by Roosevelt on a number of notable occasions . His career may have been replete with instances of saintly generosity and unbounded concern for his fellow human beings; if so, he was certainly a classic example of schizophrenia. The case of his refusal to cooperate with President Hoover on the idea of a banking holiday while depression desperate citizens were losing many millions in life savings during February and early March of 1933 was cast starkly against his declaration of the Bank Holiday immediately upon becoming President—and accepting the hero's acclaim while allowing Hoover to shoulder the undeserved blame. At Teheran he assured Stalin he would not oppose his reoccupation of the Baltic nations, and made great concessions on future boundaries for Poland on the condition that his doing so remain secret so that he would not lose millions of Polish votes in the 1944 election.

Roosevelt's amorality and dishonesty were highlighted in the statements we have noted from—among others—Vice President Garner and Admiral Kimmel. We have studied the campaign of deceit—to the American people and other nations—whereby the President "maneuvered" the nation into war. An outstanding episode in that story was the President's orders to the navy which threatened to get our ships sunk by Hitler's submarines and his rather untruthful report to the nation in the incident of the destroyer, the *Greer*. Also, we noted his public endorsements of "peace" all the while he was striving to get into the war. We have been in on Roosevelt's following of "Magic," the intercepts of Japanese messages outlining the coming attack on Pearl Harbor, his denial of that knowledge to Admiral Kimmel and General Short, his allowing Kimmel and Short to resign in disgrace and be blamed for the entire tragedy—also the elaborate measures taken to cover up what had really happened and Roosevelt's responsibility for it. And here again we note the "guilt by association" whereby scores of thousands of innocent United States citizens of Japanese descent were brutally herded into concentration camps for the duration of the war.

Probably the sharpest indictment of the President lies in his unbridled conceit and the magnitude of his ego. With knowledge of the record of unmitigated horror of Communism in Russia and the nations it had so ruthlessly subjugated, and also that Stalin was the ultimate architect of that brutality, treachery, and dishonesty, he had the consummate gall to put the lives and welfare and freedom of so many little nations and so many little people on the line in the preposterous gamble that his great "charm" could—in a few brief meetings—reform and Christianize and democratize such a heinous fiend!

But to return to the months before Pearl Harbor. Why, indeed, did Roosevelt desire that the United States be involved in the Second World War? Let us look at the scenario of the era. With much of the earth at war, the world's headlines every day shouted the names of the leaders of the warring nations Hitler, Mussolini, Stalin, Churchill, and others. And the United States —and Roosevelt—stood on the sidelines, out of the game. Down through the corridors of history the wartime leaders' names would be echoed with those of Lloyd George, Kaiser Wilhelm II, Clemenceau, and Woodrow Wilson—leaders from the First World War. That earlier "war to end all wars" had failed tragically to achieve its purpose. And now Roosevelt was an onlooker, a spectator, while others had leading roles in the making of momentous history. Oh, the President had been elected three times to that office—more than any other man before him. But that was <u>domestic</u> news. The real news that the chroniclers of history would remember and emphasize for this time and for all the generations yet unborn was being made by those wartime leaders of the great nations. Knowing his record and his personality, I cannot imagine that Roosevelt would have been content to remain out of the picture. The opportunity to be the leader of a great nation in the greatest war mankind had ever known was a chance not to be foregone. As humans we all tend to rationalize our acts and our methods. Certainly the President could convince himself that his every measure was for the good of the country. Perhaps a few lives would be lost, but in the long run how many would be saved! And how much better for our nation and for freedom if circumstances could be "managed" before it was "too late." I am sure that the President was appalled at the devastation in lives and shipping and installations as the accounting was made after Pearl Harbor, but the objective had been accomplished and we were "in it."

Now I am certain that some—many—are angered at such a speculation. I come to this determination, however, logically. I am a strong exponent of the Sherlock Holmes school of history. When we are not presented with the "smoking gun," it behooves us to analyze plausible hypotheses and eliminate those which do not hold up under the stress of examination. Roosevelt's contentions before the 1940 election that his primary aim was to keep us out of the war might be accepted—if we did not run into the history of his orders to the fleet to sail into war zone seas and broadcast in plain English positions of German ships. The record of the Japanese for decades in initiating wars with surprise attacks on the navies of potential enemies, the entire story of "Magic," the Japanese Purple Code, the allocations of Purple machines, the two months of Japanese attack plot messages, the President's assiduous day-by-day following of those messages, and the President's denial of warnings to the commanders at Pearl Harbor—all lay out a mosaic of Roosevelt's eagerness to get into the war. And the facets of his revealed character and personality traits argue for the reasons why. We cannot hold that he just wanted the fleet at Pearl Harbor to be destroyed. It was a means to an end—war. And he now had his opportunity to be a great wartime leader. I have not heard of anyone who has taken the facts of history and tried to come to an interpretation of "Why?"–except this member of the Sherlock Holmes school.

Once in the war the President had a springboard for projecting himself into the forefront of decision making and leadership—and he had a vehicle of leverage which gave him unprecedented power to compel the fear of enemies and the adherence and compliance of allies to his views. When Armistice Day brought an end to World War I in 1918, the heavier-than-air "flying machine" was more youthful than the war's youngest conscript. It had been less than fifteen years since the sons of Bishop Wright, on December 17, 1903, had flown their rude contraption at Kitty Hawk. Their longest of five flights that day had been 852 feet—had been in the air just 59 seconds. The first crude wartime uses of planes featured pilots dueling it out with pistols in their awkward, slow-moving craft and experimentally dropping artillery shells on targets. Before war's end, however, machine guns were being mounted in planes. But this was only a dim foreshadowing of the mighty use of airpower that would characterize World War II.

In the Second World War the United States shifted into high gear with the greatest industrial machine the world had ever known. No other nation could approximate it. We produced millions of military automobiles and other vehicles, many thousands of tanks, millions of guns and artillery pieces, thousands of naval vessels of all kinds and sizes, and hundreds of thousands of planes with speeds in the hundreds of miles an hour. And we produced bombs. The British had a single bomb they utilized that weighed 22,000 pounds. Our individual bombs were not that huge, but our big bombers carried enough blockbusters so that eleven hundred plane raids over single German cities dropped as much as 2,000 to 5,000 tons of bombs. We also were producing one quarter of the world's food.

The conference at Teheran came almost a full two years after the United States entered the war. In that interim before he was to have his first face-to-face meeting with Stalin, President Roosevelt had ample time to formulate a plan for leadership in the war. His plan, as we know, was the "Great Design."

Now, it is notable that the "Great Design" calculatedly had as its only prime mover Roosevelt, himself, and only Roosevelt. It was not a plan that allowed for continuity in the person of any successor President. FDR, I believe, would have been the first to recognize the fact that there was no one else who could have dreamed of carrying out the plan.

Of course, the massive might of the United States industrial power was translated through lend-lease into potent leverage over friend and foe. But when he had the opportunity to bring that great weight to constructive use, the President opted not to utilize it when it represented United States power during the earlier and ensuing stages of the war; he did not bargain for positive changes in Soviet actions and behavior which would advance the cause of freedom while aiding Russia with materiel imperative for her defense. He elected instead to wait until the end of the war when—if the "Great Design" were crowned with success—the power would belong to him personally. This is the only viable explanation for his not using other obviously far superior alternative plans—because they would not have left only him as the "savior" of the world. As he proceeded through the days, months, and years of war he systematically "burned all his bridges behind him" which might have allowed for any possible uses of lend-lease power for any alternative plans. And time was his confederate in the burning of those bridges because opportunities that would never return were inexorably—relentlessly—slipping away, etched beyond recall in history's unyielding stone.

Instead, as reported by Forrest Davis in those *Saturday Evening Post* articles personally edited by Roosevelt, at Teheran the President "conducted a seminar" for Stalin in the "Good Neighbor Policy," a term he had appropriated to himself to describe measures of Pan-American cooperation and friendship begun by his predecessors. He outlined to the Soviet dictator projections that at war's conclusion would establish the United States as paramount in the Western Hemisphere and Russia paramount in Eastern and Northern Europe. We have seen the details of the vast concessions of European territory promised by the President to Stalin at that conference.

He, however, had not been able as yet, by the time of Yalta, to get Stalin into the war against Japan—along with the additional gifts in territory and influence which the President hoped would solidify his sway over the Russian dictator and bring to fruition his hoped-for softening and reform of "Uncle Joe." But he was met with the abject offer of Japanese surrender. This must have placed the President in a quandary of "so near and yet so far." The only thing to do was to reject the Japanese offer—with some snide remarks about the political naivete' of General MacArthur who blessed the proposal. The only reason for such a decision was the advancement of <u>his own plan</u>.

Roosevelt obviously never entertained thought of the possibility that he might not be around after the war. He had calculatedly betrayed our friends and deliberately worked for the elimination of any democratic leaders who might be rivals for postwar control. Elliott, the President's son, in his book of unadulterated adulation, *As He* Saw *It*, pp.114-116, provides a primary source for Roosevelt's unbounded ego and passion for power. After talking with DeGaulle at the Casablanca Conference, the President told Elliott that DeGaulle "made it quite clear that he expects the Allies to return all French colonies to French control immediately upon their liberation. You know . . . . I'm by no means sure in my own mind that we'd be right to return France her colonies <u>at all ever</u>, without first obtaining in the case of each individual colony some sort of pledge, some sort of statement of just exactly what was planned, in terms of each colony's administration.'

> 'Hey, listen, Pop. I don't quite see this. I know colonies are important—but after all they do belong to France . . . how come we can talk about not returning them?'

He looked at me. '<u>How</u> do they belong to France? Why does Morocco, inhabited by Moroccans, belong to France? Or take Indo-China. The Japanese control that colony now. Why was it a cinch for the Japanese to conquer that land? The native Indo-Chinese have been so flagrantly downtrodden that they thought to themselves [The President had ESP?]: Anything must be better than to live under French colonial rule! Should a land belong to France? By what logic and by what custom—and by what historical rule?'

'Yes, but . . . .'

'I'm talking about another war, Elliott,' Father cried, his voice suddenly sharp.'I'm talking about what will happen to our world, if after the war we allow millions of people to slide back into the same semi-slavery! . . . . When we've won the war, I will work with all my might and main to see to it that the United States is not wheedled into the position of accepting any plan that will further France's imperialistic ambitions, or that will aid or abet the British Empire in its imperialist ambitions.'

On p. 207, Elliott (<u>Op</u>. <u>Cit</u>.) observes:

Father had been successful in demonstrating over the conference table . . . that our function would be to integrate, in the future organization of the United Nations, the disparate views of the Europe-minded British and the Communist-minded Russians.

And on p. 213 Elliott records the President as proclaiming (modestly):

'The United Nations . . . ' he said to me that last night, with great satisfaction . . . 'After the war—then is when I'm going to be able to make sure the United Nations are really the United Nations!'

There seems to be no pretense at equivocation as to who would be running the show!

Robert E. Sherwood, in his *Roosevelt and Hopkins, An Intimate History* (New York, Harper and Brothers 1950), on pp. 789-790 remembers:

Sometimes during the Teheran Conference Roosevelt drew three circles, which represented his conception of the basis of the United Nations Organization. The center circle was marked 'Executive Committee,' the one on the right was marked '4 Policemen' [U.S., Great Britain, Russia, and China] and the one on the left '40 United Nations' (The General Assembly) under which came 'I.L.0. Health—Agriculture—Food. This, so far as I know, was the first crude outline of the U.N. structure put down by Roosevelt who, unlike Hopkins, loved to draw charts.

In what might well be called the Forrest Davis-Roosevelt articles about Teheran, Davis writes that the President desired to withhold from publication his specific "ideology" about the setup of the United Nations until a successful second front had been launched on the continent of Europe—presumably across the English Channel. Davis reports that the President chafed at the constitutional restrictions of his four year tenure of office while leaders of other nations could plan without such time limitations. He also expressed to the writer his confidence that Stalin would respect the freedoms of the Scandinavians and of the areas and peoples of the Baltic states and the Baltic Sea. It would have been interesting at that point if Mr. Davis had uttered a single simple three letter word—"why?" He might have been so bold as to say, "Are you kidding?!" But he might not have wanted to risk the loss of a Presidential scoop. Certainly, however, there was not one scintilla of historical evidence to support such a preposterous thesis—and an awesome abundance of fearful facts shouted it wasn't so.

However, Roosevelt gave to Mr. Davis—and explained—general diagrams of the postwar U.N. organization with markedly detailed plans—his alone of three general branches (legislative, judicial, and executive) and the powers and jurisdictions of each.

> As for the structure of the United Nations' permanent organization, he draws largely on his own experience . . . .As I understand it, the President envisages an executive committee [cabinet?] at the top, a legislature in the form of world-wide conferences at regular or irregular intervals, and a high court, and perhaps subsidiary courts for specific purposes. The bureaucracy he would pretty much confine to a number of continuing commissions . . . . The [executive committee's] members must, however, be within easy reach by telephone or air communication.

(It is of interest to venture speculation on the question of whom the President had in mind to be the initiator of the communication—certainly not DeGaulle!)

The President in the months that followed refined his concepts as to the structure of the U.N. He seems not to have made them a matter for public consumption, though he is alleged by various sources to have expressed to confidants in or out of government, visualizations of an organization modeled in a fashion after the government of the United States or of each of the 48 states of that period. He had been Governor of New York and now was the President. It should not be a surprise to find his thoughts running along the lines of a government with three branches—executive, legislative, and judicial. In some measure, various organs of the United Nations as eventually composed corresponded in function not without similarity to the President's cabinet: Economic and Social Council, Labor, Food and Agriculture, Court of Justice, International Bank and Monetary Fund, Civil Aviation, Military Staff and Armed Forces,

Universal Postal Organization, World Health Organization, etc. We are not as yet privy to the specific designs that Roosevelt considered. The United Nations, however, was in a measure a homonym, designating at once all of the nations that were fighting in opposition to the Axis Powers, and, as the war drew toward its end, proposals for a postwar international organization to improve upon the earlier League of Nations. It should be kept in mind that in the latter sense it existed before war's end only in various ideas and proposals. At Yalta, for example, it was still an expedient in FDR's "Great Design" as he assured Stalin he might have three votes in the proposed General Assembly to only one for each other nation, including the United States. Suffice it to say, Roosevelt (as we have seen from his earlier statements quoted by his son Elliott in *As He Saw It*) had made quite clear that the U.N. would be his organization.

In the case of the 1933 Bank Holiday Roosevelt had found it to his political advantage to refuse to concur with Hoover's compassionate plan to come to the rescue of hundreds of thousands—perhaps more—who were victims of depression change-of-administration panic runs on banks. Then after so many had lost their savings he himself declared a banking holiday using the plans of Hoover—and taking all credit.

In 1940 when he was campaigning for election to an unprecedented third Presidential term he made it a cardinal point to promise that he would keep the nation out of war; and he got elected again. It would seem that he coveted a historic role as leader of a great nation in a great world war, for he worked dishonestly in an earnest endeavor to provoke war with Germany. When he was unsuccessful on that score—and always proclaiming peaceful intent—he turned to Japan, finally successfully "maneuvering them into firing the first shot." And now he was leader of a great nation at war. It would be at a price of more than a million casualties—American dead and wounded; but Roosevelt again was accomplishing his own personal aim, and others would take the losses.

As for Pearl Harbor itself, the President had managed that it would be brought about by denying vital warnings to the base. He had accomplished his own personal ends; it had been at a cost of more than 3,400 casualties—2,326 of them slain. But he did not have to take any blame. That was borne by the hapless Admiral Kimmel and General Short.

Now the question does persist—Was it not necessary for the United States to get into the war, after all? This may very well be. But the nation was not being alerted by President Roosevelt. His every motivation was getting elected to a third term. And since he was of the opinion that the vast majority of the electorate in 1940 desired us to stay out of the war, he chose to tell them what they wanted to hear—and he was successful.

Once he had won the 1940 election, the President had the war urge—if not before. The plots to thumb our Atlantic Fleet's nose at Hitler were ingenious and insidious—and in secret. Why was this, if it was imperative for us to get into the war? Roosevelt, the politician, had promised peace. Now he must stay true to the promise, even if it were to the nation's advantage for him to announce the necessity of our going to war. It therefore was exigent for him to be dishonest with the American people. And finally it was necessary for him to let Pearl Harbor be attacked, our Pacific Fleet smashed, with 3,435 casualties. It should be noted that, in each case, it was not the good of the nation that was to be considered; it was what was good for President Roosevelt.

Back again to that odious accommodation with Stalin at Teheran when the President (in addition to promising the Russian dictator that the 7,000,000 or so inhabitants of the little Baltic States would not be defended by us from Russian bondage) "consented to Russian annexation of a large part of Poland's territory on condition that the deal was not officially discussed before the 1944 election. The President frankly admitted in this private conversation with Stalin that he did not wish to risk losing the 6 to 7 million votes of citizens of Polish extraction."

Now, take note of what has transpired. Upwards of twenty million people—perhaps more—have been betrayed by our President into the ravenous grasp of the all-devouring Stalin. And what is Roosevelt's only concern?—Keeping it quiet so that he won't lose potential votes in the next election!

Take heed—these accounts are not myth, they are history. I do not delude myself, however, nor would I delude readers. There are those who will scorn the incontrovertible evidence and fly in the face of fact. They are not of the Sherlock Holmes school of history. No, they are irreconcilable, die-hard, partisans of the Tooth Fairy—or Santa Claus—or Easter Bunny schools of history. When eight year old Virginia 0'Hanlon in 1897 wrote to the *New York Sun* her query, "Is there a Santa Claus?," Francis P. Church penned his historic editorial in reply. It was a beautiful answer, and it expressed some abiding values for readers of all ages. I trust that the young Virginia found therein some comfort, and that eventually she was able to grasp the deeper truths it contained. But I would hope that the young lady by the time she was 42 had developed a new perspective about jolly old St. Nicholas. And we, for our part, must be about the realities of history.

But some will say "Yes, but he was such a good man and peerless leader otherwise." I am reminded of the verse from Second Kings, Chapter 5, which to me has always represented the epitome of dramatic irony:

> Now Naaman, captain of the host of the king of Syria, was a great man with his master, and honorable, because by him the Lord had given deliverance unto Syria: he was also a mighty man in valour, <u>but he was a leper</u>.

Naaman was by all odds a commendable personality, and the negative factor in his description was certainly not of his own choosing.

By contrast, a parallel description of Franklin D. Roosevelt following the outline given above might very well conclude:

> Now he was a good man and a peerless leader, but he subjected many thousands of depression era families to loss of their bank savings so that he might profit politically, he permitted the loss of several thousands of dead and wounded at Pearl Harbor because he chose not to give adequate warning, and he condemned millions to the loss of freedom and—in some cases—slavery and death because he was trying to win the favor of Stalin.

Unlike Naaman, Roosevelt was the author of his own negative determinants.

Now let us repeat possible construction Number 8, which I have posited as one of the conceivable explanations for the "Great Design." FDR was actuated by motives which grew out of his particular individualism and which are traceable to the patterns of personality he had manifested long before and continued to manifest all during the course of the war.

This is the only explanation which answers the why's of every step and every nuance of the perpetration of this incredible, monstrous crime against mankind. We have observed that Franklin Delano Roosevelt was afflicted with amorality, that he was dishonest if it served his ends—taking credit due to others and willing to let others shoulder blame rightly belonging to him, that he was lacking in compassion and reckless of the welfare of others, that he was an egoist in whom a deadly combination of conceit and lack of depth led him to think that he could soften and convert the obdurate and diabolic Stalin, that he was of unbridled ambition and consumed with desire for power.

To the President the "Great Design" was as yet incomplete. He had worked diligently to remove any democratic (Christian, and freedom-loving) competitors for postwar leadership and control. There was only Stalin—in the regions of the world that Roosevelt and his "Great Design" had assured him the ascendancy—who would remain. Now if Roosevelt could just complete his mastery over Stalin with his conversion to the principles of Christianity and democracy, who would be the only logical choice to be the First President of the World—or whatever the title might be? And then he could "straighten out" any unfortunate "accidents" that had happened along the way! I ask you to retrace the steps and see if it doesn't all fit like a jig-saw puzzle.

Or if there is another explanation that takes into account all the elements that have to be reckoned with, it needs to be revealed.

Outlandish, you say? Well, the "Great Design" was an outlandish scheme—and, most assuredly, the rationale is far more substantially founded on irrefutable fact than the "Great Designer" ever fabricated in his "Greatest Dreams!"

Chapter VII

The "Sin" of Postwar Anti-Communism and the Blameless Righteousness of the Left—Particularly in Vietnam

As the war began its grind to a halt, Communists and their left-hand men in Russia and America, too, stirred and shook from them their unwonted sheep's clothing and began to reassert their natural lupine characteristics—the snarls of the wolf. Gone was the pretense of amity. The American Communist Party resumed its name again, and all its utterances stripped bare its traitorous aims. The United States must give the secrets of atomic energy (and the bomb) to Russia because capitalism could not be "trusted" with it; only Socialism could be relied upon to use these for the benefit of all mankind. The armed forces of America must be reduced. The "Cold War" was blamed on the departure of the West from the "spirit of Yalta." The U.S. was the "most disliked power" in all of "liberated (a euphemism for 'conquered by the Communists') Europe."

Truman's new Secretary of State, James F. Byrnes in his book, *Speaking Frankly*, which has been referred to earlier, recounted how Molotov, Stalin's Foreign Minister, at the 1945 Paris Conference accused the United States and the United Kingdom of "enriching themselves" during the war, of collaborating with "Fascists," of "enslaving Italy," and "subjugating" weaker nations. The following year, at the Paris Peace Conference, Mr. Byrnes was subjected to Vyshinsky's tirade that the U.S. was trying to "dominate the world" by its "handouts"—to the lusty applause of the delegates from Communist Czechoslovakia, whose government was to receive $50 million at only 2 and 3/8% interest. At about the same time an army transport plane containing 7 Americans, 1 Swiss, and 1 Turk lost its way in hazardous mountain flying over Communist Yugoslavia, and was attacked by two Yugoslavian fighter planes and forced down in a wheat field at great peril.

These events were a foreshadowing—omens of things to come.

Meanwhile, let us repair to the periphery of China, which itself was becoming the periphery of the encroaching tide of Russian Communism—like nature, abhorring the vacuums created for it by Roosevelt with his "Great Design." At Yalta the 38th Parallel had been set up across Korea to divide Korea between the Soviet occupation in the North and the U.S. forces in the South. The United Nations was to supervise elections for all of Korea. When, in 1947, the U.N. sent a commission to Korea to arrange for elections, Russia would not allow them into the North. The following year a constitution was written and adopted by South Korea and put into force. Dr. Syngman Rhee was elected president. The Russians had been arming the Communists in the North since 1945. In June of 1950 they invaded South Korea, and the three year Korean War began with United Nations forces led by General Douglas MacArthur opposing the Communists. The integrity of South Korea as a nation was established, the threat of Chinese Communist entry was bandied about (notwithstanding that the U.S. maintained at the time overwhelming atomic superiority over Russia). It was in the ensuing heated dispute over policy that President Truman fired General MacArthur, and for the first time in the postwar era the United States "blinked."

And now, in the immortal words of Shakespeare's Hamlet: "Vietnam: ay, there's the rub–"

We observed much earlier a number of the achievements under the French leadership in Indochina during the nineteenth century and prewar twentieth century. Lumber—notably teakwood, abundance of rice, tea, and numerous other agricultural products were found in quantity, as well as fish, silk, rubber, petroleum, phosphates, coal, iron ore, gold, silver, tin, manganese, lead and zinc, tungsten, chromite, molybdenum, and precious stones. There was provided a system of hospital care, infant mortality had been greatly reduced, and life expectancy raised. The ministering Christian missions, predominantly of the Catholic persuasion, provided churches, schools, and orphanages, as well as hospitals.

There came a fly in the Oriental ointment in the person of Ho Chi Minh, a gentleman of undeniable leadership abilities who "got in with the wrong crowd" by joining the fledgling French Communist Party soon after the end of the First World War. He turned out to be ubiquitous wherever Communism spread its vulture wings in that era. He soon showed up in Moscow to meditate on Marxism under the masters. In 1925 he formed a revolutionary organization which later became the Indochinese Communist Party.

In World War II when the Japanese occupied Vietnam, Ho formed the Red-dominated Vietminh from several different independence groups. By 1945, with 10,000 soldiers in northern Vietnam, the Vietminh took over the government and declared independence. Soon they were fighting against the French in the South. President Roosevelt had set this stage for Communist domination in the vacuums that we have been studying, created by the crippling of French, British, and Chinese Nationalist spheres of influence and the establishment of powerful Communist domination in Manchuria in his projected plans. He then refused American aid to the French forces as they endeavored to reestablish their erstwhile orbits as the war began to draw to a close. Finally, a tenuous French control was reinstated by March 4, 1946.

Late in that year Ho reactivated his rebellion, and the French, to counter his appeal, began negotiations with former Emperor Bao Dai in August of 1947. An agreement was signed in March, 1949, whereby the French-educated and French-speaking Bao Dai became head of the French puppet government. At the time of the Korean War Ho's forces were receiving considerable aid from Russia and the new Communist government in China. Utilizing appeals to nationalism, together with terrorism and murder against civilians in the population, the rebels fought the French and pro-French Vietnamese troops to a standstill and captured the strategic Dienbienphu camp on May 8, 1954. Not to be overlooked as a pernicious factor here was the failure of resolve by government and citizens on the home front in France. A cease-fire signed on July 21, 1954, set the 17th parallel as the dividing line between the Communist North, with some 13 million population, and South Vietnam with a population of 12 million. Elections were to be held for all Vietnam within two years; they were never held. Laos and Cambodia were to be independent. S.E.A.T.0., the Southeast Asia Treaty Organization, was formed in 1954, consisting of the United States, United Kingdom, France, Australia, New Zealand, Pakistan, Thailand and the Philippines.

On October 26, 1955, Prime Minister Ngo Dinh Diem proclaimed the Republic of Vietnam as the interim government for South Vietnam. In *Civilization - Past and Present*, Vol. II, by Wallbank, Taylor, and Carson, p. 583, we find:

> Ignoring the 1954 Geneva Agreement, Communist guerrillas, the Vietcong, from North Vietnam began to terrorize the country. Their attacks increased in strength and boldness . . . . This country, together with its unstable neighbors Laos and Cambodia, would be the logical springboard for Communist expansion southward and westward, menacing all of Southeast Asia." Nearly a million North Vietnamese fled into the South, creating a desperate situation so far as jobs were concerned. Diem helped establish villages for these refugees, many of whom were Catholic. (In 1963 Diem was assassinated.)

In 1961 the Kennedy Administration decided to increase aid to South Vietnam. There resulted more scientific aid to agriculture, to expanding industries, hospitals, schools, textbooks, plans for irrigation, hydroelectric power, flood and water control, as well as military supplies.

Meanwhile, Edward Graff and Harold Hammond have given us a contemporary view of what was going on in Vietnam (*Southeast Asia—History, Culture, People*, p.126):

> The Vietcong terrorize and kill government officials in the villages if they refuse to join the Vietcong. This terrorism by bombing has also been carried into Saigon, where thousands of civilians have been killed. Those terror tactics may be the reason for the support the Vietcong have received from the peasants.

It is good to remember this and other similar accounts when research occasionally leads us to descriptions of the "spontaneous popular acclaim and following of the gentle, kindly old Ho Chi Minh."

President Eisenhower in 1959 had emphasized the vital importance of defending Southeast Asia:

> Strategically, South Vietnam's capture by the Communists would bring their power several hundred miles into a hitherto free region. The remaining countries of Southeast Asia would be menaced by a great flanking movement. The loss of South Vietnam would set in motion a crumbling process which could as it progresses have grave consequences for the forces of freedom.

And President Kennedy went to the heart of the matter when he observed:

> This is a struggle of will and determination as much as one of force and violence. It is a battle for the conquest of the minds and souls as much as for the conquest of lives and territory . . . we cannot fail to take sides.

On August 7, 1964, the United States Congress passed the Tonkin Resolution authorizing presidential action (President Johnson) in Vietnam after North Vietnamese boats in the Gulf of Tonkin reportedly attacked two U.S. destroyers on August 2nd. This was the official beginning of what is generally referred to as the Vietnam War.

The government of South Vietnam was beset by instability, in some part due to coups and assassinations. In 1965 Air Force Commander, Nguyen Cao Ky became Premier after a military takeover. A new constitution was adopted and provisions were made for free elections. In 1967 60% of those eligible to vote did so, though disrupting Communists murdered, kidnapped and wounded hundreds. Nguyen Van Thieu was elected President, and Ky was made Vice

President. That voter turnout and under those conditions is enough to shame many in our country.

It is not our purpose in this place to fight the war in detail. It suffices at this point to outline sketchily some check points—a skeleton view, if you will (if skeletons can view?). We will anon be furnishing these bones with flesh that is fundamental to a true understanding of what the war was all about.

The *World Almanac* recounts the final outcome of the struggle:

> A cease fire agreement was signed in Paris, Jan. 27, 1973, by the U.S., North and South Vietnam, and the Vietcong. It was never implemented. U.S. aid was curbed in 1974 by the U.S. Congress. Heavy fighting continued for two years throughout Indochina.

The surrender of South Vietnam came on April 30, 1974; On July 2, 1976, the country was reunited under Communist control. The *World Almanac* again:

> . . . and first steps were taken to transform society along communist lines. All businesses and farms were collectivized.
>
> The U.S. accepted over 165,000 Vietnamese refugees, while scores of thousands more sought refuge in other countries . . . . Displaced war refugees in South Vietnam totaled over 6.5 million.

Before we proceed further, it is imperative that we again take note of the fact that it was the president of the United States, President Roosevelt, whose planning and desires had resulted in the evisceration of the erstwhile French control in Indochina and the enervation of the vast Asian holdings of Britain. We have observed his oft-expressed passion that the long-time predominances of those two nations should be terminated in the postwar world, and — if possible—before. We have seen how, behind Chiang Kai-shek's back, he had promised Stalin vast Chinese (notably Manchurian) and other strategic Oriental holdings which presaged the inevitable turning over of far-reaching controls to covetous Communists in Russia and in China. On the one hand he had worked to create colossal vacuums where democratic friends had once held sway; on the other hand he had whetted the rapacious appetites and magnified the malevolent might of the evil forces who hovered, like vultures, salivating while contemplating the prey.

We Americans are a people peculiar in this world. We love our country, and we are proud to be Americans. We are proud that we are the most productive people, and thus the wealthiest people on the face of the earth. We are proud of our heritage, which includes the values of the Judeo-Christian tradition. And in that tradition we claim the majestic gift spoken of so eloquently by Jefferson:

that we "are endowed by [our] Creator with certain unalienable rights, that among these are life, liberty, and the pursuit of happiness." It is not wealth that fills us with our greatest pride; it is the birthright of freedom. And though we find ourselves on occasion prone to take all this for granted—which is to say, without the requisite appreciation—we recognize that by no other nation in the world are all of these qualities so abundantly displayed, and we are proud. And, furthermore, we assume without question that it is our responsibility as Americans to defend all this that we hold dear.

Have I described our condition accurately and with unerring insight? I detect a mood of disquiet. May I note that the foregoing paragraph is an unquestionably true characterization of our people a generation or two ago. I would also, however, make bold to observe that today, as well, this description is in focus for the vast majority of our nation's citizens; and most of us wince and are resentful when we encounter Americans who make it a practice to detract from our nation by word or by deed. You will note that I have scrupulously avoided the imputing of shame to our reactions—though I am certain that we are deeply ashamed of the detractors.

Why, then, the vilification?

Well, there is the well-known axiom: "You can't please everybody." And in the words of Grandpa in Jo David Brown's *Stars in My Crown*: "Some dogs just love to howl." But it is not, alas, that simple.

Hark back to those years of 1939 to 1941 during the Hitler-Stalin "Nonaggression" Pact when American Communists found it advantageous to be—loudly—for peace when they knew the United States would not consider going to war on the side of Russia and Germany against the democracies of England and France. I have earlier traced the nauseating campaign of that era which reached even into the programs of church youth groups. Impressionable youth in some cases swallowed the line unquestioningly, some "heroically" daring to lead in this new crusade. The war years saw the promotion of and indoctrination in the fiction of U.S.-Soviet amity and supposed congruence of our national aims, in accordance with one of the cardinal points of our leader's "Great Design." In many quarters there was spread a euphoria as to the aims of Russia and of the Communists.

As the reality of the divergence of Soviet interests began to be revealed, some die-hards turned to feelings of guilt and self (or American)—flagellation. And there were those who just desired to be different—or nonconformist. It was "fashionable" to be anticapitalist—to be socialist or collectivist. They could agree with the Communists on so <u>many</u> things, and they tended to discount the disparities with gullibility. The Communists just <u>had</u> to be "good guys" and those who opposed them or accused them of malefactions had to be "bad guys"—to the point of blissful irrationality.

Many youthful college professors of the postwar era were products of the unsettled times just described. Most were not Communists, but there was a predisposition to be anti-capitalist and anti-American when one had to choose sides. There seemed usually to be a "Yes, but–" reaction when the United States or its actions were extolled. Actually it was the case that, as the postwar colleges and graduate schools settled into the pro-socialist mold, the "young radicals" on campus became those who were the defenders of capitalism and who were pro-American. As is always true, leaders were in the minority. A scant few stood up to be counted as most degree seekers floated along with the tide and chose not to "get involved." Students who were there at the time can attest to the accuracy of this description. This was really, in essence, the prelude to the sixties.

I think that an account of an actual case in point is relevant here. I'm thinking of a young infantry veteran of four years—43 months in the Southwest Pacific area. He taught in the Spring of 1946 in the Kentucky high school from which he had graduated. A talented singer with much experience in the service, he went in the fall of 1946 to New York to study voice with the great Frantz Proschowski on the G.I. Bill of Rights. It was necessary, in order to be eligible for subsistence while studying voice, for him to pursue a masters degree in music at Teachers College, Columbia University. With college majors in English and history, he chose all the history electives he could get.

One of his courses was Problems in American Life, taught by a young socialist Ph.D. Each Saturday morning there was a fifty minute lecture followed by a break, then fifty minutes of question and answer and discussion. The young veteran did much reading and intensive research—and much courteous but effective disagreement with the professor.

Our veteran was presented his M.A. in June, 1947, and investigated enrollment for a masters in History. He was informed that he could not do that, but that he should take a degree above the masters in the Teaching of Social Studies. Already planning toward a Ph.D. in history and social studies, he took and passed the French examination for the doctorate with almost perfect papers. He took the doctors candidate's G.E.D. (General Examination for the Doctorate) taken by several thousands each year. He was gratified to learn that his grades were so high on that exam that only 2 out of 40 applicants ever receive higher. Meanwhile he entered all three summer sessions, taking maximum loads. In August he returned to Kentucky to acquire a bride and return immediately with her to New York, where she worked in the office of Nursing Education. They lived in a sixth floor walk-up apartment with one room, kitchen and bathroom privileges, five other people, and too many roaches to mention. That year the veteran sang professionally as tenor soloist in a succession of three churches to augment the G.I. Bill.

Our veteran took courses now similar in nature to the one previously described. Aware that at that time one in twenty American Ph.D.'s were products of Columbia, he felt that those in classes should hear the "other side" of questions. He continued courteously, but effectively, to make his case. He often read twenty hours a day. Often other students (who had not spoken up in class) stopped him afterwards to express agreement. But they also would say: "They'll never let you get your doctorate!"

In August of 1948 an additional member joined the family—"Junior." The veteran left New York with his family to teach in Florida. They returned to New York the following summer, enrolling for full loads in three summer sessions. Back to Florida at summer's end, he began to sing as a church soloist, and in addition to his teaching of high school history classes, he began teaching voice. After the first of the year he took over a job as director of music at one of several churches he had been importuned to serve. It was back to New York in 1950 for a similar summer schedule.

In the spring of 1951 he received an ominous letter from the department head at Columbia. It said that the question of his doctoral candidacy had arisen in meetings of the department and that he should submit copies of papers he had written in department classes. These would be reviewed and he could have an appointment to discuss them when he returned to Columbia in the summer. Our veteran had an outstanding 16 year old soprano pupil whom he took with the family that year. Dr. Harry R. Wilson was so impressed when she sang for him that he had her appear as guest soloist with his 300 voice summer graduate school chorus in the magnificent "Requiem Aeternam," from Verdi's *Requiem.*

He had sent the best papers as well as the worst he had for the review. When his interview came, the first young Ph.D. happened by the office. The head of the department commented casually: "What are we going to do with this young man? He's obviously brilliant." The reply was noncommittal. The department head returned the papers, commenting that they were excellent masters level papers for the most part, which was indeed the level on which they had been done. His critique continued. He said that the veteran had a tendency to devote too much time and effort in the assembling of facts, and he needed to spend more time on the synthesis where he drew his conclusions and made recommendations for action, etc. Now, one fact stood out with this analysis. If our doctoral candidate had been careless in research and actuated by prejudice the diagnosis would have been just the opposite. He would have tended to slight the careful gathering of facts and details and would have rushed on to his preconceived one-sided conclusions. He did not bring that up in the discussion.

He proceeded to make A's in all of his courses that summer, returning to Florida as the fall fell over the land. It was on the ghostly goblined threshold of Hallowe'en that the axe came hurtling through the myriad miles from Columbia University, Teachers College, the Department of the Teaching of History and Social Studies. The letter had been written by the head of the department, but our veteran surmised that other members of the department had had much to do with the hurling of the axe that unerringly found its mark in the back of our veteran's neck.

He now had received two graduate degrees from Teachers College and had a total of four years of graduate hours. He could have taken one-third of the hours for H-credit, that is attendance only without doing the class assignments—hearing credit. He had done four years of full credit, and on a perfect scale of 4, singing professionally much of the time and carrying heavy loads, he had a 3.28+ average. He now lacked only one language exam, one seminar course and the thesis.

The epistle acknowledged the outstanding quality of his work, but it said that in discussions among the members of the department the question had been raised that his personal political views were so strong that they "might get in the way of objective research in the field." No instance of such a failure was cited. As a matter of fact, the critique of his papers submitted for analysis had been diametrically opposed to such a conclusion. The letter ended with the observation that "no member of the department will agree to co-operate on any project conducted by you." He apologized for their having to make such a decision, saying that perhaps it was wrong—but in any case it was final. Best wishes and all that sort of thing.

Our veteran remembered the, "They'll never let you get your doctorate!" He had considered the possibility, but had decided he would prefer to risk that in order that all those Ph.D.'s being turned out by Columbia might hear another side along the way.

You have probably surmised before this time that the young veteran whose story you have read was I, George W. Seevers.

As we moved into the decade of the 1960's many young college instructors were practiced in their deprecation of traditional American values in general—

and at times obscenely iconoclastic. Good professors have had methods of stimulating discussion and dissent with respect for the dissenter. I call to mind a young instructor at the University of South Florida during the period in question who countered a female student's disagreeing query with the arrogant rejoinder, "Does your shit stink?" Such was not conducive to constructive thought, it might appear. Another instance of shining scholarship found a puerile pedagogue advertising his atheism by suggesting to a nun who took issue with him that he have intercourse with her on the floor of the classroom. In neither case, we "divine," was the instructor cursed with an overabundance of humility. Of course, criticisms were met by other faculty and students loudly defending the malefactors on the grounds of "academic freedom." I would theorize that, being apprised that the first amendment's contemporary interpretation forbids the classroom recitation of the Lord's Prayer but protects such displays of "academic freedom," the reaction of the founding fathers would be—unbounded disgust.

My college freshman American history professor on the threshold of World War II was Dr. Keith, who also doubled as Dean of Men. A colorful personality, he was six feet five and weighed about two sixty. He had been a Rhodes scholar at Oxford, and had pitched baseball for the old St. Louis Browns back before the First World War. Behind his back we called him "Bull" Keith. His lectures were sprinkled liberally with "damns" and "hells," but obscenities were never deemed necessary to make points.

One day early in the school year Dr. Keith stood before the class and admonished us:

> Most, if not all, of you have come here with some kind of faith. It may have been given to you by an old minister or by your mother and dad—or maybe your grandparents. They may have given you a good foundation, or they may not have done such a good job. Before you have been here very long, that faith is going to come under attack by some of your friends or some of your professors in the name of science, or logic, or common sense—or just because you 'should go along with the crowd.' I want you to remember this: before you let anybody take that faith away from you and smash it, be sure he's going to give you a better one than it in its place!

Particularly from the decade of the sixties, the faiths and many important values were taken from much of our youth, as well as other segments of our population—but no one bothered to give them better ones in their place. The only abiding value was "me." And if the guideposts of society have been negated and one "follows the crowd," in which direction are the pilots going to lead in such a vacuum? Youth often experience rebellion, but they are truly lost when the focus of rebellion has the low ceiling of self-satisfaction—the "me generation."

But, alas, the Communists and their fellow professionals are never in the least confused about where they want to go—and in which direction they desire to lead the rudderless flock who are "going with the crowd." The dupes go, too, helping to lead along whatever routes have been skillfully charted by the professionals—with the guise of spontaneity. Most of the followers are truly—and eagerly—deceived into a belief that they are participating in wholly (or holy) spontaneous demonstrations, or walks, or marches. But always there are the same old names organizing and leading—pouring blood on draft records, burning or, urinating on or defecating on the flag, handcuffing themselves to fences, allowing themselves to be carried off as limp dead weights, or contriving to get themselves arrested in the cause of "peace." They well have learned to utilize the psychology and the hysteria of a mass rock concert to achieve their ends. And always there are the media, skillfully used and played upon like the roll of drums to publicize, to exhibit, and exaggerate their much ado. Too often "religious leaders" are among the professionals who lend a false sanction of righteousness to the ostentatious display. With the well-knit leadership cadres in control and available, it is no mystery that we have "demonstrations on demand"—or to cite a currently popular T.V. beer commercial: "It's show time!"

I quote from a Nick Thimmesch column about the Kent State case (*Tampa Times*, July 7, 1977). There are details here that give a new illumination to what many people thought was the situation. (Of course, the sensational photo carried in papers and on T.V. across the world —of a young co-ed kneeling beside a stricken student in dramatic appeal turned out not to be a co-ed at all, but rather a runaway teenager of questionable reputation who had joined the crowd for the thrill of it all.)

> Two nights after the Cambodian invasion, hard-core, antiwar activists led a parade down the main streets of Kent, Ohio. The marchers turned violent, smashed windows in a recruiting office and then ran to the Kent State campus where they burned to the ground a building occupied by the Reserve Officers Training Corps (ROTC).
>
> It was antiwar activists who began the violence at Kent State. Gov. James Rhodes, mindful of other campus violence in the U.S. resulting in the deaths of professors, and destruction of research and buildings, became excited, and called in the National Guard. The guardsmen were very young, many no older than the students themselves. Some were still tired from a stint of riot-control duty at the site of a violent teachers' strike.
>
> The guardsmen dispatched to Kent State were green troops, and when

> confronted with rock throwing, lost their composure and fired into a seething mass of students. Four fell dead, and nine others were wounded.
>
> This became known as the Kent State Massacre. Families of the dead have filed and lost suits against the guardsmen.

Reformed Vietnam War protesters Peter Collier and David Horowitz, were the authors of an article quoted from the *Washington Post* which appeared in the *Tampa Tribune* on April 21, 1985: "The Road from Radical Chic to Ronald Reagan." They observe that the Marxist Dictator of Ethiopia, kept in power by a force of 20,000 troops from Communist Cuba, had conducted a "Red Campaign of Terror" which had slaughtered thousands of people. The writers note Leftist claims that the Soviet Union virtually always sides with downtrodden liberationists.

> Where were [the Leftists] to point out the moral when capitalist America rushed in 250 million metric tons of grain to help allay the Ethiopian starvation, while the Soviets were managing to contribute only 10 million metric tons? Where are those now that [Ethiopian dictator] Mengistu withholds emergency supplies from the starving provinces of Eritrea and Tigre, because the people there are in rebellion against his tyranny.

Some of the problems of agitation during the Vietnam War are stressed in the foregoing article by Collier and Horowitz when they note that Afghanistan is not likely to become "Russia's Vietnam" because no reports are allowed of Russian brutality to peasants and children, no body bags of Russian boys on T.V.— to Russia or to the rest of the world. There is no media coverage, so

> no protests on Soviet campuses and in Soviet streets, no clamor to bring the boys home . . . . At the height of the Vietnam War there was a noncombatant army of foreign journalists present to witness its conduct. In Afghanistan they are forbidden, as are the Red Cross and all other international relief agencies that were integral to what happened in Vietnam . . . . In Vietnam we waged a war against ourselves and lost. The Soviets will not let that happen to them.
>
> The Left's memory can be as selective as its morality . . . . The attitude toward Soviet penetration of the Americas is a good example . . . Many of us began our New Leftism with the Fair Play for Cuba demonstrations. We raised our voices and chanted, 'Cuba, Si! Yanqui, No!

Then there's good old, sure-fire, Gary Trudeau, who won (this is the way things are tilted in the world of journalism these days) a Pulitzer Prize for the cartoon (?) strip, "Doonesbury," honoring the content about the time of the Vietnam War. I don't know specifically which of his offerings merited the prize, but I am going to quote from one in which he chose to pick on President Carter. (His drawing certainly attains the nadir of artistry, and the subject matter treatment is more suitable for the editorial page rather than the milieu of Snoopy and Charlie Brown and Funky Winkerbean—if you are amenable to that sort of—well—amongst your editorials.) In the first panel we see the White House, and a call is coming in to President Carter from Cuba's Communist dictator, Fidel Castro:

> Senor Carter, I am a troubled man. I am told that you have called again for more human rights in Cuba. You must forgive me, Senor, but I do not understand. You must tell me. What does Cuba have to learn about human rights from a country which has known racism for centuries, which has waged a criminal war in Vietnam, which was capable of Watergate—a country which continues to support totalitarian regimes around the world? (Carter) Mr. Premier, that is an excellent question. And I'll be honest with you, I don't know. But I will have our moral experts look into the matter . . . . Do you still have political prisoners? That could be it, but I'm not sure.

And so we have set in stark detail the evil record of the United States as opposed to the righteousness of Castro. Ha Ha Ha! for those comics!

What I am reviewing here in these pages is the nature of the controversy which swirled around our efforts while we were attempting to conduct the war in Vietnam. Perhaps that needs to be pointed up more sharply before we go on.

A crucial few months at the center of this era involved the Presidential election campaign of 1968 and the media coverage. Edith Efron (*The News Twisters*) devised an innovative method to chart such coverage statistically. She had her technicians record the half hour national news coverage each evening of the three major networks—ABC, CBS, and NBC. Then she timed how many minutes were devoted to each viewpoint—for or in opposition to our government's policies in Vietnam. Surprise!

> In general, those who might have supported the Administration's side of the controversy were not to be seen or heard. There was no public opinion in support of the war on any of the three networks.

A "clean" bombing is one that surgically avoids damage to civilians and to civilian areas, concentrating on military targets. Our bombings of Vietcong supply bases and reinforcement areas across the border in Cambodia were eventually demonstrated to have been almost unbelievably "clean," with civilian dwellings and other such areas virtually unmarked while military bases across the road were demolished (Smith Hempstone column, *Tampa Tribune*, January 13, 1973). In the United States, however, as well as the rest of the world, the only published accounts at the time came from a Japanese Communist news service, accepted uncritically with its horrifying tales of civilian area destruction and the slaughter of women and children.

Many millions of Americans and viewers the world over saw the picture of a South Vietnamese army officer shooting a supposedly helpless Vietcong prisoner. The executioner was General Loan, and the picture was widely used to demonstrate the depravity of the side we were supporting in the war. The true story was a decade in being revealed, but it was related in Nick Thimmesh's column which was carried in the *Tampa Times* for November 8, 1978. It spoke of the

> South Vietnamese general who had the bad luck to be photographed and televised while executing a Vietcong prisoner during the 1968 Tet offensive . . . [General] Loan's own officers came back to their barracks and found their wives had been attacked by Vietcong that day and had their legs cut off. There were many such atrocities committed by Vietcong in civilian garb and thus eligible to be classified as 'unlawful combatants' in international law.

The "balanced" propaganda treatment of the war I had a first-hand opportunity to observe when American history classes I was teaching in a Florida secondary school were required to participate in nine weeks reading labs. There were numerous tapes of information which they were provided for exercises along the way. The one about the Vietnam War was narrated and "explained" to students by a deserter who went to Canada to escape the service. I'm sure that would have gone over big with the thousands of men who served during the war—sort of like having a tape of Benedict Arnold to explain the American Revolution!

Readers can well remember the blatant actions of numerous left-wing entertainers and activists, of whom Jane Fonda was probably the most repulsive—even going to North Vietnam to show common cause with our enemy and to bedevil American Prisoners of War. She was more subtle than Abbie Hoffman who showed his American concern by urinating and defecating on the American flag. She has been quoted by a number of sources, among them Nick Thimmesch (Tampa Times, October 2, 1979): "I would think that if you understood what Communism was, you would hope, you would pray on your knees, that we would someday become Communist."

Thimmesch continued in that column:

> But Fonda is around, unrepentant, and she provokes. As long as I live I will never forget that under Communist' auspices she went to Hanoi in 1972 and in propaganda broadcasts praised the Communist people's war of the Vietnamese people' at a time when American soldiers were being killed by her sponsors.
>
> She also condemned American officers as 'war criminals' guilty of fighting in a war which was 'the most terrible crime that has ever been created against

humanity.' The U.S. prisoners of war languishing and being tortured in nearby prisons could only grit their teeth.

Only the fact that technically we were not formally at war—by declaration—kept Fonda's actions from being treason. She and husband, Tom Hayden, returned home, declaring that American captives were well treated by their Communist captors.

Hank Whittemore, writing in *Parade* (April 19, 1987, "Fear Can Be Your Best Friend"), tells the story of Major Leo Thorsness, an Air Force fighter pilot captured after being shot down over North Vietnam. Said Thorsness of the "peace activists":

> 'When the delegations came . . . .We were forced by the Vietnamese to memorize answers to the questions we'd be asked. They would "bend" us. And either you bent or you died. One time they brutalized me so badly, in the face and arms, that they became too embarrassed to put me before a delegation.'
>
> 'I think those who came to Hanoi were ready to believe whatever they were told or shown. They weren't objective to begin with. And they were manipulated.'

Navy Captain John McCann refused to have his picture taken with an actress who was "working for peace," and he was punished by being incarcerated for four summer months in a 6 by 3 foot cell. (George Will, *Tampa Tribune*, April 16,1979, gave the dimensions of the cubicle as 5 by 2 feet.)

To return to the Whittemore account:

> Thorsness, now 55, doesn't even remotely resemble a Hollywood hero . . . . But he is a real hero, and he knows the meaning of courage as well as any man alive. Although his shoulder blades were separated, and he was 'bent in half' and then hung from a ceiling by the ankles, he continued to resist his captors' demands that he make public statements against the war . . . . 'When you were being tortured, you looked ahead only a minute. You prayed you could pass out before they could break you . . . . Very few of us felt that, because we'd been captured, our war was over.'

They kept up their resistance and "'paid dearly for it.'" They realized, said Thorsness, that "'for every freedom, there's an even or matching responsibility. When you were finally given a mirror to shave with, the first thing you did was look yourself in the eye. Were you satisfied with what you saw?'"

By 1972 there were more P.O.W. "shoot downs."

> Some guys had been on college campuses in the 1960's when we had been prisoners, Thorsness says . . . . They said, Why in the world should we be

> tortured to say things that everybody in the States is already saying? They knew what the story was back home.

And Fonda has made millions on her workout routines. The P.O.W.'s might have given her some new ideas for workouts with the "bent in half" routine.

James J. Kilpatrick (*The Washington Star*, May 8, 1980) tells of some discussion which supposedly took place relative to a post-Vietnam G. I. Bill. It would not have been out of place with some of the attitudes we have observed:

> An infamous colloquy made the rounds.
> How did you lose your arm?'
> Lost it in Vietnam.'
> Serves you right.'

And now let us review a few representative details about the methods of the Vietcong which were somehow overlooked by virtually all of the news media at the time. The first was in a letter to the *Tampa Tribune* by John Hurley on January 14, 1972. The writer does not give the source of his information, but it does fit the picture which comes from official sources.

> As most people know, one of the favorite VC tactics is to decapitate the village chief in front of his village and family. This encourages support for the VC. Another well known tactic used on uncooperative families is to cut a hand or foot off one of the children.

So much for the "kindly lovable old leader of the Viet Cong," Ho Chi Minh.

I am going to quote from the official "Report on the U.S. Senate Hearings" entitled *The Truth About Vietnam*, San Diego, Greenleaf Classics, Inc., 1966. The page numbers cited are from the published volume, but the official report was outlining testimony by the dates of occurrence. These records are in the public domain, as are all Congressional proceedings, with rare exceptions.

On page 282, the testimony of General Maxwell D. Taylor, February 17, 1966: "Terror is a regular tactic that the Vietcong employ against the civilian population . . . ." Senator Lauche:

> I read to you of an event that happened in June 1965 following the Battle of Dong Hoa. The Vietcong left behind about 1,500 of a total of 3,000 population dead, injured, maimed, or orphaned. These 3,000 people were simple Vietnamese peasants.

On page 82, U.S. Senate Foreign Relations Committee Hearings, February 4, 1966, report from the Department of State on Vietcong atrocities from 1962-1965: 53,292 civilians assassinated, wounded, or kidnapped in an organized program of violence.

On August 24 (1965), U.S. troops entered a Montagnard village 15 miles east of Pleiku to discover that the Vietcong had just executed the aged village chief and the village chief's youngest son. The village chief's wife was still alive but the Vietcong had tortured her by carving flesh from her body and cutting her arms. The Vietcong had also shot the wives of two of the Montagnard soldiers from the village repeatedly in the fleshy parts of their legs trying to force the women to disclose who, among the villagers, supported the Government.

On page 277, February 17,1966, Senator Russell B. Long, of Louisiana:

In one year alone they (the Vietcong) killed 456 mayors in little villages . . . . Do you know how many civilians the Vietcong have killed—innocent men, women, and children who are not combatants at all? . . . The last time I looked at it the figure exceeded 50,000.

On page 313, also February 17, 1966, Senator Symington, citing a report

about what the Vietcong did when they went into a village. They took the chief and his wife, and the four children . . . . First they disemboweled the smallest, in front of everybody, then they disemboweled the second, then the next older and the next older, then the wife in front of the chief, then the chief himself. I asked Nha Trang, the man who would know: 'That story couldn't possibly be true,could it?' And he said, 'I knew the village and I knew the chief.'

And last we have a report from C. L. Sulzberger in the *Tampa Tribune*, January 13, 1973, of

Saigon's official statistic of 5,800 persons slaughtered, principally by throat-cutting or burial alive, during the Communist occupation of the South Vietnamese city of Hue in February, 1968.

Nick Thimmesch, in his column which was carried in the Tampa Tribune April 18, 1975, told of an interview with a cavalier member of the staff of Senator Abraham Ribicoff (D.-Conn.): "'Thieu [leader of South Vietnam] . . . jailed newsmen and suppressed people. Thieu's a Fascist. The Vietnamese are better off under Communism.'"

But the columnist continued with the description of actual conditions:

Under Ho Chi Minh and his successors, the North Vietnamese have murdered several hundred thousand and these are not military casualties; they are old-fashioned executions. One most Americans are familiar with is the Hue massacre during the 1968 Tet offensive. When the Communists were finally forced out of Hue, some 5700 of the city's residents were missing. One year later mass graves were discovered, and when they were all opened some 2750 bodies of missing civilians were found; they had been clubbed, stabbed, and shot to death.

CHAPTER VIII

The "Triumph of Virtue"

General Maxwell D. Taylor, testifying before the Committee on Foreign Relations of the United States Senate, observed about the French leadership that they possessed strong military forces in Vietnam that were not involved at Dienbenphu, but the French government had already made the decision that they would not continue the fight. General Taylor referred to the Communist leaders in Hanoi:

> They have not forgotten that the Vietminh won more in Paris than in Dienbenphu and believe that the Vietcong may be as fortunate in Washington. They doubt the will of the American public to continue the conflict . . . . In a contest of patience they expect to win.

Senator J.W. Fulbright noted, as Chairman of the Committee:

> I think there is no question that if we wished to bring all of our power to bear we can completely annihilate this small country. [Note—It was not our aim to destroy Vietnam; we should have been extinguishing the forces who were endeavoring to destroy its freedoms and make it subject to powerful Communist neighbors.] There is no industrialization of any consequence. They do not make planes, missiles, tanks, anything of that character, and I am sure we could completely crush them to dust and rubble if we wished to do so.

General Taylor replied with a quotation from the ancient Greek historian Publius, writing 125 years before Christ: "It is not the purpose of war to annihilate those who provoke it but to cause them to mend their ways."

On March 31, 1975, the *Tampa Times* carried a column by Jeffrey Hart which bore the title "Vietnam Massacre is Gift from U.S. Liberals." I quote a portion here:

> The assumption behind the Paris accords worked out by Henry Kissinger in 1973 was that Saigon would receive sufficient aid to fend off the Communist invaders. The Secretary of State now says that had he known then that Congress would slash aid the way it has, he could not in good conscience have

> conducted those negotiations. No wonder. Hanoi now deploys, for example, triple the number of tanks it used in its big 1972 offensive. During the past year, the Soviet Union has doubled its aid to the North . . . . Reasonable men can argue about our entire approach to the Vietnamese conflict . . . . My own opinion is that it was the height of folly to put large numbers of American draftees into the rice paddies. Instead, we should have dealt drastically with North Vietnam in 1966, dealt with it massively with B-52's from a height of 30,000 feet. That would have made the necessary point about the rewards of aggression . . . . It is perfectly obvious that the present Communist offensive resulted from a clear perception of U.S. weakness, not material weakness but a weakness resulting from a collapse of political will.

Mr. Hart concluded—rather plausibly—that the lack of commitment of Congressional liberals had undermined the resolve and credibility of the United States so far as the prosecution of our aims in Vietnam.

John Chamberlain, in a column carried March 1, 1967, in the *Tampa Times*, noted:

> There's a lesson for U.S. 'Vietnicks' in the Third Punic War . . . . When the Vietniks counsel surrender in Asia, let Hannibal's words be thrown in their faces: 'If you gain a victory even those who hate you will hold to you; if you are defeated even your friends will leave you.'

The *Tampa Times* of May 10, 1981, had a column by George Will which was headed "Defeat from the Jaws of Victory" which cites and quotes from an article in the Washington Quarterly (Georgetown University) by John Colvin, consul-general at the British Mission in Hanoi during 1966 and 1967. He describes North Vietnamese war vehicles (from China)

> 'amphibious vehicles, artillery, armored fighting vehicles, Sergeant surface-to-air missiles on flatbeds, saucily parked even outside the British and Cambodian missions. By August and September (1967) there were none at all . . . .'
>
> When Colvin left for England in September, North Vietnam 'was no longer capable of maintaining itself as an economic unit nor of mounting aggressive war against its neighbor.' This judgment, he says, is not refuted by the strength of the Tet offensive five months later because 'most of that equipment had been in South Vietnam or en route there before the summer air offensive in the north had even begun.'
>
> Effective air strikes didn't allow time to make repairs.
>
> Thus the persistence of the campaign that 'had sapped North Vietnam's endurance was discarded. And at the end of March, 1968, all bombing of North Vietnam north of the 20th parallel was discontinued. Victory—by September, 1967, in America's hands—was not so much thrown away as shunned with prim, averted eyes.'

> The 'lesson of Vietnam' that defeatists have drummed into us for five years has been that American power is so limited that we cannot help imperfect allies who are far away resist subversion or takeover,

wrote William Safire (New York Times News Service—the column appearing January 1, 1979, in the *Tampa Tribune*).

> But the real lesson of Vietnam being driven home today, is that the perception of America's weakness of will invites aggression; that Moscow is willing to use its client states to bring about a Pan Sovietica; and that there is no turning away from our allies anywhere without the danger of a cost in lives and human freedom everywhere.

And Mr. Safire observes cogently:

> The advocates of cutting off military aid to Saigon assured us that the 'falling domino theory' . . . had long been discredited. Now we know what happened after congressional doves pinched off the lifeline: South Vietnam collapsed; Laos soon became a Vietnam puppet; Cambodia fell first to the savage Khmer Rouge, and then to Vietnamese regulars; now real fear is felt in Thailand and Malaysia. The domino theory, in Asia as in the Mideast, is not all that discredited anymore.

To quote from Jeffrey Hart again (*Tampa Times*, October 14, 1977): "Hanoi Celebrates a Victory in New York." Well, important elements of the so-called 'Peace Movement' have now come out of the closet, and the moral stench is so strong you need a gas mask.

"At the Beacon Theater in Manhattan, some two thousand cheering people welcomed the new communist Vietnamese U.N. delegation." (Present were: Cora Weiss, former Attorney General Mark Clark, Sam Brown—head of Peace Corps affiliate, ACTION, Pete Seeger—leftist folk singer, and Congressman David Dellinger.) It was obvious that "these members of the Peace Movement were not interested in peace at all but in a Hanoi triumph." For most their motivation was "sheer hatred of the United States."

Considerably more than two years before the "paragons of peace" congregated in Manhattan to rejoice in the fruits of their labors, one of those distinguished dominoes that "wouldn't happen"—happened. The United States had withdrawn its aid to the anti-communist government of Marshal Lon Nol in Cambodia, and the Communist Khmer Rouge, under Premier Pol Pot, had marched into power in April of 1975. The game of international dominoes was just beginning. It is inconceivable that they who revelled in the triumphal entry of the Vietcong into the United Nations, as though strewing palm branches before the asses of the victorious delegation (a deft bit of word transposition there might make a more piquant simile), they whose consuming interests had so embroiled them in southeast Asia—inconceivable that they were ignorant of what was transpiring in Cambodia. I want to look briefly at several news accounts in point. The dates of some of these reports were well before the Beacon Theater bash; others are of dates a bit more recent, but are retelling events already well-known before the "faithful" gathered for their exercise in jubilation.

I use as my sources the following items:

Seymour M. Hersh, "Pol Pot Regime Nearly Destroyed Cambodian Society," *Tampa Tribune* (from New York Times News Service) August 10, 1979

Michael J. Himowitz, "Photos Show Horrors of Past Still With Us," *Tampa Tribune* (from *Baltimore Evening Sun*) April 29, 1983

Norman Kempster, "Flirt With Him and You Will Die" *Tampa Times* (from the *Los Angeles Times*), September 2, 1978

Andrew McLeod, "His Mission-Establishing a Historical Memory of the Pol Pot Regime," *Tampa Tribune* (from U.P.I.), April 21, 1983

Martin Woolacott, "Warnings of Cambodian Massacre Should Have Been Heeded," *Tampa Times* September 10, 1977

"Reds Killed 1.2 Million, Digest Says," *Tampa Tribune* January 24, 1976 (UPI)

Kempster tells of official U.S. Government interviews with 22 refugees which resulted in a 300 page report to the U.N. on human rights in Cambodia. The reports told of long hours spent digging in the fields. A worker would be reprimanded if he were late to work the first or second time. "On the third occasion, he would be beaten to death with a bamboo pole, the most common method of execution." Spies reported any complaint about the food—shortness of it, seasoning, the way it was cooked; the penalty often being execution. (Can you imagine a U.S. Army mess hall with such rules!)

> Once or twice a year we had a 'mating period.' For two days, while also working, young men and young women were allowed to talk with each other . . . . Except during the mating period [they] were not allowed to talk with each other, day or night . . . . Aside from the mating period you cannot tell a girl that you like her.

You had to tell the village chief, instead. Mass marriages were held about every six months. Immediate execution for both the boy and girl caught flirting was the Khmer Rouge resolution.

Entire families were—at the whim of the Khmer Rouge—taken out into the fields and beaten to death. One refugee had escaped after being left for dead.

The Hersh account, written after a ten day visit to Vietnam, tells of interviews with United Nations and Red Cross officials who related their own observations in Cambodia where two and a quarter million Cambodians "were facing imminent starvation." Pol Pot was attempting to "purify" the nation of all foreign elements. The population—children, babies, the aged, the sick—were driven out of the cities, many to die on the roads and in the fields. Social welfare and relief facilities were "left in shambles." hospitals, schools, water supply facilities, and sanitary systems "were demolished." Officials reported 10,000 orphans in Cambodia—with no attempt at immunizations. A Roman Catholic cathedral had been razed without a trace in Phnom Penh, as well as the city's central market. All the automobiles had been destroyed. "The proliferation of rats and other vermin has caused outbreaks of plague and other diseases."

> Intellectuals were systematically purged . . . . Survivors reported that all persons who were known to speak English, French or other foreign languages were hunted down, imprisoned and, in some cases, beaten to death with sticks, they said.
>
> The possession of eyeglasses might mark one as an intellectual and bring punishment. Only 40 of 500 practicing medical doctors have been found.
>
> The rest are presumed to have been slain or to have died while working in the fields in the last four years.
>
> The relief officials also said that during their visit to Cambodia they had seen evidence of systematic torture in chambers operated by the Pol Pot government at a prison near Phnom Penh. Members of the Pol Pot regime, they said, carefully logged the names and titles of their victims and the types of torture each suffered. The officials said they knew of one large burial site where the remains of perhaps hundreds of the torture victims had been found after the Vietnamese invasion.

A photographic record of the carnage is described by Himowitz:

> The skulls, thousands of them, form the top of the pyramid, with thousands of leg bones, arm bones and the rest of what was once a small city's worth of people piled neatly around the base.
>
> If the photograph is reminiscent of pictures from the Nazi death camps 40 years ago, that's fine with David Hawk, a former director of Amnesty International . . . . As part of its revolutionary plan, the Khmer Rouge evacuated the cities, forcing the population into the countryside where as many as 2 million may have died of starvation and disease.
>
> Hundreds of thousands were executed outright, as the new government killed virtually anybody in any official position in the old regime, then set about destroying ethnic minorities and virtually the entire Buddhist priesthood . . . . Hawk's photographs dwell at length on the infamous prison called Tuol Sleng, a converted school in Phnom Penh where an estimated 15,000 Cambodians were tortured into confessing crimes against the state and then murdered.

McLeod's column bore the title: "His Mission—Establishing a 'Historical Memory' of Horrors of the Pol Pot Regime":

> Gregory Stanton remembers the day he looked into a mass grave in Cambodia and saw the bodies of 5,000 Buddhists. He remembers the stench and revulsion . . . . No precise death count has ever been established for how many of Cambodia's 8 million population died during Pol Pot's 3 1/2 year reign, but a Western diplomat in Thailand said most estimates range between 1.2 million and 2 million, although some have suggested the death toll reached 3 million.
>
> They died in executions, as a result of forced evacuation of cities, forced labor and lack of medical facilities, the diplomat said . . . . The amazing thing about the genocide in Cambodia was they killed their own people . . . . People were starving and they had mass graves all over the country.

The United Press column which was carried in the *Tampa Tribune* tells of John Barron and Anthony Paul, editors of the *Readers' Digest*, who in research for a book about the Cambodian horror interviewed more than 300 refugees who were fleeing from the Communist regime in their homeland. They, too, set the minimum number of deaths—men, women, and children—at 1.2 million. Many were killed methodically.

> They said one such killing occurred at a plantation of Mong Kol Borei on April 27, 1975:
>
> Weeping, sobbing, pleading for their lives, the prisoners were formed into a ragged line, the terrified wives and children around each head of the family. One at a time, each official was thrust forward and forced to kneel between two soldiers armed with bayonet-tipped Ak47 rifles. The soldiers then stabbed the victim simultaneously, one through the chest and the other through the back. Family by family, the communists proceeded methodically down the line.
>
> As each man lay dying, his wife and children were dragged up to his body. The woman, forced to kneel, also received the simultaneous bayonet thrusts, then the children and babies. An eyewitness remembers that a terrible stillness descended over the plantation, the Khmer Rouge saying nothing, the blood like water on the grass.

[I might point out here that in describing Communism much earlier I called it a "sadistic urge for power."]

Woollacott's column reports that in the Spring of 1975 "There were stories of Buddhist priests beaten to death with hammers and children laid out in rows with their throats cut."

The writer notes a foolish and frightening consistency of the American—and Western "liberal" establishment. "Concentrating on the corruption and incompetence of the Lon Nol government and on the many deceits and stupidities of the Americans in Cambodia," and regarding the murderous Khmer Rouge with forgiving—rationalizing and eager to justify every discordant fact, they persuaded us that it would be "better" if the Khmer Rouge took over.

We are always so much more demanding of incipient democracies faced by bloodthirsty communist alternative forces. We demand that they "grow up already," easily forgetting that in most cases they do not start with a background of centuries of maturing democratic tradition nor of respect for the sanctity of the individual. We would be satisfied with nothing less than the springing forth of full-blown Republican and Democratic parties with national conventions and all that goes with the dream. We, of course, are always disappointed. And so in China we helped the Communists to replace the Nationalists, we allowed the imperfect South Vietnamese government to be supplanted by the bloodthirsty Vietcong, and the Lon Nol era in Cambodia to be overthrown by the cutthroat Khmer Rouge.

The similar sacrificies of our sympathizers nag at our historic memory. The Shah in Iran was replaced by the ferocious insanity of the Ayatollah Ruhollah Khomeini, and in South Africa we weight the scales in behalf of Marxists and their barbarous "ring of fire."

Richard Nixon, in his *No More Vietnams*, gave details of the procedure we followed in South Vietnam with Diem:

> The Kennedy administration, increasingly frustrated with President Diem, encouraged and supported a military coup against his government. This shameful episode ended with Diem's murder and began a period of political chaos in South Vietnam that forced us to send our own troops into the war.
>
> President Diem stablized South Vietnam as a Keystone holds up a dome. Political forces converged on him from all directions. But by balancing one against another, he locked all of them into place. And just as a keystone's importance is not apparent unless it is removed, Diem's vital role became clear only after his demise, when the entire South Vietnamese political system came crashing down.
>
> What the coup supporters in the Kennedy administration should have known all along now became painfully clear: The choice in South Vietnam had not been between Diem and somebody better but between Diem and somebody worse.
>
> Whatever his faults, Diem possessed a significant measure of legitimacy. He was a strong leader of a nation which desperately needed strong leadership. With him gone, power in South Vietnam was up for grabs. The administration officials who had so eagerly hatched the plots against Diem soon

> discovered that their South Vietnamese collaborators were hopelessly bad leaders. Skills needed to overthrow a government are not useful for running one. Leading a coup and leading a government are two entirely different jobs. The chaotic leadership crisis that followed in South Vietnam was a direct consequence of the overthrow of President Ngo Dinh Diem.
>
> For two years, the gates of the presidential palace were a revolving door. South Vietnam endured 10 changes of government, and even more in the military high command. Intrigue became Saigon's form of government. (Quoted from the *Tampa Tribune-Times*, April 21, 1985)

Well, the Khmer Rouge came to power, and Woollacott also quotes from Paul and Barron:

> The corpses of babies and of old people bloated by the roadside as the population was herded from the cities to the countryside, the field near Mount Tippadei strewn with the twisted and bloody bodies of army officers in full dress uniform and decorations.
>
> The heads of 40 young women, buried up to their necks and then knifed in the throat, sticking up out of the ground like a crop of cabbages; the bayoneting to death of civil servants and their families by numbers—the men first, then the wives, then the children.

In a falling out among fellow felons, early in 1979, the Vietcong rulers of Vietnam invaded Cambodia, overthrew the Khmer Rouge, and set up their own government.

"Even worse than Hitler's treatment of the Jews"—that is the way one of the founding members of Vietnam's Communist Party characterized the Vietnamese treatment of ethnic Chinese after he defected to China in the summer of 1979. China had been an ally of the Vietcong, but the friendship was a thing of the past now. This is from a news account in the *Tampa Tribune* of August 10, 1979. Hoang van Hoan added also that ordinary Vietnamese now suffer "a life of humiliation and repression." He did not mention the Soviet Union by name, but he continued by saying that "his country has become 'subservient to a foreign power economically, militarily and diplomatically.'" This report might be discounted as a product of a falling out among questionably honest Communist "friends." However, William Safires's column (*Tampa Tribune*, November 6, 1979) reports: "genocide in Vietnam: The men in Hanoi were pushing tens of thousands of ethnic Chinese living in Vietnam out to sea to drown."

Smith Hempstone's column (*Tampa Tribune*. May 13, 1982) was headed "Viets Join Soviet Slave Trade," and it continued:

> Thousands were executed in South Vietnam after the fall of its anti-Communist government, hundreds of thousands have been confined for years to 'reeducation' camps in the jungles and 1.4 million others have fled, braving the threat of drowning, hunger, thirst and pirates to avoid a similar fate.
>
> And now the Vietnamese and the Russians reportedly are engaged in a brutal and cynical slave-trade that ought to be an affront to every civilized person: the 'sale' of Vietnamese workers to the labor-short Soviets as repayment for part of Hanoi's $3 million debt to Moscow.

"Vietnam's Desolation" was the title of a November 11, 1986, editorial in the *Tampa Tribune*:

> Here is what the Communists have accomplished since their victory in 1975: An estimated one-third of Vietnam's 60 million people are unemployed. The annual average income is $150. Shackling Vietnam with the worthless doctrine of Marxism not only ruined its economy but prompted hundreds of thousands of South Vietnamese to flee their homeland. What that loss represented in intellect and productivity can be seen in the extraordinary success the Vietnamese refugees have enjoyed in their adopted countries.
>
> And, irony of ironies, Vietnam itself became mired in a guerrilla war by invading Cambodia in 1978. The invasion and Vietnam's ruthless 'scorched earth' strategy prevented the planting of Cambodia's 1979 rice crop, resulting in a famine that killed tens of thousands, perhaps hundreds of thousands, of Cambodians. Such tactics, including indiscriminate chemical attacks, have turned Cambodians, who initially welcomed the defeat of the brutal Khmer Rouge regime, against the Vietnamese and strengthened the guerrilla efforts. The war now appears unwinnable and Vietnam must maintain a revenue-draining army of a million soldiers.

Randolph Harrison served two tours of duty in Vietnam as an infantry officer during the war. He is presently foreign correspondent for the *Orlando Sentinel*, and in this capacity went back to Vietnam with a tour group from this country in the summer of 1987. The first of several first-hand reports on that venture was carried in the *Tampa Tribune* on August 2, 1987. His observations in part were as follows:

> Vietnam is not just poor. It is destitute . . . . But Vietnam's poverty is not just the kind recorded in ledgers. Vietnam suffers a profound poverty of the spirit that drains the soul as surely as poor diet drains the body.
>
> Since defeating the U.S.-backed government in 1975, the country's Marxist leadership has watched a reunified Vietnam plummet to near the bottom of the list of the world's poor countries. Average annual wages are less than $200. Inflation last year hit 700 percent . . . Malnutrition is common in this country that once exported rice and today struggles to feed itself . . . so Vietnamese decide to have more children than ever.

Vietnam's population has doubled since 1970, from 30 million to more than 60 million today. The country must produce 600,000 additional metric tons of grain each year just to stay even with the population surge—a race it has not won for years.

Yet with all these problems, Vietnam has the world's fourth-largest military establishment . . . . Twelve years after reunification . . . 1.6 million men in uniform . . . .

Vietnam still has its 'reeducation camps,' where thousands . . . [of intellectuals and political dissidents] were sent after 1975 . . . word trickled out of Vietnam that conditions in the camps were brutal, that food was scarce and medical attention was virtually non-existent . . . . The director of an orphanage in this city's suburbs said a large percentage of her charges are children of men 'sent to the reeducation camps!'

The "Boat People"—the Tears of Asia

Patricia M. Derian, U.S. State Department, quoted by the *Los Angeles Times* News Service (*Tampa Times*, February 27, 1978): "More than 100,000 Indochinese refugees now live in small boats, temporary camps and makeshift shelters on the beaches of a dozen Southeast Asian countries," arriving some 1000 to 1500 each month. "A Cambodian told of seeing his family massacred."

Peter Arnett, A.P. Special Correspondent (*Tampa Tribune*, August 4, 1978) reported: "Eyewitness reports from surviving boat people suggest that up to 50 percent drown." W. Stanley Mooneyham, of World Vision International, was in charge of rescue efforts:

> Since the end of the Vietnam War in 1975 a total of 40,000 boat refugees have landed in Thailand, Malaysia, the Philippines, Indonesia and Australia, most of them in the past 12 months. There are 21,000 waiting in camps for resettlement, and the flow continues unabated.

Before U.S. efforts began, Western shipping had been encouraged to pass them by without stopping to give aid.

A *Tampa Tribune* account of July 23, 1979, and datelined by the Associated Press Manila, Philippines, tells of what must have been not an unusual occurrence in which 85 of 93 Vietnamese refugees (20 men, 20 women, 45 children) whose boat had been grounded on a small island were slaughtered by Communist Vietnamese troops using mortar and Russian AK-47 rifles. Survivors swam about three miles to another island. "Diplomatic sources confirmed there was such an attack."

Joan Baez, singer of anti-Vietnam War fame, was shaken (*Citizens for the Republic Newsletter*, July 3, 1979): "To the 'tortuee,' whether it's imperialistic torture or socialistic torture, it really doesn't make any difference."

Joan sent letters to 350 former anti-Vietnam war activists asking them to help sponsor newspaper ads to "the Socialist Republic of Vietnam." The ad said the number of political prisoners was between 150,000 and 200,000, and described such atrocities as forcing people to squat bound wrist to ankle, suffocating them in boxes, and using them as "human mine detectors."

Jane Fonda and her husband, Tom Hayden, declined to reply.

The headline caught my eye—"These Kids Paid Price." It was a *Chicago Tribune* report carried July 5, 1987 in the *Tampa Tribune*. It told of Vietnamese children who are undergoing great danger, experiencing excruciating hunger, thirst and suffering as they are sent out on the open seas in crowded fishing boats. Many of them perish. One boy squatted in one spot in the bottom of a boat—without food—for a solid week.

> The effort left his legs so curled up and paralyzed when he was lifted out of the boat that for days he could not walk . . . . Tri Tran, 16 says: 'I was 14 when my grandmother told me I was going to leave the next night on a boat with my little sister. My grandmother told me there was no future in my country for me. She told me when I got here to study . . . . and not to forget her.
>
> Do I know the price for freedom? I think so.'

These pages about the unfolding sadness, the blood, the brutality, the fear, the hunger, the hopelessness, and death that have been and are Vietnam, Cambodia, and their environs in Southeast Asia have not been pleasant to chronicle nor to contemplate. I must recognize that some—perhaps many of those who have protested and demonstrated for "peace" as opposed to the military and diplomatic campaigns and policies in the region—have been sincere. This is particularly true of the youth who—ignorant of the realities—have sought illusory dreams, tilting with the windmills of a world of wishful thinking. Some there are who have found unpleasant truth thrust upon them, and have reacted by symbolically clapping their hands over their ears—shouting loudly to try to drown out the intrusion. There are others who have been shocked into crash landings into the real world, and the transformations of life and outlook that can mean.

And then there are the cynical old pros who know well what they do; and they must never be misconstrued as friends of peace.

Historians and leaders are caught in a dilemma. If they insist upon defending President Roosevelt, and maintain that he is to be lauded for his courting of the Communists, they cannot disavow the results of those policies. I think it is not fitting simply to say, "Oops! Missed that one!" and walk away—

as though one had merely muffed catching a pop fly in a softball game at the Sunday School picnic.

On January 27, 1973, President Nixon attended a service at the Key Biscayne, Florida, Presbyterian Church—a service to give thanks for peace in Vietnam. The minister, the Rev. John Huffman, quoted a statement whose source he did not know. I find it is paraphrased from an original quote from Air Force Major Al Brunstrom who spent nearly seven years as a prisoner in North Vietnam, during which time he was regularly forced to undergo periods of excruciating torture:

> War is an ugly thing, but not the ugliest. The worst and most miserable thing is the man who thinks that nothing is worth fighting for, and who depends on better men to defend his freedom.

Chapter IX

Assessments and Determinations

I have kept to the path; I have resisted the temptations to diverge along labyrinthine lanes of allurement to this side or that; I have not wandered off in quest of wild flowers to the right or to the left;—I have kept to the path.

The thesis is this: Franklin D. Roosevelt promised the American people unequivocally in the 1940 election campaign that the United states was not going to enter the war in which the democracies of Europe and our Nationalist friends in China were opposing the totalitarian aggressions of the Axis powers—who at the time could claim as collaborators with Hitler in Eastern Europe the also totalitarian hordes of Stalin's Soviet Russia. Secretly, however, the President worked diligently—first in the Atlantic against German forces, and finally in the Pacific against the Japanese trying to instigate a naval "incident" that would ensnare us in the war. He utilized incendiary diplomacy with the government of Japan, and when our forces had broken the Japanese diplomatic codes, he followed for months every move made by the masters of the Land of the Rising Sun. As one of thirteen leaders in Washington, he received and read every intercepted message every day they were available. He knew in early October the details of the "bomb plot" communications—two months before the attack on Pearl Harbor; and he followed every move of the Japanese, egging them on by "diplomatic" thrusts to the brink of the attack. He sent the "purple" code machines to various places—the Philippines, and even to England—but denied them and their significant messages to Hawaii. He knew 22 hours before the bombs fell when they would fall, and he did not see that adequate warnings were given to the commanders in Hawaii.

Once in the war, Roosevelt worked behind the backs of France, England, the Poles, all the leaders of Eastern Europe, and the Chinese Nationalists—utilizing much of our massive lend-lease aid and vast diplomatic and territorial concessions to see that the Communist forces of Russia and China replaced our erstwhile democratic friends in their former spheres of influence in Eastern and East-Central Europe, in Africa, in Southern and Southeast Asia, and in China.

And, alas, the tragic, deathly, unspeakable, inevitable results of those preposterous policies were certified in the ugliness of a wall in Berlin and in thousands upon thousands of tortured corpses in Vietnam, and Laos, and Cambodia—and in scores of thousands of fleeing refugees tossing in tiny boats on the unfriendly waters of the South China Sea.

At the semester break in early February of 1986 I attended, along with hundreds of other secondary history and social studies teachers in my county, what was purported to be a series of seminars designed to improve us in our teaching. One of the presentations was about Haiti. There was a film with a voice intoning the easily recognized standard Marxist line that was so familiar from Columbus Circle and the columns of the Daily_Worker, as well as other literary offerings of that genre. Evil, capitalistic Uncle Sam with its oppressive tactics had destroyed the prosperous idyllic life once enjoyed by the inhabitants of Haiti and had reduced the population to virtual slavery. Gone was the freedom and happy family life of yore, replaced by the harsh regimen and dominion of the Great Satan.

Dr. Doyle Casteel, of the University of Florida Staff, came in to conduct a discussion. It was quite evident that a large number of our teachers were willing to accept the film and its diatribes at face value and without question. As usual, it came up in discussion how much our nation was wasting on arms and defense when the Soviets were so willing to compromise and were supposedly in the forefront of the workers for peace in the world, in accord with the great heritage left by President Roosevelt.

I begged to demur, and took note of the vast surrenders made by Roosevelt to Stalin in the "Great Conferences." These, I said, were not foundations for peace, nor had their subsequent results proved to be steps in that direction. I commented that I was in the process of writing a book about the subject.

I will never forget Dr. Casteel's smug look and smug observation: "I will be interested to see how your book is accepted by the academic community."

Ah, the "academic community!" The closed corporation that freezes out all that it does not wish to hear—or which goes counter to what they wish to believe—or to what their professors before them have dictated to be seemly, qualified, and appropriate to be accepted. This is the reason that not a single college or high school textbook has ever mentioned the breaking of the Japanese code, nor has any included the texts of the intercepted "bomb plot" messages and any of the accompanying messages. And perish the thought that it should be remarked that Roosevelt knew about these! Roosevelt still leads a charmed life in the fairy tales—and myths—perpetuated by the "academic community."

It is always—Don't study it. Don't even read about—much less, write about it. But accept the word of those who say it isn't so.

Unfortunately, this world is real. It is best not to ignore a flashing red light at a railroad crossing when a speeding train is bearing down. Smoking in bed when one has just taken a sleeping pill is not wise—or at any other time, either. To insist on making friends with a nervous skunk is to court disaster. And it is injudicious <u>ever</u> to play the game of Russian roulette. We cannot plan prudently if we ignore all the likely untoward consequences of the foregoing situations, and as individuals and as a nation we dare not blissfully assume that everything is all fine and dandy just because we have chosen to disregard facts. Much of our experience is pleasant and happy, and I would not counsel paranoia. However, I remember the story told about a supposed foe of the great Joe Louis in his heyday as world heavyweight boxing champion. After the first round the opponent stumbled back to his corner, his left eye swollen shut, bleeding profusely from his nose. His handler patted him on the back after some doctoring and said, "Great going! He hasn't touched you yet!" After the second round he had difficulty finding his corner. His mouthpiece was gone along with two teeth. His handler shouted, "Great going! He hasn't touched you yet!" In the third round he was knocked down for an eight count and staggered back to his corner, bleeding from a gash over his right eye which was also almost shut, and he was bleeding from the mouth. His handler cried, "Great going! He hasn't touched you yet!" The hapless fighter responded, "Well, would you please keep an eye on that referee, 'cause somebody out there is beatin' the hell outa me!"

Since we have found out about President Roosevelt's egregious errors in the handling of Pearl Harbor and in the mishandling of policy due to his "Great Design," it ill behooves us to cajole ourselves and our leaders into believing that his programs were wise and unerring. That could be compared to driving in the wrong direction on a one-way street, stubbornly maintaining our infallibility as we draw nearer to a ten ton truck.

What are the specific down-to-earth realities we have faced, and continue to face, since 1945? First and foremost, the results of World War II must be measured qualitatively on a scale that comprehends on the one side of the balances the enormous expenditure of thirty-five million human lives—all lost as consequences of the waging of the war. Our side was victorious, and far more than any other leader, our President, Franklin Delano Roosevelt, was the architect of that victory. What blessings have accrued to the world as a counter to those awful costs?

Well, in 1939, at the time of the Stalin-Hitler Nonaggression Pact which served as a springboard for the launching of the war, there was only one Communist nation in the world. That was Russia, whose official census for that year gave its population as 169,519,127. Of course, the Communists were only a small minority of the whole, but their control was exemplified by the fact that they had already been responsible for a greater number of deaths of their fellow countrymen than the number who were currently members of the Communist Party. The largest Communist force outside Russia was the Red Chinese, and we have earlier taken note of how weak it was after the German invasion of Russia—though it still was connected to Moscow by the umbilical cord.

In 1986 the Russian population had grown by almost one hundred millions, not including the nearly seven and a half millions in the three little Baltic states which she had invaded and appropriated to herself: Estonia, Latvia, and Lithuania. In addition to Mongolia, on its Southern border in Asia, which considers itself in alignment with Russia (population 1,860,000), and Afghanistan (fourteen and a half million), savagely ravaged by invasion for nine years, the Soviets have added to their empire eight countries in eastern and central Europe: Poland, Hungary, Romania, East Germany, Bulgaria, Albania, Czechoslovakia, and Yugoslavia with a total population approaching one hundred forty millions.These were conquered outright or were occupied until Russia had established the rule of its own fifth column Communist Party. History records that when those Parties have been unable to maintain their strangleholds, Russia has sent its conquering armies back in to crush any resistance and occupy—remember Czechoslovakia, Hungary, and Poland as cases in point. For example, Wallbank, Taylor, and Carson, in their *Civilization - Past and Present* (Vol.2,p.577), have this to say in description of one of those:

> The [Hungarian] riots of October 23, 1956, quickly grew into a nation-wide revolt . . . . On November 4, however, reinforced Soviet forces returned to the capital, where they stamped out the flames of national independence . . . . Thousands of freedom fighters died in the struggle, while within a year upward of 200,000 refugees sought sanctuary in the West . . . a new satellite regime was propped up by Soviet bayonets.

Soviet sponsored governments, of course, exist at our doorstep in Cuba (14 million) and Nicaragua (nearly 3 million). Angola, in Africa (7,700,000). with its Russian oriented Marxist government, is propped up by Cuban troops. This makes a grand total in Russia and its dominions of nearly four hundred and fifty millions.

Communist China has well over a billion people. The other Asian Communist nations are Vietnam (nearly 60 million), North Korea (nearly 20 million), Cambodia (6,300,000), and Laos (three and three quarters millions). Other Marxist-Leninist countries in Africa are Ethiopia (34 million), Mozambique (13,413,000), Benin (3,910,000), and the Congo (one and three quarters million).

From a beginning of one Communist nation controlling fewer than 170 million people, the consequences of the policies pursued during the war have brought us to a total of one billion, six hundred twenty-five million human beings who are the subjects of Communist rule.

Along the way, in November of 1960, delegations from 81 Communist Parties around the world met in Moscow and unanimously accepted as their Statement of Purpose the aim to dominate the world—and all to be anti-United States of America. No one, of course, would ever have guessed if they could just have kept it secret!—So, our blessings overflow!

William B. Shannon wrote an article which was carried in the *Tampa Tribune* October 19, 1986: "Where Is the Outrage About Afghanistan?" In it he forcefully makes the point that—though our news media and molders of opinion have been quite effective in venting their spleen against American policies wherever we attempt to stand against the known enemies of freedom (Grenada, Libya, Cuba, Nicaragua, e.g.), they have seemed to lose their capacity for wrath and indignation when tiny Afghanistan is brutally, through no fault of its own, assailed and invaded by massive, imperialist Russia, nearly twenty times her size.

It would appear that the Soviets are currently in the process of making a staged withdrawal from Afghanistan which has taken on costly quicksand characteristics—and the victims haven't been "peacefully" hospitable at all.

The *Tampa Tribune* (November 15, 1987) also carried an article by Robert Marquand, of the *Christian Science Monitor*: "Movies and College Study Keep Vietnam Issues Alive." One of those studies at Yale, taught by a professor who was a product of the 1960's, was a source of amazement to an observer. The Vietnam War, maintained the professor, was "a conspiracy between the CIA and Wall Street." When I read that absurdity I was transported in memory back across the decades to my fourth grade class, taught by Mrs. Byrd. She told us one day of a one-room school in which her mischief-loving future husband was a student. It was Autumn, and he requested permission to journey out to the outhouse behind the school. On his return he noticed two facts of life: (1) there were walnuts littering the ground, and (2) the insufferable "teacher's pet" was sitting near the window. Never one to pass up such a temptacious opportunity, he helped to clean up the litter in the yard by depositing a walnut through the window, hoping, I presume, that it would carom off the head of the teacher's pet into the waste basket. It did hit the primary target. When the culprit finally made his way back into the classroom, the "teacher's pet" was sobbing in his seat, and a very perturbed teacher was trying to solve the puzzle of who had thrown the walnut. Up and down each row she went:

Did you throw the walnut? Do you know who did?

No one would own up to it. Exasperated, the teacher said,

Well that settles it! You're all guilty for protecting the one who did it! I'm going to have to give everybody a whipping so that I'll get the guilty one, and you'll all learn not to protect them. However, Johnny was outside when it happened, so he couldn't know anything about it. It wouldn't be right to punish him.

And she proceeded to punish everyone—except the guilty party.

The young Yale professor had similar simplistic solutions to the causes of war.

To return to that adamantine, relentless march of the legions of Communism in conquest across the world—with their massively superior conventional forces, it gives one pause to contemplate what would have been the lot of western Europe and England and the oil-rich Middle East and, indeed, what of the Americas—if the atomic bomb and the H-bomb had not cast their shadows long across the Earth since August of 1945.

But the old dependables, the "peace mongers," as Christ said of the poor, we have always with us. Long since, with a naive trustfulness, they would have had us unilaterally give up our nuclear shield, relying on a childlike faith that those who slew the Polish officers in the Katyn Forest and presently give to Afghanistian children poison-gas booby-trapped bomb toys with which to play—that they can be depended on to discard their own nuclear weapons.

Of course, we have noted this group in past periods—the Russo-German Nonaggression Pact Era, the latter days of World War II and years following while China was being betrayed, the Vietnam War era, and down to the present time. We have observed the cynical hard-nosed professionals who are always there persisting to lead—those who can never find good in the United States—and redundantly echo those sentiments, and who so easily find purity and beauty in every Soviet act—and are repetitive in those empty echoes. And then the Gullibles who stumble over themselves endeavoring to outdo the leaders in their loud delusions—they possess the same happy oblivion as that of the self-assured man with a terminal case of B.O. Theirs is always the easy way—

simple "peace;" nothing is ever required of us—no plan, no sacrifice—just give in, and give up. We don't have to defend a thing.

We are always allowing ourselves to be lured aside into the contemplation of diversions which are irrelevant to the central and basic realities which must be faced. We are suffused with a righteous glow at envisaging conferences—"Summit Conferences!" But with such meetings we always face the short circuit of the Communists themselves and of our own apologists for communism. We are constrained each time to start all over as if we were saddled with the onus of proving ourselves to the Soviets and to the world—forget the diabolical record of the Communists—forget our own quite positive record in peace and in war. Just, shamefacedly, start all over.

William C. Bullitt (Op. Cit., p.169) incisively states the case:

> World Peace cannot be established by the writing of agreements. However cleverly they may be drawn by technical experts, they will be broken by evil men . . . . There is no short cut to peace by way of collecting promises that will not be kept. The problem of peace is nothing less than the problem of creating a world-wide custom of all nations treating one another as members of a single peace group.

And until that comes to fruition, it is incumbent upon us—inhabiting a world where flames have been a way of life-and death—not to cancel our fire insurance.

We hear incessantly the phrase—as from "on high": the "lesson of Vietnam"—but we have garnered the wrong lesson from Vietnam. If such a historic incumbency should ever befall us again, our nation must win it—and not fight it with our right arm tied behind us. Those Vietnam era examples, from a clamorous minority, of abdication of responsibility and duty, of patriotism, and of devotion to liberty—the "better Red than dead" suicide of the spirit—are as nothing when cast into the balances against the mighty, overwhelming surge of the fundamental decency, integrity, passion for justice, consuming fire for freedom, and depth of soul which are the heritage from the past and the potential for the future of this great land of ours—this United States of America.

New leadership in the U.S.S.R. demonstrates possible potential for rational thought, some reforms in the erstwhile stubborn domestic unreality, and even intimations of plausibility in the SALT talks. We need to be wary in optimism. Internal conditions have evidently forced some of these reforms, and our own dealing from strength has fostered a climate of reason about our mutual aims. We must not forsake that strength as we proceed with eyes open and senses alert.

A Look at Liberty

Do we really believe the injunction of Jefferson in his eloquent Declaration of Independence?

> We hold these truths to be self-evident: That all men are created equal; that they are endowed by their Creator with certain unalienable rights; that among these are life, liberty, and the pursuit of happiness.

If this is indeed our belief, it exudes a fundamental essence that permeates the entirety of our concept of humanity and of mankind's relationship to government. We are left, in some measure, with a sense of awe a—consciousness not to be explained, but observed by experience.

I perceive here a dramatic parallel from the world of music. For the uninitiated, our *do-re-mi-fa-sol-la-ti-do* scale (and its relative minor scales) is known as the diatonic scale. It is a product of many centuries of development through a number of cultures of the Western world. It has been thought that the concept of *do*—and the octave from *do* to *do* may have been a discovery of Guido, a brilliant Benedictine monk and musical theorist of the first half of the Eleventh Century. Those amazing people, the ancient Greeks, are known to have made significant advances in the use of modal forms, or chords. Recent research, however, has led some music historians to credit the Greeks with the discovery of *do*, though this is as yet theory. Suffice it to say, our diatonic scale, as it has been used for some centuries, consists, when sharps and flats are utilized, of a succession of twelve half steps or semi-tones. We do not further divide it into quarter-tones.

Let me say here parenthetically from my long experience as a professional singer, choral director, and vocal instructor, I am convinced that anyone who can speak and who is not physically deaf may be taught to sing—with patience.

Now, many millions of people throughout much of the world—parts of the Orient, the islands, of Africa, etc. have never been introduced to our diatonic scale. In New Guinea our chaplain's assistant, Vincent Bickel, was blessed with that rare quality, absolute pitch. We often heard the natives "singing"—uncomfortable, moaning incantations that sounded reminiscent of the consumption of too many green apples. Bickel, who often accompanied me when I sang (and was somewhat impatient with me because I couldn't immediately recognize any A flat that passed by and call it by name), observed the musical efforts of the natives and noted that they utilized a three-tone scale. On Biak Island in the Netherlands East Indies, we "liberated" some Japanese records done in the traditional quarter-tone mode (or one of many such modes). Their sounds violated all that we would tend to call pleasant or beautiful. I have often wished

I might have kept one of those as an example, but my fellow GI's made quick work of them by sailing them off into the jungle.

Dr. James L. Mursell, who was my professor at Teachers' College, Columbia University, in a most interesting course in musical psychology, noted a strange case of uniformity. In the Western World, in the islands, in the Orient, Hottentots in Africa—whatever the scale they are accustomed to, whenever children wish to taunt each other they always use that same little tune—"Johnny's got a sweetheart! Johnny's got a sweetheart!"—which is really made out of our diatonic scale—*sol sol mi la sol mi*.

Let me push my exigesis a bit farther, if the musical neophytes will allow me. It is in the resolution of a dominant seventh chord that we get to the most dramatic impact of our diatonic scale, and it can be demonstrated strikingly to all—veterans and neophytes alike. It is something that we are continually hearing and experiencing, though we are not having it explained to us mentally. A simple chord consists of the simultaneous sounding of three or four (or more) tones which—though from different steps of the scale—have an effect (we know not why) that is pleasing to the ear. A most common one is *do*, *mi*, and *sol*—often referred to as the "tonic chord" because it is built on the "tonic," or *do*. Other combinations—*do*, *re*, and *mi* sounded together, for instance—have a clashing, unpleasant effect.

It is quite obvious that this interpretation would be vastly simplified if it were possible to use sounds instead of words. The problem might be compared to an attempt to use words alone to describe the taste of a succulent prime rib beefsteak to a man whose diet has been restricted to spinach.

The syllable *sol* we refer to as the "dominant," and a chord built on *sol*—*sol*, *ti*, and *re*—we call a dominant chord. However, if a seventh, or *fa*, is added to that dominant chord, it has a vivid effect on the ear—an urgency to move on to a specific following chord, the tonic. (I will not muddy the waters by dragging in a "deceptive cadence" which is irrelevant to our discussion.)

I experienced this as a member of a class in music theory at Columbia, but I have done it with my own classes in high school history where skepticism as well as unfamiliarity with the subject matter characterized most participants. To simplify, let us use the key of C for the exercise and begin with the dominant seventh chord which will be built on G—which is *sol* in the key of C. My class is seated in six rows across the room with each row starting at the front where my desk is located and stretching to the rear. After some preliminary explanation I instruct the two rows to my left to sing B (natural)—or *ti*, the two rows in the center will sing D—or *re*, and the two rows on my right will sing F—or *fa*.

All will sing on "ah." Now, I say, "I am going to sing "ah" here, and I sing the "ah" on G. I say, "I'm going to show you again where each group is to sing its note, and I will sing my note at the same time. Then I am going to keep singing but move to a different note. When I change my note I want everybody to let your 'ah' go to where you feel it should change to." (Much muttered suspicion and dubiousness.) I proceed to review their notes with them, then we all sing "ah" on our pitches. Presently I change my note from G to C.

Incredulity sweeps over the faces, but everyone who is singing B (*ti*) goes up a half step to C (*do*). Everyone who is singing D (*re*) descends a full step to C, and everyone who is singing F (*fa*) comes down a half step to E (*mi*). We have now the tonic chord—C (*do*)and E (*mi*), omitting the G (*sol*) which is not demanded to satisfy the ear here. (Composers, to achieve a full chord at the ends of verses or of compositions will have one part—other than the bass hold on to the *sol* of the key, or will lead a part from *fa* to end on *sol* and make a full chord. This is not necessary, however, for the resolution to have its powerful effect.) There is a great deal of the spiritual which is made manifest in this example and other like examples from the psychology of music; we cannot explain why it is correct—we just observe, or experience it and know that it is.

There seems, then, to be something fundamentally right about our Western diatonic musical scale that does not pertain to other musical systems. Indeed, many who have been "cultured" in those other systems who are introduced to ours find their "home" in ours—find that it satisfies their psychological demands. They had not felt before a dissatisfaction, but now their musical experience in their previous culture is no longer fulfilling. They come in time to accept ours and to reject theirs. Presently the old falls as unpleasantly on their ears as it does on ours. There seem to be no cases where those "cultured" in our Western scale have rejected it and come to find quarter tone scales or others "right" for them. It is a one-way street.

Let me interject an observation here. Possibly the most appealing and irresistible force in our musical system is the presence of meter and logical plan. It lends an aura of progression from a start to a finish, or from a variety of starts to a diversity of endings—a feeling of progression, or progress within a composition following well-ordered rules and melodies and harmonies. This lends feelings of psychological satisfactions which are peculiarly pleasant and exalting. However, some of our "contemporary" musicians and composers have persuaded themselves that to be "progressive" demands a flouting of all the rules and traditions that have characterized the superiority of Western music, just as in art and sculpture we find most hideous drawings and paintings and piles of rusting scrap masquerading as the successors to Michelangelo and da

Vinci. Some acclaim this music and this art as masterworks. As for the music, it possesses a distinctive quality—studied boredom. It lacks that satisfaction of plan. It could more aptly be labeled "satisfiction."

I have been amused, as well as nettled by the program planners for some symphonies recently who have found themselves with a growing problem. They have been playing the works of the traditional masters on the first half of the program before the intermission, and then in the second half infusing a diet of the "contemporary" persuasion. But audiences have been "voting with their feet" and tending not to return after intermission, leaving the orchestras to perform for a vastly depleted cadre of listeners. The planners have decided to postpone some of the works of the great masters, placing them at the end or interspersing them throughout the listings—thus trapping the concert-goers who "don't know enough to appreciate" the new offerings. I could not help seeing a parallel to the Mother saying to little Johnny, "Eat your spinach—it'll be good for you! You can't have any desert until you eat every last bit of your spinach!"

I really don't think that anybody truly likes the extreme "contemporary," but some feel that they're supposed to like it. They fabricate an ersatz love for it with great ostentation. I am reminded of the fable of the Emperor's New Clothes, and the lovers of the extreme "contemporary" in music are no more convincing than the misguided Emperor "in the raw."

I would be derelict in my duty were I to omit reference to another degradation of music in the here-and-now Western world. Not every attempt at composition in our culture has been reminiscent of Mozart or Handel or Verdi, but by and large the movement—and the appreciation—across the centuries has been upward and toward enhancement of beauty, variety, and depth. There have been greater and more exacting demands on voices and instruments. I pointed my vocal students often toward the mastery of operatic arias because, I explained, operatic composers more than any others—almost without exception—had set out to exploit just how much the human voice could do.

One of the myriad examples of beauty is "Meditation" from Massenet's "Thais." Powerful musical rhythm under control is represented by the waltzes of Strauss, the marches of Sousa, and the "Toreador Song" from Bizet's "Carmen." No better examples of harmony exist than the male quartets of the S.P.B.Q.S.A. or their feminine counterparts, the "Sweet Adelines"—or the rich chordings of the great Negro spirituals. Deep pathos has been brought to us by Puccini in "Madame Butterfly;" and humor (as well as underlying meaning) permeates the operettas of Gilbert and Sullivan. Songs of love and devotion have been the expressions of composers of classical and popular writers through the decades and through the centuries. Stirring songs of pride and patriotism have thrilled us from age to age: "America the Beautiful," "Battle Hymn of the Republic," and "The Star Spangled Banner" (when it is not being slaughtered by some "great popular star" who has his or her own ideas about crooning it and desecrating it). Richard Llewellan has given us in *How Green Was My Valley* a matchless description in poetic prose of the singing by the people in that Victorian Welsh mining valley of "God Save the Queen." We have a rich heritage of music—spiritual, uplifting, joyous, songs of praise and worship: Lewandowski's "Psalm 150," "Silent Night," "Go Tell It On The Mountain," "Judas Maccabaeus," "Gloria in Excelsis Deo," "All Hail the Power of Jesus' Name," "Dona Nobis Pacem," Handel's "Messiah" with its "Hallelujah Chorus,"—and all those others from different sectors of the Judeo-Christian Tradition that you have thought of and looked for here on this list that I need far more space to include.

But, alas, the current musical sickness called rock and roll is a deterioration—a retrogression—that turns back on all the great progress and uplift through which we have climbed, to work instead a subversion of the values we have held dear—melody, harmony, variety, and the historical experience of developmental expression of all the vast range of human insight and elevated feeling. Now, let it be noted that there are exceptions even in the realm to which we refer that retain some of the qualities which have been considered positive, but they remain just that—exceptions. Indeed, in general most of our achievements are undone by the tyranny of rhythm and beat that prostitutes all else—a monotonous, erotic throbbing that conquers melody and meaning and harmony and words. No one is ever so bold as to appropriate the adjective "beautiful" to describe this. Some time ago I was mesmerized by a number carried on someone else's radio. It consisted of a man's voice shouting "I like music!" (pause) "I like music!"(pause) "I like music!"(pause) "I like music!" (pause)—over and over again. I harked back to the injunction, "Do not use vain repetitions as the heathen do." So often it is like that, mindful of a tribal war dance of clashing cacophony. And it is loud to begin with—to the highest decibel, then radios are turned up to their maximum volume besides. I think we have all had inflicted on us the instances of those altruistic souls who drive around with all windows rolled down and radios "rolled up," the automobiles fairly leaping into the air, the full blast rapaciously invading and overwhelming all other sound. The appeal is not uplifting, but convulsively sensual; and the performers writhe salaciously, endeavoring to shake off any semblance of virginity that may still cling to them. Love songs have in great measure given way to songs that either talk about or insinuate intercourse. There is a vast divide between "Believe Me If All Those Endearing Young Charms" and "Do It To Me One More Time!"

I have felt it imperative while outlining an exposition of the compulsions of our Western musical psychology to deal with these aberrations which are throwbacks or contrived departures from the attainments which we have been noting.

Now back to the observable premise that our Western diatonic musical scale—(though other scales are used by many millions)—seems to possess an inherent true and natural "rightness" that all who know it or who come to know it recognize. Once party to that experience, one is never satisfied with any other types of musical expression, but is strongly desirous to return to what one's deepest soul and keenest ear cries out is the "real thing."

All right, now—the parallel to freedom. We reiterate with Jefferson those awesome phrases from the Declaration of Independence about liberty and the source of our liberty—our Creator. But, just as a large portion of the world's people have never experienced our Western diatonic scale, and do not miss it unless and until they are introduced to it, so also freedom (or liberty) would appear to be the natural—the basic—the "right" estate of mankind upon the Earth, even though most of the people in the world today and in all of history have never tasted what it is like to enjoy freedom—to be participants in a condition of liberty. A relative few have thought it through and come to a comprehension of the blessings of liberty on their own, whether or not they ever personally came to know those blessings themselves. This might well be called experiencing through insight.

However, for the vast majority of those who have not been personally immersed in the advantages of liberty, who know it not through firsthand acquaintanceship and comprehension, its blessings are unmissed. History catalogues the records of peoples who have undergone slavery or oppressive monarchical rule or tyranny, who overwhelmingly outnumbered those who had lordship over them; but they have submitted and conformed with meek, passive, obedience and docility. The long record of Russia under the czars (who were, indeed, a varied lot) demonstrates how a people accustomed to rigid regimented rule were ready prey for the stern strictures of the totalitarian absolutism of the Communist State. And the story of Germany under the Kaisers demonstrates how control was actually molded into intense loyalty and pride in an impersonal government machinery which, through the humiliation of defeat in the First World War, formed the dais for the Nazi Party and a little man with a little mustache and a big voice and an evil mind.

We could recount the myriad tales of almost unquestioning acceptance—often, to a degree, contentment—among peoples who have never enjoyed the feast of freedom or the light of liberty—and who have failed to feel its want.

(We make note in passing of the rare exception when some churl is ready to surrender freedom in exchange for wealth or for power over others. Or this—freedom involves decisions, and the uncommon one there may be who would sacrifice the uncomfortable responsibility of making choices, and forego there-with the alternative of freedom.)

When, however, people anywhere who are not "tone deaf" to liberty have ever tasted freedom—have come to know liberty as their personal estate—have experienced it for themselves –, then they undergo miraculous transformation. They have found the natural, the "right" estate of mankind; and they will <u>never</u> be content with any other condition!

I must say something here by way of the definition of a well-known word. Several years ago I was working in my room at school during the hour that was laughingly referred to as my "free" period. I overheard a young teacher across the hall explaining to her class: "Courage," she said, "is not being afraid in the face of danger." I did not interrupt her class and embarrass her, but a day or so afterwards I had an opportunity to tell her about it privately and to disagree. I said this: "Courage is being scared to death and going ahead anyway and doing what has to be done!" That definition needs to be borne in mind when we survey the things I am getting ready to recount.

For those who come to know freedom and claim it as their birthright possess a qualitative difference now. If anyone deprives them of liberty, or if liberty stands imperiled they will

> . . . work and toil or suffer pain, and starvation, and torture (as our prisoners of war have done)
>
> . . . dare death, though unarmed, facing tanks and machine guns, as in the 1956 Hungarian uprising, when possibly as many as 30,000 met their deaths before a Russian army of 200,000 troops
>
> . . . flee into and through West Berlin, as did 200,000 in the last year before the building of the steel and concrete Berlin Wall
>
> . . . or crawl through barbed wire and broken glass, floodlights, machine guns, and vicious dogs—or crash speeding automobiles through guarded gates as have thousands who have struggled to freedom—or died in the attempt—since the infamous wall was built
>
> . . . fly their families in frail balloons lofted by night many miles across territory held by Communist bastions below
>
> . . . by the scores of thousands, individuals and families, forsaking all their worldly goods, commit themselves to tiny boats tossing on pirate-threatened unending sunny "deserts" of salt seas

. . . boldly, as did Martin Luther in 1517, affix his *95 Theses* to the church door at Wittenberg; and presently stand alone before the Assembly of the Diet of Worms and declare: "I cannot and I will not recant."

. . . launch out in the frail Mayflower, as did the 102 stouthearted separatist Pilgrims (31 of whom were children), sailing thousands of miles across the uncharted Atlantic to seek freedom of worship on a strange wilderness continent inhabited by a sometimes savage people [The amiable and tolerant Pilgrims are not to be confused—as often happens—with the strait-laced, intolerant, witch-hunting Puritans who later came to Massachusetts Bay.]

. . . sign the eloquent and unequivocal Declaration of Independence, as did more than fifty men who had the most to lose—sign beneath that culminating phrase: "And for the support of this declaration, with a firm reliance on the protection of Divine Providence, we mutually pledge to each other our lives, our fortunes, and our sacred honor."

. . . go with Washington and his 2400 troops that dark, bitter-cold, Christmas night in 1776 as he crossed the Delaware River to take Trenton from the hired Hessians—through the huge boulders of ice carried downstream by the on-rushing current

. . . or trudge hungry and unshod through freezing iciness of Valley Forge, leaving bloody footprints in the snow

. . . bravely, night after night, be Harriet Tubman, with a $40,000 price on her head, leading, in all, more than 300 slaves to freedom through the "Underground Railroad"

. . . being born into slavery, then soon orphaned, work your way through high school and college, become a college professor and in time director of the Department of Agricultural Research at Tuskegee Institute. The former slaves were now in large measure share-croppers raising peanuts and sweet potatoes. To increase the values of their product, Dr. George Washington Carver developed nearly 300 different substances from the peanut—including peanut butter—and from the sweet potato nearly 120

. . . strike, as the American doughboys in 1918 France, when all else had failed, stopping the massive "victory" drive of the Germans in their tracks. Nevins and Commager provide a spine-tingling description in their *A Short History of the United States*

They came just in the nick of time. First at Mondidier and Cantigny and then at Belleau Wood, they proved their mettle, and the German Command, which had discounted American help, reluctantly admitted that "the American soldier proves himself brave, strong, and skillful. Casualties do not daunt him." But the great crisis was still ahead. On July 15th the Germans launched their longawaited offensive on each side of Rheims, designed to crack the last Allied line and open the path to Paris, only fifty miles away. At first successful in the West, they poured across the Marne where they ran into fresh American

> troops. "Right here on the Marne," wrote the German Chief of Staff, Walther Reinhardt, "we well-nigh reached the objectives prescribed for our shock divisions. . . . Especially all divisions of the Seventh Army . . . achieved brilliant initial successes, with the exception of the one division on our right wing. This encountered American units. Here only did the Seventh Army . . . confront serious difficulties. It met with the unexpectedly stubborn and active resistance of fresh American troops. While the rest of the divisions . . . succeeded in gaining ground and tremendous booty, it proved impossible for us to move the right apex of our line, to the south of the Marne, into a position advantageous for the development of the ensuing fight. The check we thus received was one result of the stupendous fighting between our 10th Division of Infantry and American troops." And he added ruefully, "The Americans appear inexhaustible."

We see, thus, a compelling parallel between natural "rightness" in our music and the natural estate of man in the liberty bestowed upon us by a beneficent Creator.

I saw recently a brief presentation on television. It showed a young woman in Independence Hall in Philadelphia standing in what she told us was "one of the most important rooms in America." It was here, she said, that the founding fathers signed the Declaration of Independence "which guaranteed for us our freedom and independence." We have noted the great and eloquent observations of the language of the Declaration. Majestic—yes, but they did not "guarantee" for us our freedom and independence. A war had to be fought and won—a war that had already been in progress for over a year and would yet continue for five years more. The crossing of the Delaware and Battle of Saratoga and Valley Forge lay ahead, as well as King's Mountain and many other battles—and patriot deaths. And those resolute fifty-six signers had only begun their sacrifices. Britain ordered its armed forces to hunt down the "traitors" and their families.

Nine of them fought and died from wounds and the rigors of war. Five were captured and cruelly tortured by the British. Two lost sons in the fighting, and one had two sons captured in battle and gravely mistreated. Wives, sons, and daughters of many were jailed, mistreated, and impoverished. The mother of one was imprisoned. One was driven away from the deathbed of his wife, pursued relentlessly by the royal forces, and never again saw his children. Twelve had their homes burned by the British, and one suffered the complete destruction of his rice plantation.

An uncomfortable question rears its head. I have tried to present a background for the premise that liberty is the natural estate of mankind—not totalitarianism and restrictions of freedom. Our founding fathers believed deeply in liberty; and we are the heirs of their beliefs, their eloquence, their courage, their struggles against seemingly insurmountable odds, and their sacrifices oft to that "last full measure of devotion." And "four score and seven years" after the signing of the Declaration of Independence our nation was engaged in a bloody campaign, a partial aim of which was to make the blessings of liberty universal in our land.

Is it, then, our appointed mission as twentieth century Americans to clasp this luxury of liberty to our selfish breasts and to deny it to or destroy it for others? The errors that were made at the great wartime conferences we were not privy to, but history records that for a generation, whenever our basic policy has been called into account, it has been infinitely difficult to determine what is its real orientation. In a democracy such as ours it has been possible traditionally in a time of war to focus a unitary national foreign policy to achieve positive ends. (It is of course true that the Soviet-serving goals of Roosevelt's "Great Design" were kept from the public—yea, even from most of our leaders—until the war was over; it would indeed have been difficult to foster enthusiasm and sacrifice for such aims, as evidenced by the President himself in his concern about Polish voters in the 1944 Election.) We must weigh the procedures whereby we arrive at our choices—thoughtfully.

It has seemed that democracy in peacetime loses the options of a unitary foreign policy directed toward the preservation of national values, and substitutes in their place a lowest common denominator of decision which magnifies exaggerated fears of conflict toward a paralysis of action. Must "all agree" before we put plans into operation? Or is it true that democracy is incapable of leadership for peace; is it the case that democracy can plan for war in wartime, but is unfitted to plan for peace in peacetimes? (I must enunciate with clarity that the latter does not mean unilateral disarmament.)

It is imperative at this point that we note that the terms "freedom" and "democracy" are not interchangeable. I often read authoritarian pronouncements in "Letters to the Editor" that "We do not live in a democracy; we live in a republic." This is analogous to stating, "I don't live in Illinois; I live in Chicago." For "democracy" refers to the source of power—the people, while "republic" describes the structure of government—a representative democracy. "Pure democracy" is exercised in a number of organizations such as the New England Town Meeting, a church's board of stewards, or a labor union local. These operate on a small enough scale to allow all members to meet together and have their say and to vote. It would be unwieldy to have a meeting of more than two hundred million citizens to make decisions. Where would we meet? And the proceedings of some of those examples of "pure democracy" are in too many instances seemingly interminable! So we adapt our democracy to fit the practical invention of the ancient Romans—the structure of the republic. We choose officials at local, state, and national levels to carry on the day-to-day business of government. The check by the popular source of power is always the next election.

But, again, "freedom" is not the same as "democracy"—or "one man-one vote." True it is that democracy has tended to be more protective of freedom and liberty than any other system—but not necessarily. When I moved with my family to a large Southern city just before 1950 no blacks could eat in restaurants downtown, and blacks rode in the rear of the bus—which meant that most stood, even when there were vacant seats in the front. The electorate in the city were about 85% white, and those rules had been made by big majorities, and by "one man-one vote" decisions. But it is not the source of power that protects liberty—it is the limitation of power. That understanding is imperative to a comprehension of our aims.

Now, do we really feel that the power of the example of liberty and democracy is inferior to the death of the soul under totalitarian Communism? Is "better Red than dead" the "Gospel truth?"

We are the victims—most of us—of a system gone awry. Many of our legislative leaders are quite willing for our processes to be sabotaged; others are caught up in the messiness or the inefficiencies and stand by in helplessness while the law-making mountain labors, time after time, to bring forth a mouse. Conscientious and far-seeing leaders are frustrated as plans fall prey to unproductive practices.

There comes to mind an unpleasant memory from my experiences when for a time I was a teacher of American history in a junior high school. Faculty meetings sometimes were held at the end of a long day, and we were tired to begin with—desirous of getting away from there and out to fight the traffic that lay between us and home. It was an unwinnable school policy that chewing gum was verboten in class—not the least reason being the vandalism that resulted from gooey Juicy Fruit on desks, maps, in textbooks, in seats, on walls, and in Mary's hair. We fought a ceaseless and thankless battle, dealing with it as best we could—some of us more assiduously than others. It is an undisputed biological fact that every junior high school student was born with a wad of chewing gum half the size of a golf ball in his mouth. All of our teacher discussions would not alter one whit the biblical pronouncement: "Ye have the chewing gum always with you." So many times when the faculty meeting, after a tiresome hour, seemed to be drawing to a merciful close, some benighted soul would raise a hand and say: "What are we going to do about all this chewing gum?"—and we were in for another half hour.

Opponents of defense policies are skillful at raising points as irrelevant to the real question as the chewing gum issue: "Another Vietnam!," "million dollar commode handles," "the Bomb is going to get us!," "military-industrial complex," "one jet bomber uses more fuel than all the automobiles in New York State," "We could feed all the starving in Ethiopia, India, China, and downtown Burbank," "Another Vietnam!," "We could better spend the money to buy tricycles for poor children in America," "If we would spend only half that amount to fight poverty in Mexico." "Another Vietnam!," "But the Sandinistas are so reasonable!," "But it's so far away!," "But Gorbachev is so reasonable!," "But our side is so unreasonable!," "Another Vietnam!" And we know well that there are always those instant picket lines who were born with these very picket signs in their little hands. And the effect on reasonable debate is as though we were stepping in that chewing gum.

The use of the term "intellectuals" very closely parallels the "academic community" of which we took note earlier. Norman Podhoretz comments on their claim that Communists "no longer believe in Marxism." But Podhoretz observes that Communist leaders are victims as well as beneficiaries of the system that gives them their power and are not about to bite the hand that would strangle them if they so tried. But the gullible and predictable intellectuals are ever willing to blame all woes on the evil Americans. A typical case was Susan Sontag who in 1982 described the "utter villainy of the Communist system"—but still professed "passionate support" for Communist rebels in El Salvadore opposing American "tyranny." Also, in the *New York Times*, when Lon Nol fled Cambodia and the savage Khmer Rouge began their bloodthirsty rule, Sydney H. Schanberg's article was headlined "Indochina Without Americans: For Most a Better Life." Anthony Lewis's reaction was: "What future possibility could be more terrible than the reality of what is happening to Cambodia now?"

The classic example of such eager credulity I found in a Colman McCarthy column in the Tampa Tribune for December 11, 1987, headed "A Fresh Approach to Peace by the Soviets": (Gorbachev) "The Russian who currently rules the Soviet state appears of late to be involving citizens less in violence than in its opposite, peace."

He has sanctioned 57 year old Cenrikh Borovik to lead the Soviet peace Committee. Borovik

> has stories about everyone from Ernest Hemingway, with whom he went fishing in 1960 in Cuba, to Joan Baez, who welcomed the Russian in

> California . . . . A commuter airline [has been] shuttling Western peace groups invited in by Borovik for peace seminars

and the Leningrad to Moscow peace march in June, 1987,

> in which 320 Americans and Soviet citizens walked . . . . While in Washington, Borovik invited Linda Smith, the president of Mothers Embracing Nuclear Disarmament, to visit Moscow to explore a way of opening a MEND chapter for Soviet mothers.

Borovik quotes American writers

> on peace—that it cannot be achieved by military force, only by understanding—and suddenly we realize the irrationalities of past myth-fed anti-Soviet hatreds . . . . "We are not an evil empire," Borovik said . . . . "We are good people. We don't want to conquer anybody, whether it is Western Europe or the United States . . . . So let us speak about the future. Let's not blame each other for our former mistakes" . . . glasnost and perestroika are as needed by Americans as by Russians.

(Afghanistan, Cuba, and Nicaragua didn't get touched on in the Pollyannaish rose-colored conversation.)

"Intellectual" chewing gum again —to step in!

It has been malignantly effective. James Burnham has written a monumental volume in description of the results: *Suicide of the West*. Joseph Sobran, in a column which appeared December 18, 1986, in the *Tampa Tribune*, summed it up well. Of Communism and detente he wrote:

> Our differences were negotiable, so there seemed no point in extending, much less repeating, the agony of Vietnam . . . . We didn't fret—we hardly noticed—as country after country either went communist or turned bitterly anti-American: Vietnam, Cambodia, Laos, Angola, Ethiopia, Libya, Mozambique, Rhodesia, Afghanistan, and, of course, Nicaragua and Iran. We quickly resigned ourselves to a passive role in the world.

Aleksandr Solzhenitsyn, whose authoritative voice should be hearkened to with awe, put it this way in *Time*, February 18, 1980:

> Communism stops only when it encounters a wall, even if it is only a wall of resolve. The West cannot now avoid erecting such a wall in what is already its hour of extremity.
>
> Meanwhile, however, 20 possible allies have fallen to Communism since World War II. Meanwhile, Western technology has helped develop the terrifying military power of the Communist world.
>
> The wall will have to be erected with what strength remains. The present generation of westerners will have to make a stand on the road upon which its predecessors have so thoughtlessly retreated for 60 years.

Winston Churchill, in August of 1945, had this to say about our nation:

> The United States at this minute stand at the summit of the world. I rejoice that this is so. Let them act up to the level of their power and responsibility not for themselves but for all men in all lands—and then a brighter day may dawn on human history.

We were at that time just learning to spell "Hiroshima" and "Nagasaki." No one else possessed the awesome power of the atomic bomb. In the two decades that were left in the life of Churchill, I have a feeling that he was less than overjoyed as he observed the way we shouldered our burden. We have not led decisively; our critics within have prevented us from a frank and honest reading of the historical record—and it is upon that, and that alone, that our leadership is predicated. We are importuned to embrace Communist leadership wherever we find it—"as is." We are never to take cognizance of the fact that United States leadership represents not just military might, but, preeminently, democracy, economic well-being—and liberty. The result has been abdication, confusion, and chaos—and a lack of respect for and faith in our nation and freedom at home and in the world. Our policies too often have appeared to be lack of "involvement" while the Kitty Genoveses of the Earth have been raped, tortured, and murdered.

And just why should it be the lot of our nation to lead at this time in the history of mankind? Well, a very important consideration is this: It was our President, Franklin D. Roosevelt, who got us into this tragic state of affairs for our nation and the world with his disastrous "Great Design"—and who schemed knowingly to remove any other potential competition for primacy as the champion of liberty and democracy. It was that "Great Design," also, that had laid the foundation for the formidable power of Stalin and the Soviet Union and the potentials for the growth in power and in evil of international Communism with its well-spring centered in Russia. Who else could lead for liberty? It is the U.S. vs the U.S.S.R., and any decision we make—whether positive or negative—is a positive one in the ramifications it has for the lesser nations of the world. We are like the elephant in the henyard saying, "Let's dance!"

It was Jefferson again who penned in his Notes on the State of Virginia (1781-1785): "Indeed I tremble for my country when I remember that God is just."

That could well have portents for this hour.

I believe it was Red Skelton on a show years ago who was posing as a writer of a series about the adventures of the incredibly heroic Wonder Boy. He was pacing up and down while dictating to a couple of secretaries. As he ended one chapter he had Wonder Boy in a most precarious position. He was gagged and chained tightly, hand and foot, to a steel column inside a sealed steel closet outside of which burned a raging fire. Into the closet water was being pumped rapidly, and already it was up to his chest.

> "End of Chapter Twelve," said Red. One of the secretaries whispered in an aside, "This is the worst fix he's ever had Wonder Boy in. I don't see how he's going to get him out of this!" "It's impossible," said the other girl. Red triumphantly continued: "Chapter Thirteen. Once out of the closet, Wonder Boy . . . .

I do not propose that such a miraculous answer as that of Skelton's Wonder Boy awaits us. However, an acceptance of truth and reality is the best point of departure. Someone voiced a great verity when he said: "It's not enough to love flowers to have a lovely garden . . . you must also hate weeds." You cannot effectively favor the right unless you are willing to oppose the wrong. Envy is a venomous corrupter of the vision of the Third World directed toward us; while, on the other hand, there is certainly far less to be jealous of in the lack of liberty and lower living standards of the lack-luster Communist world. Our record has been a magnanimous one of generosity and aid to those less fortunate than we are; the Communist world has a catalogue of conquest, brutality, and slavery—and much of this has been to its own people. There is no Katyn Forest or Khmer Rouge Cambodia in our past. Leadership will come from the Soviet Union or the United States; and if it is to be for good it must—it will—come from the latter.

All students of history are conversant with the two hundred years of the Pax Romana which was begun under the aegis of the great Caesar Augustus in 27 B.C. and spanned the generations to the death of Marcus Aurelius in 180 A.D. It was under a relatively benevolent overlordship of the Roman Empire, and it meant a period of peace for Western Civilization in a "single peace group," as identified by William C. Bullitt in *The Great Globe Itself.* On p. 163 Bullitt finds a historic parallel in a century closer to our time:

> Throughout the period from 1815 to 1914 the British, with notable exceptions, exercised their power with a sense of fair play as well as British interests . . . . The success of the democratic revolutions in America, France, Great Britain and many lesser European countries, the spread of Christianity, and the calming influence of British sea power, made it seem before 1914 that the world was moving slowly but steadily into an era of peace based on old Greek and Roman customs, ever-expanding democracy, and ever-extending respect for Christian principles.

One of the "notable exceptions," of course, was the Crimean War; and the historical emergence of the modern nations of Germany and Italy (the Franco-Prussian War being the capstone of the former), the disintegration of the once-powerful Turkish Empire, and the Imperialist rivalries in Africa all were stepping stones to the First World War. But Britain tended to be a positive stabilizing force throughout the era.

The lesson, then, is that lasting peace can be predicated only on a foundation of constancy, reliability, and trust; and such a foundation has been provided only under the leadership of a powerful and unselfish nation who found that the advancement of its own ends was correllated and harmonious with legitimate aims of other nations. Let it be underscored that this cannot be the outcome of the selfish designs of a Mussolini, a Hitler, a Stalin—or a Roosevelt.

Archibald MacLeish has said: "There are those, I know, who will reply that the liberation of humanity, the freedom of men and mind, is nothing but a dream . . . . They are right. It is the American dream."

A notable immigrant to our land, George Magar Mardi Kian, put it impressively:

> You have been born in America; I wish I could make you understand what it is like not to be an American all your life—and then suddenly with the words of a man in flowing robes to be one, for that moment and forever after. One moment you belong with your father to a million dead yesterdays—the next you belong with America to a million unborn tomorrows.

I am thinking of a remarkable young lady. During the mid to late 1970's, our nation welcomed many thousands of refugees from South Vietnam as they fled from Communist oppression in their homeland. One such family—mother, father, two daughters, and a son—came to make their home in Ocala, Florida, sponsored by Ocala's First United Methodist Church. Huong (Hoon) Thai Le, one of those daughters, was 12 at the time. In June of 1981, Huong was valedictorian of the graduating class of Ocala's Forest High School. Her eloquent valedictory address, "To America, With Love," brought a standing ovation. I want to include a part of that message here:

> My country was never at peace during any of my childhood there. As a child growing up during a war, I longed for peace. Peace at any price. Since then I have learned that you cannot afford to have peace at the expense of freedom. Many of my people thought that way. Now they cannot even eat their meals in peace, and it is too late to throw off their oppressors. They, and I, have learned that 'peace at any price' is too high a price. There are some things worth dying for. The freedom you have here is one of those things.
>
> My friends, hold fast to what you have. I have come to appreciate the

United States as the greatest nation on earth. She is worthy of your fullest loyalty and greatest sacrifice. Treasure her. Love her. Defend her.

The price of freedom is never easy. Without vigilance and care, freedom can be easily lost. That must never happen. Your Patrick Henry put it better than anyone I know: 'Is life so dear and peace so sweet as to be purchased at the price of chains and slavery? Forbid it, Almighty God. I know not what course others may take, but as for me, give me liberty, or give me death.'

Chapter X

Precepts and Prescription

One day, some years ago now, a guest speaker addressed a high school assembly in a city in one of our more populous states. In an inspirational vein he likened the trials, encounters, and challenges of life to a game of football with obstacles and vicissitudes representing the opposing team—not altogether a novel approach for such an audience. He stressed that they must prepare diligently for the contest with their best efforts in school. He warned against the pitfalls of overconfidence and noted that often the cheers would be drowned out by the jeers. He reminded them that much of the game is involved in the hard work of grinding out gains a little bit at a time.

Then he waxed eloquent. He besought them to shake off that big opposing center—slothfulness, to block out those huge twin tackles of doubt and fear. He admonished them to bull right over the gigantic nose guard of adversity and to fake out the big left end of fatigue. He called on them to plow through that mammoth linebacker, disappointment. Take in stride, he exhorted, the great corner backs of discouragement and despair. And finally, he urged them, with grit and determination, to outrun that persistent safety man called impossibility. This was the recipe for success and happiness.

In the question period that followed a thoughtful and perceptive senior boy brought a needed perspective when he rose. "Sir," he said respectfully, "Where are the goalposts?"

Constraints on human behavior come from two directions: from without, and from within. Basically the first take the form of laws or of the threat of punishment. There are those of us who willingly conform to a system of legal "rules of the game" which in its highest sense we recognize as the great rule of Law. Others there are, however, who submit to laws on a reluctant, piece-meal basis, actuated only by convenience or by fears of consequences—choosing to depart when they can—or when they think they can—"get away with it."

The constraints from within are rooted in what we call moral code. The earliest such code was the Ten Commandments, imparted by Moses to the wandering tribes of Israel nearly fifteen centuries before the time of Christ. It exerted a powerful force, molding relationships between individuals in their families and in their communities, in their tribes, and in their nation. And at the center was their paramount relationship with God as individuals and as a nation. This constituted an ennoblement of mankind, as each person was to be honored and respected and protected as an individual with dignity within the group. Such was not the status of their contemporaries in savage or pagan societies.

The Ten Commandments, we should note, was given a new qualitative setting by Christ in the Sermon on the Mount when He said, "Therefore all things whatsoever ye would that men should do to you, do ye even so to them."

Emphasizing the values of the Ten Commandments and the precepts of the Sermon on the Mount, William C. Bullitt (Op. Cit. p.155) observes:

> The ethical teachings of religion have done far more than any other influence to lift men from savagery to civilization. Moses, Buddha, Confucius and Mahomet, each in his own way and on his own level, led men toward the light. And in the teachings of Christ the light itself was present.

A recent Associated Press headline from Amherst, Massachusetts, told of the parents of an eighth grader who were quite put out that their daughter's history textbook was "too conservative." They were quoted as complaining:

> The book tries to glorify and resolve the issues and paint the U.S. as the tough guy fighting communism rather than teaching that . . . there are differing opinions and no absolute answers.

I submit that this viewpoint at times might have made for some interesting chit-chat among the inmates at Buchenwald, or the Polish officers slain by the Russians in the Katyn Forest Massacre, or the myriad helpless Cambodian victims of those delightful Khmer Rouge—or the happy-go-lucky cocaine pushers who have targeted your children as their next victims.

Now let me make a vital observation: there is no such thing as an effective moral code—those constraints from within—that is not associated with belief in God. Read that again: there is no such thing as an effective moral code that is not associated with belief in God. The actuation of such a code is rooted in a complete context of whole-hearted desire. Those of us who are so motivated often fail to abide by what we know is right, but we cannot shed the reproval of conscience when such an event transpires. It cannot be a decision of pragmatic convenience; our conscience knows well that the code has been broken, and no confusion instructs us that there are "no absolute answers."

What then of those who would attest to a moral code but who have no such belief? In many cases they are constrained by membership in a society which finds its moral code in such a context, and as such they are the co-beneficiaries of that context, outnumbered as they usually are. And they often are willingly so. The nature that they have militates against mendacity. But still, as history shows, a great moral code, which is deeper than a mere legal system, does not arise in a mere secular society or in a pagan community which creates its polytheistic gods to represent what people fear, or the hungers that must be satisfied for life to continue.

William Golding, in his *Lord of the Flies*, paints a frightening picture of the potentially thin veneer of civilization without a system of abiding values to sustain it. Indeed the history of our century demonstrates how a Hitler or a Stalin or an Idi Amin can dissolve that thin veneer if he achieves a position where subversion of those values is allowed to proceed.

Why not, then, avail ourselves of the vast sources of power which moral codes have provided and can provide us in an era of unprecedented stress? But comes now a judge whose edict declares that it is illegal for a school to post the Ten Commandments on its walls. This, he says, is in line with our sacred Constitutional guarantee of freedom of worship.

Let's see, though—really, how much have we heard in recent years about "freedom of worship" or "freedom of religion?" Instead, the overweening "constitutional" virtue is an absolute "separation of church and state." And this, itself, has undergone an arbitrary redefinition dictating an antiseptic eradication of any shadow of religious connection with government or government processes. Even to meditate is to contaminate. God, the new "untouchable" cowers in the shadows, crying plaintively, "Unclean! Unclean!"

Is this the fulfillment of the aims of the inspired drafters of the Constitution and the Bill of Rights? Did they in any way demonstrate an attitude of antipathy toward religion or worship as such? Or were they characterized by a deep reverence for worship and for freedom as concomitant virtues? Let's check a few prime examples.

I have heard Jefferson cited as one who was supposedly strongly "thumbs down" on the subject of theology, but it was he who in the Declaration of Independence referred to "the laws of nature and of nature's God" as the substantiation for our nation's right to independence. He asserted that "all men are created equal" and that "they are endowed by their Creator with certain unalienable rights," and he made note of "liberty" (which Webster defines as "freedom from restraint") as one of the cardinal God-given rights. He appealed "to the Supreme Judge of the world for the rectitude of our intentions," and for the support of the declaration he claimed the sustenance of "a firm reliance on the protection of Divine Providence."

James Madison, in his *Journal* of the proceedings of the Constitutional Convention, recorded words of wisdom from the aged Benjamin Franklin. It was in the midst of contention as to the rights of the large and small states that Franklin rose, on June 28, 1787, to observe:

> I have lived, Sir, a long time; and the longer I live the more convincing proofs I see of this truth, That God governs in the affairs of men!—And if a sparrow cannot fall to the ground without his notice, is it probable that an empire can rise without his aid?—We have been assured, Sir, in the sacred writings, that 'except the Lord build the house, they labour in vain that build it.' I firmly believe this;—and I also believe that without his concurring aid we shall succeed in this political building no better than the builders of Babel . . . . I therefore beg leave to move, that henceforth prayers, imploring the assistance of Heaven, and its blessing on our deliberations, be held in this assembly every morning before we proceed to business; and that one or more of the clergy of this city be requested to officiate in that service.

With such ideas, could it be that the Constitutional Convention was unconstitutional?!

George Washington was the President of the Constitutional Convention; he was also, of course, the first President under the Constitution. If his outlook was characterized by animosity toward religion and toward any sympathetic relationship between government and worship, he slyly concealed it when he issued his eloquent Thanksgiving Proclamation in 1789:

> . . . It is the duty of all nations to acknowledge the provisions of almighty God, to obey His will, to be grateful for His benefits, and humbly to implore His protection and favor . . . who is the beneficent author of all the good that was, that is, or that will be.

He noted that both houses of Congress had requested the setting aside of a national day of public thanksgiving and prayer, thus demonstrating that they, too were skillful at masking their true feelings.

It would seem obvious that in the era of the molding of our Constitutional government there was certainly no demonstration of any equating of religious observances with political leprosy. Rather, there was a warm, often eloquent, advocacy and participation.

Then what could the phrase "separation of church and state" have meant, and what possible purpose could it have been intended to serve? Of course, these words do not appear in the Constitution, though they could easily have been included had the writers intended for them to be there. We do find reference to such wording in contemporary discourses and discussion, but never as an end in itself. It was always as a means to an end, and that end was unrestricted free exercise of religion. It would be of revealing interest for our present prayer opponents to mount a quest for a single instance where the authors of the Constitution and the Bill of Rights characterized "separation" as a means to curb expressions of worship. It was rather a means to <u>prevent</u> any government limitations on such worship activities.

Is it possible for twentieth century citizens to don the eyes of eighteenth century Americans and survey the political landscape of that time? Let us try. Viewed in simple, most of the nations of the Western world were noteworthy for governments which in each case espoused a single official religion (or denomination), generally one or another version of Catholicism or Protestantism. The dissident persisted at his own risk. Preceding generations had been marked by successions of nationalized religious wars and inquisitions.

More in point, England, Mother country to the colonies, had staggered unsteadily out of Catholicism into a relationship with an entity now known as the Church of England. It must be classed as Protestant, but to some critics it appeared more in the nature of a Roman Catholic caterpillar emerging after all those years as an Episcopal butterfly. It was <u>the state church</u>, and it was supported by taxpayers—willingly or not. The personality and bent of the ruling monarch had seemed the basic factor determining the severity of the restraints—and punishments—placed upon dissenters, but often there had been severe chastisements visited upon those who had attempted to carry on worship services of their own, or who had expressed beliefs not in line with prescribed doctrine. It was often unsafe to differ in any detail, even though one might be a thoroughly loyal church adherent. What we see is a complete "marriage" between the Church and the state. The "twain" had truly become "as one."

Now, where do we find ourselves? We see among the founding fathers and those who were responsible for the adoption and exposition of the First Amendment no frowning on nor shunning of religious expressions or exercises of worship, even when they were carried out by government agents and government leaders themselves. The facts were diametrically the opposite. And when we look for a solid example of what they inferred by "an establishment of religion" we observe the specific historic condition of establishments of religion in Europe that might just as well have been termed "establishments of state," and we find the often oppressive "establishment of religion" which was the state church, the Church of England.

It is thus a state church that they were determined to avoid. Oh, there had been periods when diverse religious groups in England had enjoyed considerable latitude in their activities and services, but the threat was always there in its potential, given the legal situation. The nonconformists could never be assured of protected rights. And there were always those taxes—from everybody—for direct support of the one denomination. No, the only sure way to make it impossible for Congress ever, with whatever intentions, to establish such a state church was to include a specific statement banning such action along with the provision that there would never be any government limitation on the free exercise of religious rights and prerogatives.

If I am in error as to the motivation and intent of the authors and planners of the First Amendment, I would be interested to know the basis for a counter-diagnosis. The "marriage" between the government of England and the Church of England constituted an unholy, smothering, monopoly. However, there is a vast world of difference between a marriage and a tip of the hat to a lady in passing—or a "Good morning" on a spring day, or a gentleman's holding the door open for a lady with arms full of packages.

There are numerous acts which are incidental to primary enterprises undertaken by persons or by groups. Drinking fountains and restrooms in the halls of Congress bear witness to the fact that not everything which transpires there has to do with Roberts' *Rules of Order*. The band's playing "The Star-Spangled Banner" before a football game is a gesture irrelevant to the contest itself, but it is a parenthetic remembrance that in the varied phases of our community life we do not forget the symbol of our nation's devotion to liberty. And such was President Lincoln's interjection in his "Gettysburg Address" of the universally espoused recognition of our national religious context "this nation, under God, shall have a new birth of freedom"—since interpolated into our "Pledge of Allegiance:" "one nation, under God, indivisible, with liberty and justice for all."

The reading of a verse of scripture and recitation of "The Lord's Prayer" or of the grace, "God is great, God is good," to begin a school day or a school meal are obviously gestures in the manner of the playing of "The Star-Spangled Banner" or the repeating of "The Pledge of Allegiance"—gestures which had been engaged in for nearly two centuries of our history—until recently. Those who, not wishing to participate themselves, would forbid the participation of the vast majority who do wish to must recognize that their roll of flagrant transgressors must be headed by Washington for his "Thanksgiving Proclamation" and the addition to his oath of office of the phrase "so help me God;" by Lincoln, by Franklin and the Constitutional Convention for their daily prayers, by every Congress in our history for their opening prayers, and by Jefferson in his "Declaration of Independence." (An acceptable correction might be, "We hold these truths to be self-evident: that all men happen to be equal.")

May I ask the Absolute Separationists—and I insist upon an answer: If it is wrong for children in an elementary school lunchroom to say, "God is great, God is good, and we thank Him for this food," how can it be right for Jefferson to credit God as the donor of our "life," our "liberty," and our "unalienable rights?"

Some very sincere critics have made the point that our people are not religiously homogenious, but are instead pluralistic—a "multiplicity of diverse religions." A look at some interesting recent statistics may inject a bit of needed clarity into the discussion. Obviously, it would be impossible to achieve a definitive breakdown on the thoughts of every single individual in the nation, but we do have available figures on those who have translated beliefs into memberships in various religious denominations. Nearly 65% of our entire population are religiously affiliated. There are, of course, numerous sects and denominations—many virtually duplicating the practices and beliefs of others, but it is notable that more than 99.7+% of all memberships are in one or another branch of the great Judeo-Christian Tradition. The proportion of Jews among those is 4.6%. We shall presently give special consideration to them.

It is evident that our culture could not in truth be characterized as consisting of a "multiplicity of diverse religions" but quite to the contrary. We have been told that the Lord's Prayer is verboten in schools because it is an expression which has relevance to only one of our many sects; but a Sabbath morning eavesdrop in church sanctuaries in any American city would hear congregations everywhere repeating: "Our Father which art in Heaven, hallowed be thy name."

There are two basic elements which draw together all the various groups who carry on the Judeo-Christian Tradition, and which, with all their differences, set them apart from other religions . . . . First: in the ancient Ten Commandments and even earlier in Hebrew history we had a unique association of the concepts of good and evil—of morality—with the worship of a God who was held to be the author of such a code. And, second: rather than a deity or deities of never changing cycles—planting seasons, growing seasons, harvest time, etc.,—or irrational taboos, we see a God of history, of plan, and of purpose. And as a conjunction of that purpose and that moral code, we find a parallel between man's relationship to God and his relationship to his fellow man: "Thou shalt love the Lord thy God with all thy heart, and with all thy soul and with all thy mind. This is the first and great commandment. And the second is like unto it, Thou shalt love thy neighbor as thyself;" and "Forgive us our trespasses as we forgive those who trespass against us."

The most malignant element which has invaded these considerations is one that is entirely extraneous—the quicksand of egalitarianism. Too often freedom is the first mortal casualty of egalitarianism. In our great land marvelous achievements have been recorded in the efforts to relieve conditions where opportunities had been limited and where hope lay in the breaking of fetters. Tragically, however, some who have looked to mandated "equality" as the ultimate aim have tended to concentrate on efforts to hamper and to stifle those who enjoy success and fulfillment. If one man's vision is limited, he must blind those who see the stars; if one's lack of endeavor brings lack of achievement, compensation must be wrested from the fruits of the endeavorer. In the case of school devotionals or an astronaut's landing on the moon and broadcasting a prayer, it is "unequal"—and therefore illegal—if there is anyone present or listening who happens to be a Hindu from an obscure sect in central India.

The result is intellectual and spiritual vandalism, because the court actions are never brought by Hindus or Buddhists, etc. They are brought by secularists or by Madalyn Murrays whose motivation is not religious freedom, but rather intolerance and vitriolic hatred of *anything* or *anyone* religious. An ancient parallel is related in the First Book of Kings when two women came before wise King Solomon carrying two baby sons, one living, the other dead.

> Then said the king, "The one saith, 'this is my son that liveth, and thy son is the dead:' and the other saith, 'Nay; but thy son is the dead, and my son is the living.'" And the king said, "Bring me a sword." And they brought a sword before the king. And the king said, "Divide the living child in two, and give half to the one, and half to the other." Then spake the woman whose the living child was unto the king, for her bowels yearned upon her son, and she said, "0 my lord, give her the living child, and in no wise slay it." But the other said, "Let it be neither mine nor thine, but divide it."

"What's bad for Madalyn Murray is bad for the country!" Since I don't want worship freedom, no one else can have it, either! Swish with the sword!

The unequivocal fruits of possessing a Constitutional right should be that citizens are allowed to carry out the activities which make up that right. In the case of religious freedom that means to pray, to read scriptures, to display symbols, art works, and decorations emblematic of seasons. It does not form a Constitutional right if the legal answer is without fail that you cannot do it.

It is to be noted that Madalyn Murray's atheism, as well as that of many who claim that designation, traces literally to the Greek "a theos"—against God. This is an absolutely negative point of view. By contrast, freedom is a positive concept. We Americans may use our press freely, even to taking issue with official policies. We may speak freely, even to disagreeing with the powers that be—and in the halls of Congress. The rights to petition and to assembly may be carried out freely with no circumscription on the subjects to be covered or the places where those liberties are to be entered into. Only in judicial fiats of the last generation (and pursuant administrative directives) have the negative "against God" subversions of freedom of worship assumed the atheistic postures as to all of government's being unalterably antagonistic to any vestige of religion. Madalyn in all her fanatic intolerance must be deliriously happy—but her objective is *not* religious freedom!

Note should be taken here that some supposed religious leaders are always eager to rush into print with pronouncements that could well have been written by Madalyn—reminiscent of the scriptural injunction "If the trumpet make an uncertain sound, who shall prepare himself to the battle?"

When we speak of that precious and scarce commodity, freedom, too often we fail to appreciate its true meaning and value. Those in the history of the world who have enjoyed liberty have always been, and are now, a rare minority. We who do enjoy this blessing must ever remember that it has been won by struggle and sacrifice and by many who have given their utmost breath. It does not appear likely that its future will demand less fortitude. But, in addition we must be aware of the nature of freedom. Someone has cogently said: "The essence of freedom is this, that some things must be allowed to go on of which I personally disapprove." Roger Williams spoke of religious freedom as "a full liberty of religious concernments." And prior to the Declaration of Independence Jefferson had written: "Freedom is the right to choose, the right to create for oneself the alternatives of choice. Without the possibility of choice, a man is but a number, an instrument, a thing." What does this signify for school prayers? It can mean only that the traditional devotionals must be allowed; no one may be forced to say a prayer if he desires not to—but he cannot stop the participation of others just because he personally disapproves.

"No!" someone objects. "What if there is someone present who opposes the Bible and prayer? Shouldn't he be allowed to leave the room? Or, really, should it go on at all since someone may disagree?"

What is it about religious freedom that makes it liberty's stepchild? Does freedom of speech dictate silence if there is anyone present who disagrees—or should that individual stand in the hall till the discussion is over? Must the presses shut down till everyone is unanimous in support of a single viewpoint? Should political candidates keep silent because they have opposition? Really, is it permissable for a president to make partisan speeches, telecast and subsidized by funds which include taxes paid by his opponents? Or should the rights of assembly and petition be suspended until we are certain no one would mind? As a matter of fact, is it really right to countenance voting in elections since unanimity is virtually unheard of? The picture begins to come into focus—it is the same as that found under any totalitarian dictatorship.

I have been informed unctiously that no freedom has been lost; any pupil or teacher who wishes may still pray silently—I would assume so long as they don't get caught. Our liberty has finally equalled that of Moscow! Patrick Henry would be proud!

And that brings us again to the stepchild: Another fetter has been prescribed for worship or prayer freedom that other freedoms do not suffer; and all too often it has been promoted by sincere religionists whose naivete is being exploited insidiously by more knowing anti-religionists. Prayer, they intone, is such an intensely personal matter, and one's worship exercises are so private that it is a sacrilege for them to be carried on by a public group. One judge in northwest Florida in granting an injunction to stop daily school prayers sanctimoniously compared such activity—you won't believe this—to the Spanish Inquisition! Undoubtedly there are occasions when petitions and thanksgiving are rightly personal and private—not in the least compromised by a class recital of "The Lord's Prayer," of course; but to stipulate that they may be engaged in in no other manner but privately is again to make this "freedom" a stepchild in the arena of liberty. The efficacy of "free speech" that is limited to one's privacy would be—nonexistent; and in 1735 John Peter Zenger did not find freedom of press to be "an intensely private thing." The Pilgrims had had enough of the enforced privacy of worship when they left their English homeland; and can you imagine the satisfaction one could derive from being restricted to humming the "Hallelujah Chorus" to oneself! If it is my aim that everyone else must keep any worship manifestations private so that I will not be bothered by them, that could be called bigoted intolerance; it is quite a different thing from freedom.

Although I disagree, if the tenets of a religious minority forbid their saluting the flag, I respect their right not to participate. I will protest loudly, however, if it is dictated that such a right extends to stopping me and the rest of the group from repeating the Pledge of Allegiance.

But why box with shadows on the "protection" of supposed dissidents? The litigants have forsaken pretense by shedding their sheep's clothing and baring their wolf fangs. The same objectors have supported the suits to eradicate the "moment of silence" observed by some schools to begin their day. Can't you visualize Madalyn Murray's saying—uh—"amen!" to such a legal action! But how could any religious minority feel violated or "embarrassed" by silence—and a period during which they, themselves, are at liberty to pray or to refrain according to the dictates of their consciences? The motivation of the Madalyn Murrays could thus be no solicitude for an "oppressed" sectarian group. How could it be anything other than aversion to prayer itself and to the freedom that others have to pray? Freedom of thought may allow a misanthropist to hate his fellowman; it would not follow that he should be given a machine gun and admonished to "go get 'em!"

When the Constitution was submitted to the states for ratification after the convention, it was specified that it should go into effect when nine of the thirteen states had ratified it. Many people there were, however, who insisted that it needed a specific group of amendments to protect basic rights, and several states approved the new government with the understanding that such a "Bill of Rights" would be forthcoming for their approval. Congress passed a number of amendments, of which ten were ratified by the states in 1791-2. Can you imagine that, had it been explained publicly that the First amendment had as its intent the prohibition of any scripture verses or prayers by children in the nation's schools—then and forever—that it would have been approved? You know it would not, and this fact tends to wrap up our discussion and tie a ribbon around it. Further, the margin by which it would have failed would have been astronomical. Indeed, such balloting would probably never have occurred, because the Congressional votings would certainly have been overwhelmingly opposed to a proposed amendment interpreted in that fashion. Each basic freedom protected under the Bill of Rights was included because it was considered to be basic—important. The people would have demanded an amendment specifically and positively emphasizing worship freedom rather than worship restriction. The very fact that no such upheaval occurred is the most eloquent testimonial we could have to the fact that all considered it as it stands to be just such a positive affirmation of liberty.

Then what about public belief today? A fairly recent Associated Press article by Gregg Harrington noted: "A recent poll by the weekly *National Enquirer* showed 92.6 per cent of the respondents favored an amendment allowing organized prayer in schools." Concurrently another Associated Press correspondent, George W. Correll, observed in support: "Polls have shown most people, by about 3 to 1, want government-run schools to include religious exercises." Now, certainly, such democratically ascertained landslides do not, per se, prove the infallibility of one side in a contention; quite probably a poll taken in 1491 as to whether the Earth is flat or round would have found "flat" winning by a comparable margin. On the other hand, being on the losing end of such a smashing defeat would surely not be conducive to over-confidence!

So, acknowledging the obvious fact, that our 1790 citizens did not construe the First Amendment to forbid routine school devotional exercises, how about the chances today for strumming up a two-thirds vote of each house of Congress and a majority of three-fourths of the fifty states in support of a specific constitutional amendment which would carry out the vitriolic anti-scripture wishes of Madalyn Murray O'Hare? It wouldn't even be gambling to bet against it!

Jeffrey Hart has noted: "During the 1960's, the court 'interpreted' the founders' principle that government should not prefer one religion over another to mean the government should exert an active preference for no religion at all." Obviously true, and by no stretch of the imagination could that judicial thesis be identified with our founding fathers.

Tolerance is a virtue of finite degree. Freedom must countenance the legitimacy of a myriad shades of belief, speech and action; but the true lover of liberty can never countenance the contention that liberty itself should be destroyed.

A news account sums it up. The American Civil Liberties Union has championed many causes; for some reason it has chosen on this question to oppose freedom of worship. The *Tampa Tribune* carried an Associated Press dispatch from Washington relative to Congressional hearings on the mushrooming disgrace of child pornography. It noted:

> The (Congressional) panel is considering legislation to provide criminal sanctions for the sexual abuse of children and to ban the often accompanying practice of photographing or filming children engaging in sexual acts.
>
> Heather Grant Florence of the American Civil Liberties Union opposed the bill, saying it tramples on First Amendment Rights . . . . "Those . . . who may profit as a result of (the activity), such as a publisher, editor, distributor or retailer, are not violating the law," she said.

Now we have it: the First Amendment means, they maintain, that a publisher has a right to exploit for profit the children drawn into the web of vice and pornography; but on the other hand, a school teacher is forbidden to lead those same children in the reciting of grace at mealtime! I think the founding fathers would be nauseated.

To return to the consideration of the possibility of any nation's leading in a movement toward a prolonged period of the blessings of world peace, it is imperative that this condition be fostered in a climate of mutual faith and trust among those national members of such a "peace group." It is obvious that there are governments and leaders whose recent history does not evidence a record of trustworthiness, and certainly even our own citizenry are not 100% so qualified. It is our responsibility through democratic processes to prevent such persons from gaining leadership positions, and if we do not have faith in those processes we may as well throw in the proverbial towel now.

The only way whereby this climate of mutual faith and trust may blossom and grow strong is in the context of a moral code which is shared by the fundamental citizenry and the leaders of a society. You will observe the distinction that I make here from a mere framework of legalism, however well-ordered it may be. We endeavor to give this a basic solid foundation such as has never been attempted before. If we proceed with success and with dramatic benefit to those nations who have chosen to be members of the peace group, it is to be hoped that the values of such a community of peoples will become apparent to those nations who have not merited membership in or chosen to join heretofore in such a voluntary avowal of mutual trust. Meanwhile, the members will, of necessity and in wisdom, have maintained defensive attitudes relative to those who have not chosen voluntarily to forswear concepts of lack of trust in the moral code of the emerging society.

A national allegiance to and concernment with a moral code possesses some gratifying connotations in everyday life as well as in the international sphere. My father, who was a Methodist minister, enjoyed telling of an experience many years ago when he found himself alone midst the mingling multitudes of a huge metropolitan railroad terminal. He had a number of heavy bags with him which would have been inconvenient—or impossible—for him to take along on a quick trip to the restroom. Then he had a brilliant idea. He said, "I just took out my Bible and laid it on my biggest suitcase. When I came back nothing had been disturbed at all." I shudder when I think of what would have happened if it had been today that he chose such a solution. The Bible would have been stolen, if not torn to shreds, and all the bags would be long gone!

There was a time not so very long ago when you would have found many communities who never locked their doors during the daytime hours, and fears of intruders and looters never disturbed people's minds. Today steel barred windows and doors have come to replace those peaceful scenes of yore. Churches and synagogues once were held in awe and respect; now their fixtures, cash boxes, and P.A. systems are prize prey for plunder and vandalism.

Certain it is that the menace of the drug culture has subverted the thinking of many individuals and ofttimes made responses a more criminal and deadly circumstance. Questions of racial interaction often have taken place in settings of vitriol rather than of balm, and the mighty in finance have lost their ethical orientation. It, too, cannot in any way be a condition of comfort that a very large proportion of our newborn babies each year are born in poverty—to unwed teenage mothers. These are some of the unpleasant repercussions—the bitter fruits—of our nation's systematic downgrading of "the voice that speaks from within"—the moral code. Conditions have been far better in our past—it is too easy to get the overwhelming record.

But has our reaction to this been sound? Did we, indeed, "get smarter?"

Thus, both in our concerns with other nations (if we wish to lead) and in the quality of our everyday life we would doubly benefit if our national policies, particularly in our courts, would return to interpretations that re-emphasize the values of our moral code rather than contrary ways we have tended to explore during the generation past which have set our course as neutral to or in antipathy against such a code.

Let me stress the point that we are talking about a condition that has not prevailed before save in a limited way and over a limited span of time—a hoped-for period of peace perpetual. In his monumental volume, *Human Destiny*, Lecomte du Nouy noted (p.267): "Peace must be established by transforming man from the interior and not by erecting external structures. We have already said it: the source of all wars, the source of all evil, lies in us." And William C. Bullitt (Op. Cit., p.1) bears witness to the fateful fact that mankind's moral refinement has in no way been commensurate with his achievements in the realm of science. Arguably, the greatest single accomplishment in the latter area has been the harnessing of atomic energy with its infinite potential for the betterment of human life and the quality thereof. However, the effect has been quite the contrary: it has brought the most awesome fear the world has ever known—because of our failings in the former field.

This does not connote a universal dereliction of honor; many persons there are and government leaders there are whose moral standards are in every sense to be trusted in and relied upon. However, we are now faced with a situation in which we come short if we cannot have faith in the leaders of all nations who possess the atomic potential.

In this connection, I have heard much mention of the phrase "human nature;" and, taking issue, there are those who say that such does not exist. I want to observe that there is such an entity as human nature. It consists of all that mankind is capable of doing, thinking, and feeling from the most satanic baseness to the height of the sublime—"a little lower than the angels." It is in great measure and, in quantity, quite predictable, too. If, for example, you wear a warm coat into a theater, you may find it uncomfortable and choose to slip out of it, leaving it under you on the seat. If, absentmindedly, you get up to depart without taking the coat, when you return for it five minutes later it is likely someone will have "found" it. However, if you run out of gas when homeward bound, and stand helplessly beside the road, you can know pretty certainly that presently someone will stop to lend you aid. And, vexatiously, it may be the same guy who stole your coat! (Of course, some current news accounts come to mind of "aid-lenders" in such circumstances who instead took advantage of that golden opportunity to mug the hapless victims—a sort of Good Samaritan story in reverse. They probably couldn't bring themselves to pass up such a "God-sent" opportunity.)

Now it is the province of education (usually family, etc.), but most particularly of religion to try to see that the sublime side of human nature is dominant over its nether manifestations. No surer avenue exists than the moral code with no equivocation about whether or not there are really "absolute answers" or merely "different opinions,"—and the power of conscience which is an inevitable accompaniment of the moral code.

Du Nouy (Op .Cit., pp. 262 and 264) reinforces this:

> All these dreams, all these legitimate hopes which will infallibly materialize someday, depend on the individual development of man's conscience, on the deep penetration of the virtues of the Scriptures, on the comprehension of human dignity . . . . God grant that we are mistaken. But if we have read the signs of the times correctly, or even if we have exaggerated some of the symptoms, the only salvation for mankind will be found in religion.

And he adds: "a sound Christian religion."

Bullitt (Op. Cit. p 166) observes: "There is no record of any totalitarian state keeping any international agreement its dictator wished to break."

And he further notes (p.169)

> A world custom of brotherly dealing between nations can grow only from long repeated actions in accord with the principle expressed in the words 'do unto others as you would they should do unto you.' Aggressions destroy the growth of such a custom. Aggressors kill not only such peace as may exist, but hope of future peace, since they cut the growth of the custom of brotherly dealings.

If I have made my case for national and international dealings actuated by a moral code, I must in some measure have scored, too, with the indispensibility of its relationship to religion. A nation whose contexts of rule and decision are outspokenly and unreservedly atheist must not be surprised to find its work, its promises, and its pledges accepted on a tongue-in-cheek basis of pronounced skepticism. The record of our times demonstrates a story in which lies have constituted an integral part of policy. Those among our citizenry who would have our own nation emulate the divorce from all religious connotations of those nations to whom we refer need to consider carefully whether or not that is truly what they desire—or certainly the rest of us should—judges and justices included!

I have had numerous long and mind-expanding discussions over the years with agnostics—those who say "I do not know the answers about final causes and whether or not there is a God." I have found them almost always to be tolerant toward opinions, ideas, and beliefs other than their own. Some there may be, but I have yet to find an humble atheist—one who does not want or strongly desire the eradication of the beliefs and practices of those whose views regarding deity he opposes. Let me hasten to add that because there are such a majority who classify themselves as fundamentalists, we are prey to extremes among those who are distinguished primarily, not by what they are for, but by what they are against—and they are against most of us. They are closed-minded, prejudiced, and judgmental; and they do their cause a disservice.

A factor that is galling about the protagonists of atheism is that they claim a monopoly on reason, logic, and common sense. They tend to be by nature so self-satisfied that they could be visiting in someone's home and use those flimsy little bathroom guest towels without feeling guilty!

I want to present briefly a case for belief. Du Nouy was probably the world's foremost statistical biologist when he wrote his *Human Destiny*, and quite early in the volume he presents the incomprehensible statistical odds against the chance formation of a single molecule of a dissymmetry of the lowest scale with life potential. I would strongly commend this exegesis for anyone seriously contemplating the concept of spontaneous generation. At the latter part of his discussion (pp. 35-36 and 38) he sums up:

> Events which, even when we admit very numerous experiments, reactions, or shakings per second, need an infinitely longer time than the estimated duration of the earth in order to have one chance, on an average, to manifest themselves can, it would seem, be considered as impossible in the human sense . . . . To study the most interesting phenomena, namely Life and eventually Man, we are, therefore, forced to call on an anti-chance, as Eddington called it; a 'cheater, who systematically violates the laws of large numbers, the statistical laws which deny any individuality to the particles considered.'

With that as a springboard, let us explore some areas of reason, logic, and common sense. First, there are those who would say that the alleged deity is supposedly infinite—illimitable, and they refuse to entertain thoughts about a fairy tale which man cannot comprehend. Oh? We are living in two entities the existence of which cannot be denied and which are infinite—and which defy comprehension: time and space. We can grasp and understand only the infinitesimal portion of each which we currently occupy, and a very limited vista from there outward or forward or backward. Our minds must erect walls or boundaries—but we feel a sense of awe when we contemplate that the other side of the wall goes on forever. Infinity is not a viable foundation for disbelief.

However, let us begin with where we are in our mundane existence, and survey a simple thesis which I have found no one willing to attempt to answer. Everywhere on this earth when we find plan or organization, we always find the planner or the organizer—the intelligence or the instinct (that is, an instinct that directs) which is responsible for the plan or the organization.

Not long after Pearl Harbor I was stationed in Australia near Melbourne with my infantry division, preparing for the campaign to come in New Guinea. They used to take us on "invigorating" hikes through the countryside, and fully as amazing to us as the occasional kangaroos were towering anthills—like the trunks of large trees, five—ten—a dozen feet or more high. If you cut into one of those, besides getting to know on a close personal basis more of them than you really care to, you will find many, many, thousands of ants moving through the myriad corridors, each seeming to know where he is going and for what purpose—a highly organized, efficient organization. A brief survey in your encyclopedia will tell you that there may be as many as five separate divisions of a clearly defined caste system in any one hill, each type having specific tasks or functions to carry out. Sometimes there are slaves who seem to perform as a group without resentment. The remarkable agricultural ant seems to cultivate an expanse of grass around its nest, methodically destroying any foreign plants or weeds which appear, and storing much of the new seed to be used as food. And behind this highly complex planning we find the intelligence—or the instinct—of the ant which has brought it into being.

Then there are the bees with whose detail of organization, work, and production of honey we are sweetly familiar. A hive may contain from 10,000 to 100,000 bees, divided into three classes: a single queen bee who lays possibly several thousand eggs a day and "mothers" the entire colony, a few drones (males) whose function is to fertilize the queen, and many workers (usually females whose sexual organs have atrophied) who gather the nectar and pollen and manufacture the honey, storing it and packing it into cells in the comb and also tending the young larvae till they are able to care for themselves.

The honey serves as food for the colony also, as well as for man. Quite an intricate and efficient organization—and behind it is the intelligence, or the instinct, of the bee which is responsible for it.

The yearly migrations of the wild geese southward from Canada for hundreds of miles and their welcome return as a harbinger of spring are massively well-ordered enterprises. Who has viewed it has not been thrilled by the beauty of those characteristic V formations as they wing their way in ordered grace through the pathways of the sky? The amazing treks of the swallows in due seasons for the thousands of miles, from continent to continent, and the regular return of one contingent to Capistrano—these are disciplined, intricately organized ventures on a grand scale—and behind these we find the intelligence, or the instinct of the wild goose and the swallow.

When you climb into your automobile and turn the ignition key you seldom think about the detailed planning by many people—the inventions and improvements of the multitudinous systems that make it up: ignition, fuel, brakes, steering, shock absorbers, comfortable seats, doors, radio, air conditioning, lights, electrical system, etc.—until that morning when it doesn't start. But behind all those systems are the men or women who conceived of them and Eli Whitney who thought of standardized parts, Henry Ford who brought into being the assembly line, and all those laborers and mechanics who worked on your particular horseless carriage to bring it into being.

Or look at the system of traffic control in a large city—Manhattan Island, for instance, where a sophisticated system of traffic lights, ever-changing at timed intervals can, at various intersections, stop all east and west bound traffic and permit north and south bound to proceed, and a moment later reverse the process—so that on any day millions of vehicles can travel through the streets with a minimum of accidents and difficulty. And behind this we find the intellect of the planners who conceived of the necessary ideas or who designed the electronic lights and timing devices and brought them into being.

Coming from a small town in Kentucky, I never ceased to wonder at the magnificent efficiency of New York City's layout of subways, with local and express trains of three different systems crossing and crisscrossing over and under each other—sometimes with stations having three levels below the street. And the rider can reach any part of that vast city with ease. (Of course, in recent years trips are taken with some trepidation because of the problems of threats of muggings and other crimes, but I have already dealt with the need for a moral code.) The subway is truly a marvelous layout to observe—and behind it we have the inventors, the architects, the engineers, and the officials who planned it and over the decades brought it into being.

We have mentioned the contributions of Eli Whitney and Henry Ford, but in thousands of factories, both large and small, across our land daily the raw materials go in and an infinite variety of finished products pour forth to satisfy consumers' demands—infinite variety from the designs of a multitude of planners. (Someone, incidentally, has observed that the likelihood of life's having come about on the earth by accident is comparable to the supposition that the unabridged dictionary could have been the result of an explosion in a printing factory!)

Whenever there is an airplane crash it makes large headlines in the news. However, in 1986 in the United States our twenty busiest airports in all averaged about 25 million passengers either arriving or leaving. In total there were 6.4 million departures by commercial airlines. Incoming as well as departing planes are assigned flight levels, as well as private planes and military craft in the vicinity. In 1986 there was only one fatal accident with one fatality—truly a miraculous record for a marvelous system. And behind that detailed, intricate project are the many thousands of people who thought of all those details and the instruments necessary, and the big planners who formed the successful network to carry out those plans.

We are all aware how much work is involved in keeping a beautiful lawn. We know when it is time to mow and trim again because the natural, invariable law is that the longer it has been since the cutting the more scraggly and unsightly it becomes. It <u>never</u> goes the other way. I think that the most phenomenal work of landscaping I have ever beheld is that at Disneyworld, near Orlando, Florida. Not only are the green lawns watered and trimmed to perfection and the varied and beautiful flowers situated in exquisite array—the bushes are shaped like the characters in Walt Disney's drawings for his comic strips and animated cartoons: Mickey, Minnie, Bambi, Dumbo, Donald Duck, the Dwarfs, etc. Now, do you imagine that when the idea came that Disneyworld should be built that they sent out explorers to search the country over looking for bushes that were shaped like animals surrounded by lovely flowers and grass? No, the meticulous detail was a result of the brilliant ideas and planning of the minds who conceived of it all and brought it into being.

If you and I were to visit Macy's department store in New York a week before Christmas, I might point out the elaborate care with which the store is laid out: here is a section for women's clothing, there are men's suits, here are sporting goods, there are shoes for women and shoes for men, and in other areas we would find books, stationery, cards, TV's, radios, furniture, chinaware, recorders, perfume, haberdashery, lamps, appliances, clocks, watches, jewelry, heat pumps, hardware, etc., etc.—and in one very noisy place, toys. After pointing out the infinite detail of the arrangement, if I said to you: "This all came about by accident," you would know that I was kidding, that I was "under the influence," or that I should be committed! All of that could have come about only by the planning and hard work of the personnel of the store.

We have not tried to do the impossible and bring to mind every case where plan exists in the world, together with its planner. I am open to another impossible task—a suggestion of any case where there is plan without the planner.

Possibly the most nearly perfect plan or organization with which most of us commonly come into contact in daily life is a watch or a clock. Some watches or clocks keep virtually perfect time, perhaps gaining or losing only fractions of seconds in a year's time. They could be called, to all intents and purposes, thoroughly dependable. And behind our watches and clocks we find the planners who conceived the idea or ideas and brought them into being.

But when our watches and clocks get out of kilter, where do we go to set them right? Well, our time-keeping is more exacting than the mere (supposed) twenty-four hour journey of the sun around the earth, though that suffices for any exactitude that most of us need for our own timepieces. (I am aware, of course, that the sun does not go around the earth—what an orbit that would be!) The earth's rotation on its axis, which gives our 24 hour days, is at the same rate, specifically 24 hours each—today, this week, this month, this year, this century, this millenium, etc., etc. Dr. Jerry Bergman, writing in "Impact" (June, 1985) notes:

> If the Earth traveled much faster in its 292-million-mile-long orbit around the sun, centrifugal force would pull it away from the sun, and if too far, all life would cease to exist. If it traveled slightly slower, the Earth would move closer to the sun, and if it moved too close, all life would likewise perish. The Earth's 365 day, 5-hour, 48-minute and 45.51-second-round-trip is accurate to a thousandth of a second! If the yearly average temperature on Earth rose or fell only a few degrees, most life on it would soon roast or freeze. This change would upset the water-ice and other balances, with disastrous results. If it rotated on its axis slower, all life would die in time, either by freezing at night because of lack of heat from the sun, or by burning during the day from too much sun . . . . If the Moon were much nearer to Earth, one result would be huge tides which would overflow onto the lowlands and erode the mountains . . . . If the Earth were not tilted 23 degrees on its axis, but was at a 90 degree angle in reference to the sun, we would not have four seasons. Without seasons, life would soon not be able to exist here . . . . If it were not for the tremendous amount of water on the Earth, there would be far greater day and night temperature variations. Many parts of the surface would be hot enough

to boil water in the day and the same part would be cold enough to freeze water at night. Water is an excellent temperature stabilizer. The large oceans on Earth are a vital part of our survival!

There seems to be planning here with exactitude. It is so precise that astronomers can look through their telescopes tonight and make their computations and predict the exact times and places where solar eclipses will occur on the face of the earth far down through the years beyond the lifespan of any person now living; and they can tell us, for instance, when Halley's comet will again make us a visit on its seventy-five or so year trek through the heavens.

In our galaxy alone, the Milky Way, there are from one hundred to two hundred billion stars in addition to our own sun—many times more than the number of individual human beings who now live, or who have ever lived, on the face of the earth!

Let us step out beyond the tiny confines of our solar system—on out into the immensity of space. There and there and there we see the varied constellations, groupings of stars which man in his imagination has given names taken from his own experiences or his folklore. Seldom are they readily recognized as picturing the items for which they have supposedly been named, some notable exceptions being the Southern Cross and the Big Dipper and the Little Dipper. The last two under their classic names of Ursa Major (Big Bear) and Ursa Minor (Little Bear) would be difficult to associate with those classic descriptions. However, we do find that the constellations are emblematic of order and organization in the universe. As early as 1500 years B.C. the writer of the book of Job twice made reference to Ursa Major. There are 88 identifiable constellations, 48 of which the ancient Greeks had described before 400 B.C.—remarkable, since not all of the heavens are visible from any one spot on earth. Long before the discovery of the compass, ancient mariners had learned to sight upon Polaris, the North Star, at the end of the handle of the Little Dipper, and all else would fall into perspective. With this and memory and such crude maps as were available they were able to navigate many thousands of miles with a minimum of accident.

There we have it—wherever on the earth we find plan, we always find the intelligence of the planner, from the ant hill and the ant, the bee hive and the bee, on to the intelligence of man and his proudest plans. To me it is without reason, without logic, without common sense, to leap to the infinitely more magnificent plan of our solar system and the universe and to say, "Behind this there is no intelligence—it just happened by accident." And as an added grace we have the blessing of the vital moral code.

In this context we have a profound thought expressed by Dr. David H. C. Read, noted pastor of the Madison Avenue Presbyterian Church:

> If I were to wake up one morning and find I was an atheist with my faith in God completely gone, I think I would miss almost more than anything else having someone to thank. The loss of what we call grace, the recreating and refreshing power that comes through Christ, would of course be devastating, but what a deprivation it would be to plunge on to the end of one's days with no one to thank. I can hardly conceive what it would be like never, never being able to say in a moment of exhilaration, of, unexpected happiness, or of rescue from deep distress, "0 God, you're good to me!"

The potency and efficacious quality of thankfulness are not to be forgotten. In Chicago on a day some years ago the first blush of spring was in the air. Gone were the chill memories of winter's snows. The sky was blue. There was a balm that beckoned. The grass was green. Flowers were beginning to make their colors and their fragrance known. Birds fluttered and dived and climbed, singing as they soared. On one of the city's broad downtown sidewalks an aged blind man sat close to a building front, tin cup on the walk before him and a sign fixed to stand upright with the legend, "Help the Blind." The crowds rushed by. Few paid him much notice, and his cup held only a few small coins. Presently a little girl about ten years old came by, holding her father's hand. She paused and read the sign and put a quarter in the cup. Then she walked on with her father. They had gone only a few steps when she stopped and said, "Wait a minute, Daddy!" Running back to the man beside the walk, she took his sign and turned it over on its blank back. Quickly she took a crayon from her purse and neatly printed a new sign with just seven words and set it up before the man. Then she walked on hand-in-hand with her father. But now many passers-by stopped to pay attention, and many put money into his cup. The words the girl had printed were these: "It is Spring, and I am Blind."

No, the atheist may ridicule my belief as simple and childlike, but I find his faith in accident far more lacking in reason, logic, and common sense than could belief in an omnipotent God ever be.

And from this scale of observation we are inspired to meditate upon the magnificence of man. More than a thousand years before Christ, King David expressed it eloquently in the Eighth Psalm:

> 0 Lord our Lord, how excellent is thy name in all the earth! who hast set thy glory above the heavens.
>
> Out of the mouths of babes and sucklings hast thou ordained strength because of thine enemies, that thou mightest still the enemy and the avenger.

When I consider thy heavens, the work of thy fingers, the moon and the stars which thou hast ordained;

What is man that thou art mindful of him? and the son of man, that thou visitest him?

For thou hast made him a little lower than the angels and hast crowned him with glory and honour.

Thou madest him to have dominion over the works of thy hands; thou hast put all things under his feet:

All sheep and oxen yea, and the beasts of the field:

The fowl of the air, and the fish of the sea, and whatsoever passeth through the paths of the seas.

0 Lord our Lord, how excellent is thy name in all the earth!

One salient principle which perpetually penetrates in this particular is this: each individual—consciously or subconsciously—arrives at the evaluation of himself which determines his relationship to a standard "a little lower than the angels." If one is not touched by beauty, majesty, and depth of thought and feeling, one has drawn tight around oneself the ties and strictures that get in the way of soaring. A familiar couplet gives expression to this fact: "Two men gazed through prison bars. One saw mud; the other, stars."

Perhaps a personal reference may clarify here. In early 1942 I was a member of an infantry division being transported by an incredibly slow sea convoy from the United States to Australia. Down our eastern coast and through the unexpectedly lovely Panama Canal our ship had come, and now with the rest of our flotilla we sailed westward across the tropical Pacific. It would, reminiscent of Noah and his Ark, take us forty days before we would reach our destination.

In the tossing seas of the Atlantic and Caribbean approaching the Canal we had all had our initiation to the joys of mal de mer, which caused many of us to fear we would die—and some to fear we wouldn't. After the Canal, though, days were routine, hot, and boring. One pastime for many in various localities on the deck was poker, in which I did not partake—and in which quite a few who did came to wish they hadn't.

We had no touring U.S.O. shows to break the monotony, but almost every evening the heavens put on fantastic, breath-taking displays as the sun in all its regal pomp and splendor took its wondrous westward way. I've never seen a sunset I didn't like, but these were imposingly impressive in their awesome beauty. You don't find sunsets without luxurious rich reds, but here they were elegantly interwoven with bursts of brilliant extravagant gold. The celestial artist flung his clouds across the firmament with here a group, graceful and ornate, floating on a sea of blue; and there, and there, and there, carved Gibraltars and majestic towering mountains, shining in their sublime and stately splendor—all reflecting their exquisite eminence as though etched there with magnificent, picturesque, ever-changing strokes of scarlet, crimson, aureate, blue, white, and deep purple. And then there were the magnificent rays radiating out from the center like an irrepressible explosion of glorious Northern Lights. As far as one could see, with no land to impede the view—to the west, to the east, to north, and to south, the skies rejoiced in exalted glory and grandeur—and all was mirrored on the vast bosom of the water. At last the sun rolled on and sank beyond the western horizon in a lustrous ball of flame—and it was gone; but echoes still remained emblazoned against the reluctant gathering dusk as the evening's first bright stars made their presence known. It was a sight to be remembered with rapture—as though the angels had let us peek briefly through the very thresholds of Heaven!

And many of those fellows playing poker on the deck never stopped to look up and share any of it. They were the modern "untouchables"—those who possess not the quality of being attuned on that level "a little lower than the angels." And their concept of self, their own sense of responsibleness had divorced them from that high estate.

May I confidently predict that this literary effort of mine will never receive a Pulitzer Prize—nor any other token of accolade from those who today have responsibilities for making decisions as to what works have the merit to claim acclaim. I make this observation not because I have the temerity to place myself on a plane with Lincoln, who in that monumental misstatement from the Gettysburg Address said, "The world will little note, nor long remember, what we say here." It is just this—that among the "facts of life" right up there with stories about the birds, bees, and AIDS, it is not the "in" thing to write commending the United States or expressing pride in our nation. I do so, nevertheless.

I tend to become bored by Miss America contests—et al., but I have always been thankful that in 1957 I was tuned in when Miss South Carolina, Marian McKnight, was chosen as Miss America. I don't remember who were the other four of the five finalists, but the last hurdle came when the girls individually were brought out and asked three questions by the master of ceremonies. No one was permitted to hear anyone else's answers. The first two questions were "How did you get your hooped skirts from your home to Atlantic City?" and "What living person do you most admire, and why?" The third question was the big one: "What would your being selected as Miss America mean to you?" The answers of the other four contestants followed a predictable pattern such as: "I would like a career in motion pictures and it would give me a boost" or "I would like to use the prize money to help my parents retire a mortgage on our home," or "It would be a good start on a modeling career," or "I would use the scholarship award to put myself through college."

> Miss McKnight was the last to be questioned. She pondered a bit and then answered thoughtfully: "It would mean to me that I have been chosen as the one who best embodies all of the ideal qualities of young American womanhood, and for one year I am to represent those qualities to my nation and to the world."
>
> It just put her in a class apart—of pride in herself and pride in her country. And she was Miss America.

This is really a "call to arms," spiritually speaking, or a call to commitment—as individuals, and as a nation. This means not an exhortation to ride off in all directions, firing our guns at will. It does mean a positive appreciation of the values that have made this nation great and a recognition that our nation must be the leader in the defense of those values, and of the other nations in the Western World who share those values. We must be vigilant and alert when challenges present themselves in the form of bears in sheep's clothing. Take to heart the record and lessons of history. And of a surety we must have the discernment to recognize bears when they come in bears clothing—a place where many of our leaders have been tragically lacking. Wishful thinking when dealing with powerful adversaries is moral, spiritual and national suicide. We must be certain of our own values, and we must be assured that those values are not the values that actuated the leaders of past Marxist governments. (How many of you readers have read of new world records in track and field boasted by iron curtain countries and failed to have a question mark in the back of your mind as to whether or not it really was true?)

We must be responsible as guardians of all that we hold dear; too often persons in positions of trust are, and have been, victims of illusion in the assessment of realities in world conditions—which is like using a hose attached to a gasoline pump to put out a fire! We have surveyed in previous chapters the overwhelming advances of international Communism within the past half century due to the resolve of Communist governments—and to the lack of resolution on the part of the free nations, of whom our own country is the leader. And I speak not primarily of a choice of war or not, but of a choice to let it be known that we are adamant in support of freedom. We made that choice at the time of the Berlin Airlift, for example, and we emerged triumphant. For our generation the ringing challenge of the ancient Mordecai to Queen Esther rings true—Esther who would dare death to save her people: "And who knoweth whether thou art come to the kingdom for such a time as this?"

We shall see whether we deserve to be called "great." Someone has said that the highest reward for man's toil is not what he gets for it but what he becomes by it. And it may have been the same sage who observed:

> Great occasions do not make heroes or cowards, they simply unveil them to the eyes of man. Silently and imperceptibly, as we wake or sleep, we grow strong or we grow weak, and at last some crisis shows us what we have become.

In our nation's capital the Archives Building has emblazoned above its doors the inscription: "All That Is Past Is Prologue." Some years ago a little old lady hailed a taxi in front of it, and as she settled into her seat she looked up and read the legend to her driver: "'All that is past is prologue!' Isn't that wonderful—isn't that amazing! Uh—what does it mean?" And the cab driver, with worldly wisdom, replied: "Well, Lady, it means simply this—You ain't seen nothin' yet!" I would like, in keeping with those sentiments, to visualize a new inspiration to United States leadership and perception for a world of a just peace and morality; for if it does not result from our leadership it is not likely to occur at all.

Some two centuries ago the great Edmund Burke made a cogent comment which is certainly no less true today: "All that is necessary for the forces of evil to win in the world is for enough good men to do nothing." And it was Havelock Ellis who noted: "This world had been a much better place in which to live had it not been for the many timid friends of God."

Legend has it that the proud archangel Lucifer, later supposedly to have been cast out of Heaven for his rebellious nature and to have become Satan, came before God one day. God was talking about all the wondrous things he had planned for the world. Lucifer interrupted him with a question:

"Who is going to accomplish all these wonders?"

And God said simply: "I'm depending on Man to do it."

"But," said Lucifer, "Suppose Man doesn't do it—what then?"

And God replied, "I have no other plan."

And from the first verse of the 127th Psalm comes the inspiration of divine undergirding for great tasks: "Except the Lord build the house, they labour in vain that build it: except the Lord keep the city, the watchman waketh but in vain."

We need guard against "grasshopperitis" when we face the challenge. When Moses chose out twelve tribal leaders to go to spy out the land of Canaan, they returned with glowing evidence of the lush productivity of the area. But, except for Caleb and Joshua, they maintained that to take the land would be an impossibility: "And there we saw the giants, the sons of Anak, which come of the giants: and we were in our own sight as grasshoppers, and so we were in their sight."

Years later one of the greatest triumphs of the Israelites would come right there at the spectacular fall and destruction of the mighty walled city of Jericho, but now they defeated themselves because they gave up and gave in. Their devastation came, not because of any superiority of the Anakims, but because, as they said: "We were in our own sight as grasshoppers."

It is at times human to feel that we are the only ones resolved to stand for truth or to face the foes of freedom, and we are in danger of falling prey to the, "What's the use?" frame of mind. We can feel so deserted and alone. But think—do we really believe that no one else has found the profound and positive values which we hold dear? No, there were and are those in Poland, and in East Germany, in the Baltic States, in China, in Vietnam, in Cambodia, in the Soviet Union, in Cuba, in Nicaragua, in El Salvador, and among those who have fled for their lives from those nations where Communist tyrannies have been implanted—and the list goes on. These need to be made to feel that someone shares their burden and their aspirations.

Nearly three thousand years ago the remarkable prophet Elijah, hounded by the evil King Ahab and his vicious Queen Jezebel, and reviled by the prophets of the false god, Baal, fled into the wilderness and entreated in despair that God might take away his life.

> And he said, I have been very jealous for the Lord God of hosts: because the children of Israel have forsaken thy covenant, thrown down thine altars, and slain thy prophets with the sword; and I, even I only, am left; and they seek my life, to take it away.

And the answer came: "Go, return . . . . Yet I have left me seven thousand in Israel, all the knees which have not bowed unto Baal, and every mouth which hath not kissed him."

Roosevelt Ridge is a mountainous spine which juts out to the eastern New Guinea coast south of Salamaua, a Japanese stronghold and port until it was taken by units of the 41st Division in 1943. It was named after Lt. Col. Archibald Roosevelt, colorful, charismatic son of Teddy Roosevelt and commander of the third battalion of the 162nd Infantry. I was in E Company, second battalion. In the weeks before Salamaua fell, the Ridge and its environs claimed the lives of many men, both Japanese and American.

My company had been in constant contact with the enemy for quite a few days atop the Ridge when we were relieved by other units and pulled back behind the Ridge near the beach for some days of rest. We never knew whether they were aiming at us or were just missing the troop positions at the top of the hill—or were just blasting away in a "to whom it may concern" attack, but on one of the first afternoons of our "resting" we were hit by a rain of Japanese artillery and howitzer shells with perhaps some mortars mixed in for bad measure. I went through a number of such assaults, but this was the most deadly I ever "enjoyed."

In the movies and on television they are in the habit of using whistling sound effects to represent shelling; I found that a more representative analogy is that of an ultra-fast freight train speeding straight toward you. By the time the second one falls, you are in your two-man foxhole; you may have been less than assiduous about digging your first one, but never again. It is terrifying to lie there hearing the coming "freight train," knowing that if it decides to "visit" you there is absolutely nothing you can do. This afternoon for twenty minutes or more, shell after shell fell in seeming endless barrage. First there was deathly stillness as a "freight train" headed toward us, then all hell broke loose in a thundering crash as fragments hurtled through the air in every direction. Then a few seconds of the still, then shrieks of "Medic! Medic!"—Then the silence again as the next "freight train" gave advance notice of its arrival, and the frightful scenario began anew—shell after shell after shell—a seeming eternity of shells.

Then suddenly a familiar sound was heard deep behind our lines. It was the welcome angry roar of our own 155 howitzers and artillery rifles! We knew that their forward observers were in strategic positions, in radio contact with our big guns in the rear. We did not know whether or not they had actually spotted and mapped the guns that were tormenting us. But a tearful, joyous surge of relief swept through our battered positions. At long last someone on our side was shooting back! And presently the shelling of our perimeter ceased.

How many times I have remembered that experience when I have thought of those courageous but helpless fighters for freedom in eastern Europe, in Southeast Asia, in Cuba, in Nicaragua and El Salvador—in all those areas crushed by Communist oppression; and our Congress has been pious in its refusal to allow the "someone on our side" to have the ammunition to fire back.

And I think of that moral code that is empty unless it finds expression in the positive values we as a nation support, and in the evils we are unreservedly ready to oppose. This present generation—and in this nation only—will answer the call for responsibility in leadership that will defend freedom, and a meaningful peace. Or it will never be.

If we answer, however, we will avail ourselves of the most indomitable support that mankind has at its disposal.

Not long before the Normandy invasion in World War II, a B-17 "Flying Fortress" made its way with an armada of bombers flying many hundreds of miles from their bases in Britain deep into the heart of Nazi Germany. It was night. Dropping their bomb load, they were swinging around to head back to their base in England when suddenly they were rocked heavily with the antiaircraft fire. They began to lose altitude. The captain tried valiantly to keep the plane on course, but presently it was evident to all that it was a losing cause; they were going to crash. The captain gave the order for the men to jump.

To their consternation they discovered that the enemy fire had jammed the door mechanism of the bellygun turret beneath the plane, and the seventeen year old bellygunner was trapped down in there. They pried with every tool they had available, but nothing would do. Finally they were getting so low they would have to jump or it would be too late.

An old master sergeant, old enough to be father to the terrified kid down in the turret, had managed to ease the door wide enough to push his own forearm down through. He reached down and clasped the hand of the boy. As the last man jumped, he heard the old master sergeant say in assurance, "Take it easy, Buddy, I'm flyin' with ya!"

After the remarkable evacuation of 345,000 British and some French troops at Dunkirk on the coast of France in May and June of 1940, the Continent belonged to Hitler and his fellow totalitarian Josef Stalin, of Russia. Now the German dictator unleashed his Luftwaffe in round-the-clock devastating air raids in the hundred day "Battle of Britain." By December 19,000 civilians had been killed and 27,000 wounded. The British stood strong, however. Prime Minister Winston Churchill stirred them with his oratory, and the wonderful Spitfires of the R.A.F. and R.C.A.F. began to knock Hitler's bombers out of the skies in record numbers.

At one juncture King George VI went on the B.B.C. to try to encourage and fortify his embattled people. He concluded by reading a poem which someone had sent to him on a postcard that week. He did not know the name of the poet, but it was M. Louise Haskins:

At the Gate of the Year

And I said to the man who stood at the gate of the year:
"Give me a light that I may tread safely into the unknown."
And he replied: "Go out into the darkness, and put your
hand into the Hand of God.
That shall be to thee better than light and safer than a known way."

Bibliography - Book II

Allen, Fredrick Lewis: *Only Yesterday*, New York, Blue Ribbon Books, Inc., 1931

Buckley, William F. and Bozell, L. Brent: *McCarthy and His Enemies*, Chicago, Henry Regnery Co., 1954

Bullitt, William C.: *The Great Globe Itself*, New York, Charles Scribner's Sons, 1946

Burns, Edward McNall: *Western Civilizations*, Vol. 2, New York, W.W. Norton & Co., Inc., 1969

Byrnes, James F.: *Speaking Frankly*, New York and London, Harper and Brothers Publishers, 1947

Chamberlin, W.H.: *America's Second Crusade*, Chicago, Henry Regnery Co., 1950

Clemens, Diane Shaver: *Yalta*, New York, Oxford University Press, 1970

Dall, Curtis B.: *FDR, My Exploited Father-In-Law*, Tulsa, Okl., Christian Crusade Publications, 1968

Davies, Joseph E.: *Mission to Moscow*, New York, Simon and Schuster, 1941

Davis, Forrest: "What Really Happened at Teheran," *The Saturday Evening Post*, May 13 & 20, 1944

Deane, John R.: *The Strange Alliance*, Viking, 1947

De Toledano, Ralph and Lasky, Victor: *Seeds of Treason*, New York, Funk & Wagnalls, 1950

Du Nouy, Lecomte: *Human Destiny*, New York, London, Toronto, Longmans, Green and Co., 1947

Efron, Edith: *The News Twisters*, Los Angeles, Nash Publishing, 1971

Eibling, Harold H., King, Fred M., Harlow, James: *History of Our United States*, River Forest, Palo Alto, Atlanta, Toronto, Laidlaw Brothers, 1969

Flynn, John T.: *The Roosevelt Myth*, New York, Devin-Adair Co., 1948

Flynn, John T.: *While You Slept*, New York, Devin-Adair Co., 1951

Graff, Edward and Hammond, Howard: *Southeast Asia-History, Culture, People*, New York, N.Y., A New York Times Company, 1971

Kennan, George F.: *Russia and the West under Lenin and Stalin*, Boston & Toronto, Little, Brown & Co., 1961

Kimball, Warren F. (Editor): *Churchill & Roosevelt: The Complete Correspondence*, Princeton, N.J., Princeton University Press, 1984

Kravchenko, Victor: *I Chose Freedom*, Garden City, N.Y., Garden City Publishing Co., 1946

Lattimore, Owen: *Solution In Asia*, Little, Brown and Co., 1945

Ledwidge, Bernard: *DeGaulle*, New York, St. Martin's Press, 1982

Lenin, Vladmir Ilyich: *The Infantile Sickness of Leftism in Communism*, Collected Works, Vol XXIV, Moscow, 1920

Lippman, Walter: *U.S. Foreign Policy*, New York, Pocket Books, Inc., 1943

Miles, Vice Adm. Milton E., U.S.N.: *A Different Kind of War*, New York, Doubleday, 1967

Moley, Raymond: *After Seven Years*, New York and London, Harper and Brothers, 1939

Morrison, Samuel Eliot & Commager, Henry Steele: *The Growth of the American Republic*, New York, Oxford University Press, 1969

Nevins, Allan and Commager, Henry Steele: *A Short History of the United States*, New York, The Modern Library, 1945

Roosevelt, Elliott: *As He Saw It*, New York, Duell, Sloan, and Pearce, Inc., 1946

Sherwood, Robert E.: *Roosevelt and Hopkins, An Intimate History,* New York, Harper and Brothers, 1950

Smith, Emma Peters, Muzzey, David Saville, and Lloyd, Minnie: *World History*, Boston, New York, Chicago, Ginn and Co., 1946

Solzhenitsyn, Aleksandr: *The Gulag Archipelago, 1918-1956*, New York, Harper and Row, 1985

Spector, Ivar: *An Introduction to Russian History*, Princeton, N.J., Van Nostrand, 1969

Wallbank, T. Walter, Taylor, Alastair M., and Carson, George Barr, Jr.: *Civilization—Past and Present*, Vol. II, Glenview, Ill., Scott, Foresman and Company, 1965

Wittmer, Felix: *The Yalta Betrayal*, London, The Claxton Printers, Ltd,. 1954

U.S. Senate Hearings: *The Truth About Vietnam*, Greenleaf Classics, Inc., 1966

Index